POSTCOLONIAL BIBLICAL CRITICISM

INTERDISCIPLINARY INTERSECTIONS

Edited by

Stephen D. Moore and
Fernando F. Segovia

Other volumes in the series:

THE BIBLE AND POSTCOLONIALISM

Series Editor:
R.S. Sugirtharajah

T&T CLARK INTERNATIONAL
A Continuum imprint
LONDON • NEW YORK

Published by T&T Clark International
A Continuum imprint

The Tower Building,
11 York Road,
London SE1 7NX

15 East 26th Street,
Suite 1703,
New York, NY 10010

www.tandtclark.com

British Library Cataloguing-in-Publication Data
A catalogue record for this book is available from the British Library

Typeset by Tradespools, Frome, Somerset
Printed on acid-free paper in Great Britain by Antony Rowe Ltd, Chippenham, Wiltshire

ISBN 0567084396 (hardback)

CONTENTS

ACKNOWLEDGMENTS

This volume has been made possible as a result of the assistance and support of a good number of people, to whom we are deeply indebted and most thankful. First and foremost, thanks are due to all those who kindly accepted the invitation to serve as contributors to the project. Second, to Professor R.S. Sugirtharajah, General Editor of this series on 'The Bible and Postcolonialism', for his gracious invitation to submit the volume for inclusion in this distinguished series. Third, to Dean James Hudnut-Beumler of the Divinity School at Vanderbilt University for his unreserved backing of the project and much appreciated support toward editorial expenses. Fourth, to the Revd. James A. Metzger, who, as a doctoral student in New Testament and Early Christianity within the Graduate Department of Religion at Vanderbilt University, served as editorial assistant for the project, for his superb editing of the project. Fifth, to Lynne S. Darden, who, as a doctoral student in New Testament and Early Christianity at Drew University, served as research assistant for the project, for ably compiling the index. Finally, to the entire staff of T&T Clark International.

LIST OF CONTRIBUTORS

Roland Boer, Centre for Studies in Religion and Theology, Monash University, Victoria, Australia

Laura E. Donaldson, Department of English, Cornell University, Ithaca, NY, USA

David Jobling, St. Andrew's College, Saskatoon, Saskatchewan, Canada

Tat-siong Benny Liew, Chicago Theological Seminary, Chicago, IL, USA

Stephen D. Moore, The Theological School, Drew University, Madison, NJ, USA

Fernando F. Segovia, The Divinity School, Vanderbilt University, Nashville, TN, USA

POSTCOLONIAL BIBLICAL CRITICISM: BEGINNINGS, TRAJECTORIES, INTERSECTIONS

Stephen D. Moore and Fernando F. Segovia

The origins of the present volume go back a few years—to be precise, to the 1997 Annual Meeting of the Society of Biblical Literature and the months that followed. In the course of that meeting, the two of us discussed the possibility of launching a consultation that would bring together for mutual engagement and fertilization the discourses of Biblical Studies and Cultural Studies. We had both been working, in different contexts and from different perspectives, on such interaction, toward the development of a cultural biblical criticism,[1] and we thought that a program unit within the context of the Annual Meetings would allow us to do so in sustained and collective fashion. This idea we pursued in earnest through the remainder of 1997 and into the early months of 1998. While agreed on the overall focus for such a consultation, a beginning exploration into the nature and parameters of a biblical criticism informed and guided by Cultural Studies, the question of a specific angle of inquiry and a proper nomenclature for it soon forced itself upon us. What had been conceived in general terms had to be narrowed down.

In effect, within the Society at that time, a program unit bearing the designation 'Cultural Studies' in its title was already in existence. What had begun as a three-year consultation on Gender and Cultural Criticism (1993–1995), under the leadership of Alice Bach and J. Cheryl Exum, had petitioned, successfully, in 1996 to become a section, changing its name in the process to The Bible and Cultural Studies. While the rationale and aims of our envisioned consultation were not the same as those of this

---

1. In April of 1997, Moore, along with J. Cheryl Exum, had convened an international colloquium on the topic of 'Biblical into Cultural Studies' at the University of Sheffield, under the auspices of the Centre for Biblical and Cultural Studies. The colloquium papers were published the following year, in a co-edited volume entitled *Biblical Studies/Cultural Studies* (Exum and Moore 1998b). For this volume Moore co-authored with Exum the introduction, by the same title, with a focus on the history of Cultural Studies and its implications for biblical criticism (Exum and Moore 1998a; see also Moore 1998). In October of 1993, Segovia, along with Mary Ann Tolbert, had organized an international conference on the theme of 'Reading from This Place' at the Divinity School of Vanderbilt University. The conference papers appeared in 1995, under the title of *Reading from This Place*. Volume 2: *Social Location and Biblical Interpretation in Global Perspective* (Segovia and Tolbert 1995b). In this volume Segovia had two pieces, the introduction and a position paper, on a cultural studies approach to biblical criticism (Segovia 1995a, 1995b).

newly approved section,[2] we thought it most unlikely that the Program Committee would approve another unit under the very similar title of 'Cultural Studies and Biblical Studies', regardless of difference in description and goals. The question for us, therefore, became what to do within the ambit of our original plan, the proposed intersection between Biblical Studies and Cultural Studies, in such a way as to differentiate ourselves sufficiently, in both name and perspective, from this standing program unit. It was out of this search, then, that we came to settle on postcolonialism as the focus of inquiry.

Postcolonial Biblical Criticism: Beginnings

Indeed, it did not take long for such a solution to come to the fore: why not examine the intersection of Biblical Studies and Postcolonial Studies? The reasons for such a dialogue were many and substantial. To begin with, the reach of Postcolonial Studies in the academy at large was becoming ever broader and ever deeper, directly affecting any number of fields across the disciplinary spectrum. Indeed, introductions to, manuals for, and histories of such studies were rapidly multiplying. In addition, Postcolonial Studies could be readily considered as one of the manifold variations of Cultural Studies, so that our original intentions in this regard would be preserved in the process, in circumscribed but nonetheless effective and fruitful fashion. Lastly, both of us were by then becoming increasingly interested as well in pursuing the postcolonial optic in our respective scholarly agendas. Such a combination of academic, discursive, and personal reasons proved decisive in the end, and, by the early summer of 1998, we had arrived at a cordial agreement regarding our proposed angle of inquiry.

At the same time, such a decision happily coincided with certain developments within biblical criticism itself, where echoes of a postcolonial approach were beginning to make themselves felt. Thus, for example, already in 1996, a volume of *Semeia*, as always at the forefront of the

---

2.   The existing unit defined its mission in terms of a comparative analysis of the Bible as artefact and icon in word, image, and sound—a twofold analysis involving the impact of the Bible on Western culture and of Western culture on biblical interpretation. This mission involved interdisciplinary analysis of literary, visual, and auditory works, including the popular media. This mission also involved cultural analysis of gender, race, and class in both ancient and modern cultures. As such, its goals were listed as follows: (a) to investigate cultural appropriations of the Bible and the impact of cultural images on interpretation; (b) to encourage readings of the Bible in conjunction with extra-biblical works, from antiquity to the present; (c) to provide a forum for cultural analysis of gender, race, and class in biblical texts and interpretations; (d) to provide a forum, through the use of interdisciplinary and multimedia presentations, toward new developments in pedagogy and new areas of research in biblical criticism.

discipline, had been devoted, under the expert direction of Laura Donaldson, to the theme of 'Postcolonialism and Scriptural Reading' (1996a), about which volume we shall have more to say below.[3] Similarly, early in 1997, a series entitled 'The Bible and Postcolonialism' had been launched by Sheffield Academic Press, with the first volume, *The Postcolonial Bible*, already under way and scheduled for publication in 1998 (Sugirtharajah 1998b) and a number of other volumes under active consideration and development.[4] Moreover, for the fall of 1998, at the Annual Meeting of the Society, a panel discussion of *The Postcolonial Bible* had been scheduled as a featured session within the Bible in Africa, Asia, the Caribbean and Latin America Section (BAACLA). Even in biblical circles, therefore, postcolonialism was very much in the air. Our proposed unit would prove most timely, therefore; yet a quandary remained before us: should the unit opt for Biblical Studies in general or Early Christian Studies in particular? Substantial and persuasive argumentation could be marshaled in either direction.

On behalf of a more expansive reach, there was no question that the result would be to maximize the number of potential participants in the conversation and thus the impact of the consultation on the Society as a whole. On behalf of a more restricted reach, without doubt the result would be a more focused and integrated program. The latter option would center the discussion on the Roman Empire, while the former would have to contemplate and allow for studies ranging from a variety of imperial contexts, from Egypt, Assyria, and Babylon to Greece and Rome. A gain in scope would mean a loss in depth, and vice versa. This was by no means an easy decision to make; in the end, however, we decided to go with depth as preferable at this early stage of the conversation. Besides, such a focus, we felt, would prove more than sufficient, since we were contemplating studies regarding not only the texts themselves but also the interpretations of these texts. We thus settled on 'New Testament Studies and Postcolonial Studies' as title for both project and consultation. In any case, we thought, should a move from consultation to section be contemplated later on, once

3. Donaldson, based at the time at the University of Iowa and with broad interests in English, Women's Studies, and American Indian/Native Studies, had published in 1992 a highly influential volume on the intersection of race, gender, and colonialism (Donaldson 1992).

4. R.S. Sugirtharajah served as general editor for the series. The Editorial Board consisted of the following members: Marcella Althaus-Reid, Ralph Broadbent, Kwok Pui-lan, Sharon Ringe, and Fernando F. Segovia. Sugirtharajah, then at Selly Oak Colleges in Birmingham, England, played a key role in this project; by then, he had already written a number of articles on postcolonialism and biblical criticism, with a manuscript, bringing together some of these earlier studies and a number of new pieces, *Asian Biblical Hermeneutics and Postcolonialism: Contesting the Interpretations*, scheduled for publication in 1998 (Sugirtharajah 1998a).

the unit had run its appointed course, the question of reach could be revisited and reconsidered. Thus, a first draft of the proposal was drawn up during the summer of 1998; the membership of the Steering Committee was secured in the early fall; and a planning meeting was called for the Annual Meeting.[5]

At this meeting of the would-be Steering Committee, final touches were made on the proposal draft and a program was devised, as required, for the duration of the term. The proposal was then submitted to and approved by the Program Committee in the spring of 1999.[6] Given the rules of the Society regarding Annual Meetings, the consultation would not be able to begin its deliberations until the 2000 Annual Meeting, which would continue through 2002, leaving us a year and a half prior to our first actual gathering—much too long a wait to get going. Happily, a way was devised to begin in 1999 itself by borrowing a session from BAACLA. Both Sugirtharajah and Segovia were on the Steering Committee of this section, which, as it happened, was due to go out of existence with the 1999 Annual Meeting; our request for a special session was warmly received and approved. Thus, in effect, with the passing of BAACLA, the New Testament Studies and Postcolonial Studies Consultation came into being.

We decided to run in 1999 what was to have been our inaugural section—the immediate genesis for this volume. The Steering Committee felt that it would be wise and fruitful at the start to compare a postcolonial optic in criticism with other critical angles of inquiry at work in the discipline of similarly cultural and ideological concerns and interests. The session, chaired by Kwok Pui-lan, was drawn up as follows: Segovia would deal with the nature and parameters of postcolonialism as such; then, the contrast between postcolonialism and other discourses, with a focus on biblical criticism throughout, would be pursued as follows: feminism, Laura Donaldson; Marxism, David Jobling; poststructuralism, Moore; liberation, R.S. Sugirtharajah. This initial session proved quite successful,

---

5. We were both agreed that the Steering Committee should have broad representation, both in terms of religious studies and interdisciplinary studies; we were most fortunate to secure Laura Donaldson, Kwok Pui-lan and R.S. Sugirtharajah, all of whom readily agreed to join us in this undertaking.

6. The mission for the consultation, under the unifying focus of the New Testament and its interpreters throughout, was defined as the examination of the various representations of empire and colony and the ramifications of such constructions in the ancient Mediterranean world of the Roman Empire, in the modern world of Western imperialism and colonialism, and in the postmodern world of post-imperialism, postcolonialism, and globalization. Its goal was described as twofold: to examine the impact of imperial reality in the texts of the New Testament as well as in the interpretations and interpreters of these texts in both the modern and postmodern periods, since both texts and interpreters (and their interpretations) came out of sundry imperial realities.

with over a hundred and fifty people in attendance, and set the stage for the three sessions to follow through 2000–2002.

This initial session constitutes the foundations of the present volume. The idea of gathering these papers for publication was entertained from the first but not pursued right away for a variety of reasons. Chief among these was our commitment to see the consultation to its end before raising the question of publication. By that time, the postcolonial impulse in biblical criticism had multiplied significantly, giving rise to a steady flow of important publications, detailed in the section to follow. More than ever, therefore, we saw the need for a volume that would set forth postcolonial biblical criticism in the light of other critical angles in the discipline, and thus the idea of gathering the presentations from that first session was revived. A number of changes were in order, however.

First, Sugirtharajah had already published, in expanded fashion, his piece on liberation and postcolonialism elsewhere,[7] so we decided to include a second piece on Marxism, given the importance of this intersection not only within biblical criticism but also in postcolonial circles; for this we were able to secure the services of Roland Boer. Second, we now perceived a significant lacuna in the original round of papers, insofar as there had been no piece on racial and ethnic theory, again a most important preoccupation for both biblical and postcolonial criticisms; for this we were again able to secure the services of Tat-siong Benny Liew. Finally, the other pieces, originally written as oral presentations, would have to be significantly revised; all four individuals in question— Donaldson, Jobling, Moore, and Segovia—agreed to do so. The result is a unique volume, we believe, one that sets postcolonial biblical criticism in both disciplinary and interdisciplinary context, precisely at a point where its corpus of publications continues to witness swift expansion. Before summarizing the various contributions, an overview of this corpus is in order.

Postcolonial Biblical Criticism: Trajectories

How best to map the field of postcolonial biblical criticism? The task is already a complex one, notwithstanding the fact that less than a decade has elapsed since the terms 'postcolonial(ism)' and 'Bible' were first conjoined within Biblical Studies. The complexity arises from the difficulty of postulating where precisely it is that postcolonial biblical criticism begins or ends. Depending upon the example being considered, postcolonial biblical criticism seems to emerge out of liberation hermeneutics, or

---

7. See Sugirtharajah 2001: 203–75 and 2002: 103–23.

extra-biblical Postcolonial Studies, or even historical biblical criticism, or from all three sources at once. Three main clusters are thus in evidence.

The version of liberation hermeneutics out of which much postcolonial biblical criticism seems to flow is that relatively recent inflection of it variously termed contextual hermeneutics, vernacular hermeneutics (Sugirtharajah 1999b), or cultural studies (Segovia 2000a: 3–53). Acutely attuned to the sociocultural location of the biblical interpreter (cf. Segovia and Tolbert 1995a and b), contextual hermeneutics may be said to relinquish the central (frequently Marxist-driven) focus on economics and the universal plight of the poor typical of classic liberation theology for a focus on the local, the indigenous, the ethnic, and the culturally contingent, with the aim of recovering, reasserting, and reinscribing identities, cultures, and traditions that colonial Christianity had erased, suppressed, or pronounced 'idolatrous'.

How exactly is contextual hermeneutics related to postcolonial hermeneutics? The distance between the collection *Voices from the Margin: Interpreting the Bible in the Third World* (Sugirtharajah 1991)—an early landmark of contextual hermeneutics—and the collection *The Postcolonial Bible* (Sugirtharajah 1998b) is not considerable, but neither is it insignificant. The multinational contributors to the former volume frequently attend to the specter of colonialism, insufficiently exorcized even in the majority of nations that have officially undergone decolonization. Not surprisingly, the colonial (and the postcolonial) assume thematic centrality in a higher percentage of the essays in *The Postcolonial Bible*. Furthermore, the field of extra-biblical Postcolonial Studies provides at least some of the contributors with a fresh conceptual vocabulary and analytic apparatus with which to treat those themes in relation to biblical texts and their histories of interpretation and appropriation, unlike the earlier volume. Like most of the contributors to *Voices from the Margin*, however, most of the contributors to *The Postcolonial Bible* write explicitly out of their specific cultural locations, and this strategy, as much as the thematic focus on colonialism and its aftermath, might be said to be a defining trait of the collection.[8]

The still small subfield of postcolonial biblical criticism would be a good deal smaller still were it not for the prodigious industry of R.S. Sugirtharajah. Sugirtharajah's own relationship to liberation theology, as evinced especially by his monographs (1998a; 2001; 2002; 2003), appears to be one of obvious debt and partial estrangement. Not the least interesting feature of his work is his extensive internal critique of the liberationist tradition from a 'postcolonial' perspective (2001: 203–75; 2002: 103–23).

---

8. Further on *The Postcolonial Bible*, see the four reviews in the *Journal for the Study of the New Testament* 74 (1999), together with the response to those reviews in *JSNT* 75 (1999).

More straightforwardly rooted in liberation theology is *The Bible and Colonialism* by Michael Prior (1997), who two years earlier had published *Jesus the Liberator: Nazareth Liberation Theology (Luke 4.16-30)*. When Prior declares near the end of *The Bible and Colonialism*, a study of the multiple ways in which biblical land traditions have been pressed into service for colonial ends in Latin America, South Africa, and Palestine/ Israel, that he deems 'the ... work to be an exploration into terrain virtually devoid of enquirers' (p. 294), he is not exaggerating. His book was the first monograph on the title topic (Sugirtharajah's *Asian Biblical Hermeneutics and Postcolonialism* appeared the following year), and it has not yet received the attention it deserves within postcolonial biblical criticism. Another significant (although widely-read) work in this fledgling field is Musa W. Dube's *Postcolonial Feminist Interpretation of the Bible* (2000), which, unlike Prior's book, is a thoroughgoing example of contextual hermeneutics. Writing explicitly out of a Botswanan, and, more generally, black African cultural context, Dube enacts a 'decoloniz-ing' feminist reading of the Exodus and Conquest narratives in the Hebrew Bible, and of selected Matthean narratives, especially that of Jesus' encounter with the 'Canaanite' woman; provides a devastating critique of previous readings of the latter pericope by white Euro-American feminist interpreters; and champions 'ordinary' readings of the pericope issuing from women members of the African Independent Churches.

A second cluster of works that fit less cosily under the umbrella of postcolonial biblical criticism stand out as a group in the first instance by the recurrence of the word 'empire' in their titles, and they are located primarily on the New Testament side of the testamentary divide. The list includes *Paul and Empire* (Horsley 1997), *Matthew and Empire* (Carter 2001), *Unveiling Empire: Reading Revelation Then and Now* (Howard-Brook and Gwyther 1999), and *Jesus and Empire* (Horsley 2002). To this group belongs also, by reason of thematic focus and/or the name of Richard Horsley (a name even more prominent in this second cluster than Sugirtharajah's was in the first), such works as *Liberating Paul* (Elliott 1994), *The Message and the Kingdom: How Jesus and Paul Ignited a Revolution and Transformed the Ancient World* (Horsley and Silberman 1997), *Paul and Politics* (Horsley 2000), and *Hearing the Whole Story: The Politics of Plot in Mark's Gospel* (Horsley 2001). What all of the books in this cluster share in common is a sustained focus on the theme of empire as an exegetical lens through which to reframe and reread selected New Testament texts.

This, of course, is a lens that has always been employed by historical critics of the Bible: to reconstruct the various 'backgrounds' against which the historical critic's Bible becomes visible is, in part at least, to conjure up a succession of empires, beginning in earnest with the Assyrian Empire and ending with the Roman (cf. Moore 2000: 187–88). But whereas the more

traditional biblical scholar has tended to peer through that lens
intermittently, the particular authors in the cluster we are considering
tend to gaze through it unrelentingly. Despite a shared preoccupation with
empire, however, members of this cluster also differ from each other in at
least one significant respect. Whereas some of them seem solely interested
in the ancient imperial contexts in which the biblical texts were generated
(as is the case, for example, with the collection *Paul and Empire* or
Horsley's *Hearing the Whole Story*), others are intent on keeping the
ancient imperial contexts in tensive dialogue with the contemporary
contexts in which the biblical texts are appropriated (so, for example,
Howard-Brook and Gwyther's *Unveiling Empire* or Horsley's *Jesus and
Empire*). This preoccupation with reception is shared by certain authors in
our first cluster—consider Prior or Dube, for example, or, more especially,
Sugirtharajah (whose predominant preoccupation throughout his many
publications is with the history of biblical interpretation as a subset of the
history of colonialism and of resistance to colonialism)—suggesting that
the boundaries we are establishing here in this mapping of the field are, in
the end, highly permeable.

The mapping problem is further exacerbated by the fact that exceedingly
few of the authors in the 'X and Empire' cluster evince any interest in
affixing the label 'postcolonial' to their projects. Indeed, the most explicit
statement of location in relation to postcolonial studies in this body of
work, that of Sze-kar Wan introducing his contribution to *Paul and
Politics*, is a cautious one, and should induce a corresponding caution in
the cartographer: 'My reading here is not strictly postcolonial, but in some
aspects it does coincide with the goals of postcolonial studies in which
ethnic integrity, self-determination, anti-colonial and anti-imperial concerns are all inextricably intertwined' (p. 192, n. 5). Since cartography has
had a largely unfortunate connotation in the history of colonialism,
however, a map of postcolonial biblical criticism that disintegrates even as
it is being drawn is not altogether inappropriate.

Pressing on, we note a third cluster of works, this one distinguished by a
thoroughgoing engagement with the field of extra-biblical Postcolonial
Studies, in contrast to the light engagement characteristic of the first
cluster and the non-engagement characteristic of the second (although
there are exceptions in both camps). There is, of course, no shortage of
such work to engage, the past decade and a half having witnessed a small
stream of works on colonialism and imperialism, postcolonialism and
neocolonialism swell into a torrent and eventually a flood, most especially
in the field of Literary Studies. Leakage from this field, indeed, more than
any other single factor, might be said to account for the origins of
postcolonial biblical criticism. The first volume on the Bible and
colonialism to appear was *Postcolonial Literature and the Biblical Call
for Justice* (1994), edited by Susan VanZanten Gallagher, a Professor of

English, although it seems to have had little impact on postcolonial biblical criticism. More influential was the next such collection, *Postcolonialism and Scriptural Reading* (1996a), edited by Laura E. Donaldson, a Professor of English and Native American Studies.[9] It would be misleading, however, to relay the impression that all the essays in this eclectic collection—which range over topics as diverse as colonial Yehud under the Persian Empire; *El Evangelio de Lucas Gavilán*, a modern Mexican paraphrase of the Gospel of Luke; African-American spirituals; and the *faux* Australian Aboriginal novels of B. Wongar—are thoroughly rooted in extra-biblical Postcolonial Studies: some are, while others are not.

Notable among critics whose primary training was in Biblical Studies but who have achieved fluency in 'theory' as a kind of scholarly second language, not least postcolonial theory, are Erin Runions, whose *Changing Subjects* (2001) draws upon the analytic categories of the postcolonial theorist Homi Bhabha, bringing them to bear (against all the odds) upon the book of Micah; and Roland Boer, whose *Last Stop Before Antarctica* (2001a) ranges more eclectically across the theoretical landscape, and also ranges from the books of Exodus and Daniel to the journals of nineteenth-century European 'discoverers' of Australia. No less eclectic in inclination is Tat-siong Benny Liew, who harnesses a broad assortment of theoretical resources, not least those of Bhabha, to resituate Mark's story of Jesus in its multilayered imperial framework. Like Dube, but unlike any of the authors in our 'X and Empire' cluster, and also unlike classic liberation hermeneutics, Liew is sharply critical of the ideology of the biblical text he is considering. In Liew's work, as in Dube's, postcolonial biblical criticism meshes seamlessly with (is, indeed, an instance of) that other recent development in Biblical Studies known as 'ideological criticism' (cf. The Bible and Culture Collective 1995: 272–308).[10]

It is certainly no accident that Boer, Donaldson, and Liew are all contributors to the present volume, for, as the volume's subtitle implies, the particular version of postcolonial biblical criticism that it is most interested in exploring is the version that is most thoroughly interdisciplinary (not because we deem it to be intrinsically superior to the other versions we have considered but simply because it remains, as yet,

---

9.   Roland Boer's edited collection, *A Vanishing Mediator?* (2001b), can be considered the obverse of the Donaldson collection: instead of a literary scholar assembling a team largely composed of biblical scholars to ponder the Bible's intersections with empire, we have a biblical scholar assembling a team largely composed of literary scholars for the same task.

10.   Other significant volumes that we have been unable to weave into our narrative include Sugirtharajah 1999a; Segovia 2000b; Dube and Staley 2002. There are, of course, a considerable number of relevant individual articles and essays in addition that we have not discussed. Especially interesting is Lee 1999, which is followed by four response articles in the same issue, and a reply from Lee.

somewhat underdeveloped). To a description of the essays that make up the volume we now turn.

Postcolonial Biblical Criticism: Intersections

Biblical Criticism and Postcolonialism
In the first essay Fernando Segovia examines the juncture between Biblical Studies and Postcolonial Studies signified by postcolonial biblical criticism. This study thus sets the stage for the others to follow, providing a vision and configuration of this criticism prior to any consideration of it in light of other recent critical approaches. For Segovia, such criticism represents a type of ideological criticism, along the lines of various other such angles of inquiry at work in the discipline, among which feminist and liberation as well as minority and queer criticisms feature prominently. All such approaches, he argues, foreground relationships of domination and subordination, that is to say, uneven relationships of power. Each type highlights one such relationship in particular; for example: gender construction and interaction in feminist criticism; economic systems and class divisions in liberation criticism; ethnic/racial classification and stratification in minority criticism; sexuality and sexual orientation in queer criticism. For Segovia, then, it is the realm of the geopolitical that postcolonial criticism foregrounds—the uneven relationship of power at work between the imperial and the colonial. This claim of specificity is immediately qualified, however, to allow for a multiplicity of concerns in and intersections among all such approaches. Thus, for example, in addressing the geopolitical, postcolonial criticism would remain keenly attentive as well to issues of gender and class, race/ethnicity and sexual orientation, and any other such categories—all would be seen as imbricated and interacting. The same, of course, would be true, *mutatis mutandis*, of all other such approaches as well. The foregrounding in question is thus at once distinctive and convoluted.

Segovia undertakes the analysis of postcolonial biblical criticism from the perspective of biblical interpretation. As with any proposed disciplinary juncture, such criticism, he argues, must have a well-grounded and well-informed grasp of the postcolonial discussion. Toward this end, therefore, he sets out to establish the meaning and scope of the postcolonial problematic as advanced in such studies. This he does by way of a review of the literature encompassing a variety of critical genres: from brief surveys of the field in general introductions to critical movements, through a manual or general overview of the field, to detailed mappings of the field. The findings reveal an area of studies that is not only highly diverse but also highly conflicted. Given such a broad spectrum of opinion and such sharp intensity of debate, a number of fundamental decisions regarding what is understood by postcolonial criticism and what is the reach of such criticism are imperative in any application to biblical criticism.

With regard to object, five issues are identified as essential to any definition of the field: the force of the term; the nomenclature to be adopted; the terrain to be surveyed; the referential boundaries; and the nature of the encounter. To begin with, concerning the meaning of the term as such, a psychological or social reading is favored: the postcolonial as conscientization of the geopolitical problematic regardless of actual historical and political conditions. Second, regarding the meaning of imperialism and colonialism, a spatial understanding of such nomenclature is preferred: imperialism as referring to the center and colonialism as pointing to the periphery. Third, with respect to the terrain of inquiry to be pursued, a balanced view of the postcolonial is advanced: analysis of both cultural production and material matrix. Fourth, regarding the referential reach of the imperial–colonial relationship, a broad understanding is preferred: analysis of the periphery not only in terms of the center but also in its own terms. Finally, concerning the nature of imperial–colonial contact, a multifarious mode of encounter is favored: acknowledging and theorizing similarities and differences within (between center and periphery in any such formation) and among (between centers and peripheries in different formations) imperial–colonial structures. With regard to scope, two issues are singled out as essential to any determination of range in the field: a sense of proper comparative application and a sense of proper underlying frameworks. In terms of operative breadth, a view of the postcolonial as far-reaching is advanced: analyzing imperial–colonial formations across historical periods and cultural contexts, from antiquity to the present as well as both inside and outside the West. In terms of foundational context, a view of the postcolonial as wide-ranging is proposed: embracing a variety of political and economic frameworks, inside as well as outside those of modernity and capitalism.

In sum, Segovia sees ample room in Postcolonial Studies for a view of its envisioned range as transhistorical and transcultural and of its proposed task as highly comparative in nature. Thus, from the point of view of disciplinary parameters, the application of the postcolonial angle of vision to biblical criticism emerges as entirely warranted. Similarly, from the point of view of disciplinary meaning, such application can be readily formulated and executed along the major lines of reference outlined above. The result is a properly grounded and properly informed postcolonial biblical criticism. Thereby, Segovia concludes, two significant lacunae in Postcolonial Studies can be directly addressed: its lack of attention to the realm of antiquity (critical focus on imperial–colonial formations in the biblical contexts) and its omission of matters religious (critical focus on the religious realm by way of cultural production and material matrix).

Postcolonial Biblical Criticism and Poststructuralism
Stephen Moore's piece opens with an examination of the relationship between the two 'post-'terms of the title—postcolonialism and postmodernism. These terms should not be treated as virtual synonyms, Moore argues, notwithstanding the fact that colonialism was an enabling facet of modernity. Postmodernism, conceived at its broadest as the global culture of late capitalism, is less a synonym for *post*colonialism than for *neo*colonialism, and as such in need of postcolonial critique. Within academic culture, a third 'post-'term, namely, poststructuralism, regularly mediates between the other two. Postcolonial theory, in particular, epitomized by the work of Edward Said, Gayatri Chakravorty Spivak, and Homi Bhabha, is poststructuralist through and through. Moore proceeds to rehearse, and respond to, some of the scathing attacks that have been launched against postcolonial theory.

Moore then turns to a protracted discussion of Bhabha's 'Signs Taken for Wonders: Questions of Ambivalence and Authority under a Tree outside Delhi, May 1817', a text in which postcolonial studies, poststructuralist theory, and biblical interpretation interface and interlace. Bhabha's essay, one of his best-known, improvises upon an anecdote from an 1818 issue of the *Missionary Register* that describes a dialogue between an Indian Christian catechist and representatives of a throng of five hundred 'poor and lowly' Hindus that has assembled outside Delhi to read and discuss some translated Bibles earlier distributed to them. What interests Bhabha about this encounter is the way in which 'the English book' par excellence, at once the book of mission and of empire, redolent with immutable meaning and authority, is effectively rewritten in the process of being reread, its presumed univocity and universality thereby being deconstructed. Discussion of the issues raised by the essay nonetheless leads into the thorny question of agency in Bhabhan theory. Where do the forms of resistance to colonial domination that most preoccupy him—forms encapsulated in the terms ambivalence, mimicry, and hybridity—actually occur? In the consciousness of the individual colonial subject? Or in his or her subconscious, or unconscious? Or in the tide of discourse that ebbs and flows between colonizer and colonized, with erosive effect?

Postcolonial Biblical Criticism and Feminism
In her introduction to *Postcolonialism and Scriptural Reading*, Donaldson described postcolonial criticism as oppositional reading, a 'reading like Canaanites': a rescue of voices in the text silenced by dominant readings of the text (Donaldson 1996b). Such oppositional reading she further characterized as multidimensional in nature, keenly attentive to the intricacies of the colonial situation in terms of culture, race, class, and

gender. Her contribution on postcolonialism and feminism in this volume is very much in line with the vision offered in that earlier programmatic statement.

Here the work of Gayatri Chakravorty Spivak functions as point of departure in various respects. First, in terms of her proposal for a new postcolonial model, planetarity, meant to encompass all those missing in the dominant social texts of global studies. Second, by way of her strategy of ethical singularity, whereby an ethical relationship is established with a single figure, so that the realm of the ethical can function at the level of relationship rather than knowledge. Third, in terms of her notion of spectrality, which allows past histories to interrupt the hegemonic in the present. Thus, Donaldson agrees with a move beyond the old postcolonial model, singling out in particular its failure to include gender and sexuality within its angle of vision, thereby relegating women to the category of the colonized. Similarly, she sets out to establish an ethical relationship with a specific figure from the Gospel narratives, a female character systematically passed over in interpretation. Finally, in so doing, she lets herself be haunted by this figure in terms of disability and indigeneity. The study constitutes, therefore, the rescue of a forgotten voice of distinct complexity.

The figure in question is the demon-possessed daughter of the Syro-Phoenician and Canaanite woman in the Gospels of Mark (7.24-30) and Matthew (15.21-28). While the character of the mother has drawn attention from feminist and postcolonial scholars in recent times, displacing traditional interpretations and yielding anti-colonial readings of the story, that of the daughter has not. Doing so, Donaldson ventures, will serve to displace and reconfigure, in turn, anti/postcolonial readings of the story. Donaldson develops her ethical relationship with the daughter in steps. First, through the issue of disability—she cannot speak on her own behalf and has no say over her healing. The Bible, Donaldson points out, systematically engages in the erasure of disability by presenting all such characters as objects in need of divine action, not only dehumanizing them but also depriving them of their own fresh view of reality. Consequently, instead of approaching the daughter as a body out of control, an example of individualism run rampant, Donaldson argues for a view of her as a disturber of social order, an agent of transformation. Second, through the issue of gender—she shows, when compared with the Gerasene demoniac, that possession itself is constructed in gendered terms. Thus, the presence of stereotypical male and female attributes in possession resist any simple collapse as the colonized. Finally, through the angle of indigeneity—she, taking a cue from the Matthean account, is a 'Canaanite' and hence associated with the original inhabitants of the land, an indigenous woman. From this perspective, Donaldson suggests, her silence may point to shamanism, involving an altered form of consciousness and yielding a sacred and special site of knowledge. This last step in the relationship is expanded through the invocation of an earlier ghost: the figure of the Medium of Endor from 1 Samuel 28.3-25, a story that bears similar witness to the persistence of the indigenous and the shamanistic under a situation of occupation and domination.

In the end, this ethical relationship has produced what Donaldson characterizes as a biblical hauntology. The ghosts traced in and through the figure of the demon-possessed daughter point in a different interpretive direction than those followed by feminist and postcolonial versions of the story. Such haunting surfaces instead considerations of disability, gender, and indigeneity—all of which serve to disrupt and reconfigure postcolonial criticism. That, in turn, emerges as the distinctive contribution of feminism to postcolonialism: a reading that is at once oppositional and multi-dimensional, allowing for the rescue of all silenced voices everywhere and thus in keeping with the vision of planetarity advanced by Spivak. For Donaldson, as her work clearly demonstrates, such a model of planetarity should be at work in postcolonial biblical criticism, and toward this end feminism can play a key and indispensable role.

Postcolonial Biblical Criticism and Ethnic/Racial Studies

Tat-siong Benny Liew's study begins by surveying scholarship on the crystallization, or possible creation, of race as an ideology in the modern period. Liew then ponders the fortunes and potential futures of race in a postmodern and globalized world, invoking—although not without caution—Paul Gilroy's Utopian vision of a postracial, planetary human-ism. Turning to ethnicity, Liew surveys attempted definitions of the term and reflections on its relationship to race. Ethnicity turns out to be an extremely fluid and elusive concept, subject to recurrent temporal and cultural mutations—not that race can be conceived in contrast as a fixed or stable concept, as Liew is careful to note. Proceeding to examine the historical and conceptual links between race/ethnicity and colonialism/postcolonialism, Liew argues that each pair of terms is intimately intertwined with the other. Yet the two pairs should not simply be allowed to collapse into each other, since colonialism can operate outside the parameters of race and even ethnicity. At the same time, an adequate understanding of much that falls under the purview of post/colonialism requires a correspondingly adequate understanding of race/ethnicity.

Within New Testament studies, race or ethnicity have received little theoretical attention even from scholars who engage explicitly with them, most proceeding as though these terms are immediately or intuitively transparent. Furthermore, scholars who have used the terms as inter-pretive categories have tended not to adduce the categories of colonialism or postcolonialism in addition. There are, however, exceptions to the rule, and Liew proceeds to review their work, before turning to distinguish several different strategies for reading New Testament texts in relation to race/ethnicity and/or post/colonialism. Continuing this taxonomic thrust, Liew isolates and ponders several topics and/or problems that he sees as being of particular importance for such work: the vernacular (which he considers in relation to 'exotic essentialism' or nativism); diasporic identity; sexuality; psychoanalytic theory; community; and biblical authority. His final substantive section consists of an extended reflection on Theresa Hak Kyung Cha's Asian-American novel *Dictée*, a work that Liew sees as simultaneously a consummate racial/ethnic and postcolonial text and—more unexpectedly, since it is work of fiction—an illustration of cutting-edge biblical scholarship.

Postcolonial Biblical Criticism and Marxism (I)
Roland Boer's study represents a sharp indictment of postcolonial theory in general and postcolonial biblical criticism in particular on the grounds that both largely ignore the contributions of Marx and the Marxist tradition to the analysis of imperialism and colonialism and that, in so doing, both turn their backs on their own history. In response, Boer offers, by way of Ernst Bloch and the Christian–Marxist dialogue of the 1950s and 1960s, a vision of a postcolonial biblical criticism that takes to heart issues of political economy, class divisions, and class conflict.

    The shift away from the Marxist tradition in postcolonial theory Boer traces to the way in which such theory has dealt with its precursors— theorists prior to the emergence of theory itself, from the foundational figures of Karl Marx and Vladimir Lenin to later critics of colonialism in the Marxist tradition. What distinguished this tradition, Boer argues, was its combination of analysis of imperialism in terms of capitalist expansion, study of cultural production in the local context, and level of political involvement. The process of detachment from this tradition, then, involves a separation of key aspects of Marxist theory from Marxism and the resultant negation of their political potential. It is a process, he observes, that can be readily observed at work in Said, through Spivak, to Bhabha. In the case of Said, it was the result of reading Antonio Gramsci in the light of Michel Foucault: a view of power as diffuse rather than centralized, leading to a watering down of the concept of hegemony as forged in the Marxist tradition. With Spivak, it was due to a reading of Marxism with the lens of Jacques Derrida: a deconstructive exposé of incoherence at the core of dominant discourses, opening the way thereby for the marginalized but also yielding a de-fanged portrait of Marx along the lines of leftist liberalism. In the case of Bhabha, it was the result of reading Mikhail Bakhtin in the light of Jacques Lacan: a psychoanalytic approach, in itself idiosyncratic and problematic, that surfaced hybridity, leading to a toning down of the concept of dialogism as developed in the Marxist tradition. To be sure, Boer concedes, postcolonial theory proved successful in creating an alternative history by rescuing a wealth of resistance; at the same time, he wonders whether, in leaving Marxist theory aside, such work can account for the struggles of liberation or rather renders all such resistance powerless in the face of imperialism.

Such eschewing of the Marxist tradition, Boer continues, can be readily detected as well in postcolonial biblical criticism, where references to Said, Spivak, and Bhabha abound but not to Marx or Marxist critiques. An analysis of the works of R.S. Sugirtharajah and Mark Brett brings the point home. On the one hand, Sugirtharajah explicitly portrays postcolonialism as the proper successor to Marxism and liberation, given the failure of socialism, the rise of global capitalism, and the loss of political momentum in the Third World. Thus, Marxism has ceased to be a viable alternative in terms of political economy, opposition to capitalism, or political option for the Third World. Similarly, liberation is no longer applicable, given its excessive focus on texts, its disregard for major and popular religion alike, and its homogenization of the poor. It is postcolonialism, therefore—a postcolonialism grounded not in the major discourses of the First World but in the imaginative literature of the Third World—that can provide a proper praxis for liberation today. For Boer, not only is such liberation demarxified but also such grounding deprives postcolonialism of tools for resistance available within imperialism itself, including Marxism. Brett, on the other hand, approaches Genesis from a variety of theoretical perspectives, identifying postcolonial theory as a main source of inspiration and without any direct reference to Marx or Marxism. The result is a reading of Genesis through Bakhtin as interpreted by Bhabha: two voices at work in the text, one dominant and one subversive, assigned to different authors. For Boer, a Marxist reading would show that both voices come from the ruling class itself and represent but different positions within it.

In light of such developments and omissions, Boer argues, it is imperative for both postcolonial theory and postcolonial biblical criticism to recover their theoretical and enabling history in the Marxist tradition. For this purpose, the figure of Ernst Bloch is offered as an exemplary resource: a Marxist with an interest in the Bible and biblical criticism and with a dialogic strategy of reading cast in economic and class terms. In effect, for Bloch the Bible is a text riven with class conflict and hence the category of class becomes indispensable for criticism. Thus, within the Bible one finds, in highly complex and ever-shifting fashion, traditions that convey the ideology and power of the oppressor and traditions that reflect subversion or rebellion on the part of the oppressed. As a result, the task of criticism becomes, through careful attention to textual layers and turns, that of properly sifting between such conflicting traditions. Indeed, criticism emerges thereby as a political tool—an unearthing of alternatives to the dominant system. It is precisely such work, now far more attuned to the complexities and shifts of the text, that Marxist criticism can and must bring to biblical postcolonial studies. In the end, however, Boer proves less than hopeful in this regard: first, on account of his belief that the voices of the oppressed are not as evident throughout the Bible as Bloch would have it; second, in light of the deleterious impact of the events of 1989–1990 on the fortunes of Marxism as a whole.

Postcolonial Biblical Criticism and Marxism (II)

David Jobling's essay certainly shares in the indictment of postcolonial theory and postcolonial biblical criticism advanced by Boer, but to a much lesser extent. The former's occlusion of Marxist history and critique, operative in the latter as well, is both granted and softened: such obliviousness, Jobling comments, while indisputable and detrimental, may not be as intentional or thoroughgoing as portrayed, nor should the lack of Marxist history in postcolonial contexts or the collapse of the global center for Marxism be underestimated. However, rather than pursuing such lines of thought (rereading the foundational figures of postcolonial theory, addressing the historical absence of attention to social class and social conflict in regions of the world, or theorizing the fall of communism from a Marxist perspective), the essay launches in a different direction altogether. In effect, what Jobling does is to project Marxism and postcolonialism as options within a dialectic of liberation encompassing the local and the global. This balancing relationship is elaborated as follows: on the one hand, a myriad of local sites, each engaged in a particular struggle for liberation; on the other hand, a variety of global discourses, each providing an ideological framework to local sites for direction and support in the struggle. Such discourses include, among others, Marxism and what he calls the Bible/Christianity, and now, Jobling would add, Postcolonial Studies as well. In this view, moreover, these ideological options relate not only to the local venues but also, and in so doing, to one another as well, thus intersecting and challenging one another. For Jobling, therefore, postcolonialism ultimately challenges Marxism, just as Marxism challenges postcolonialism.

As point of departure, Jobling chooses a local site: not his own, but the South Africa of the late 1980s, still engaged in the struggle against apartheid, as analyzed by Takatso Mofokeng. This is a situation portrayed as having limited ideological options at its disposal: Marxism as too far advanced; traditional African religions as too far behind; the Bible/ Christianity as appropriate for the time being. Such analysis Jobling describes as characteristically anti-colonial in nature, yet devoid of postcolonial theory. On the one hand, he points out, the latter was still in its formative stages at the time—postcolonialism would not emerge as a discourse until the early 1990s. On the other hand, he observes, even if it had been available, it would not have been of much use—when it did emerge, it was in the academic centers of the metropolis, away from local contexts and decidedly global in tone. If postcolonialism, then, is to function as a viable ideological option—alongside other such global discourses as Marxism and the Bible/Christianity—in and for the struggle, it has to bring together the untheorized aggregate of local scenes and the theoretical apparatus of postcolonial analysis, still, admittedly, insufficiently theorized. Indeed, Jobling warns, a fundamental danger facing postcolonialism lies precisely in distancing itself from and forgetting the local sites of struggle.

For Jobling, the importance of Marxism and the Bible/Christianity for the local goes without question. Both provide historically global ambitions and connections—in some respects, problematic, given their traditional penchant for domination (and, in the case of the Bible/Christianity, its collusion with colonialism); in other respects, useful, given their worldwide structures and influence. Thus, the local can readily and effectively call upon international socialism or the worldwide church for orientation and assistance in the working out of its agenda. Throughout, however, it is the local site that drives the agenda and chooses the appropriate ideological option, or combination of options, for the situation in question, thus channeling such an agenda along specific ideological lines. As another such option, Jobling argues, postcolonialism could play a very significant role in this regard as well.

This question is pursued from the point of view of postcolonial biblical criticism—how can such criticism be conceptualized and exercised for this purpose? The answer is as a crossroads of the Bible/Christianity, Marxism, and postcolonialism. To begin with, such criticism should have a broad conception of biblical interpretation, one that encompasses not only the domain of the academy and its professional practitioners but also all modes of interpretation present in the churches. This is what Jobling means by the Bible/Christianity—in effect, Biblical Studies writ large. In addition, such criticism should avoid easy comparison between imperial–colonial frameworks across history and adopt instead a Marxist analysis based on mode of production at work in different historical periods. Thus, for Jobling, what constitutes resistance and liberation in one mode of production, say, slavery in the Roman Empire, cannot be translated willy-nilly to another mode of production, say, globalization in present-day late capitalism. Finally, such criticism should take to heart the postcolonial critique of Marxism itself as a grand colonial narrative and the postmodernist concern with subsystems of domination, largely ignored in traditional Marxism. At the same time, it should avoid dangers inherent in postcolonialism: not only aloofness from the local, but also turning faddish, adopting a binomial opposition between developed and undeveloped areas, and avoiding self-criticism.

In the relationship between the local and the global, Jobling argues, postcolonialism stands above all in need of hybridity. This would be true as well of all other ideological options, including the Bible/Christianity and Marxism. Global discourses must make themselves serviceable to local sites in ways that will vary from site to site, from time to time, and thus hybrid relationships are of the essence in attending to the local. Thus, hybridity should be at the heart of postcolonial biblical criticism as well. Its goal should be to bring together—in shifting fashion, as the situation may require—the triad of biblical interpretation, Marxist history and tradition, and postcolonial analysis. By way of conclusion, Jobling returns to the problematic between Marxism and postcolonialism. Toward this goal of hybridity, Marxist analysis would supply such criticism with a mode of production that would encompass both past and present, allowing critics to examine not only the world of antiquity but also the location of criticism itself. Indeed, Jobling concludes, postcolonial biblical criticism could conceivably serve at present, in the aftermath of the fall of socialism, as a means of acquainting readers with Marxism in contexts where no history or tradition of it is to be found or where such tradition and history have been considerably weakened—a Marxism, to be sure, duly filtered through the critique of postcolonialism and postmodernism.

Postcolonial Biblical Criticism: Concluding Remarks

The preceding summary of contents shows how postcolonial biblical criticism may be conceived and practiced not only in terms of postcolonial analysis as such but also in the light of other critical discourses at work in biblical interpretation. The former dimension reveals the range of formulation and application possible within the proposed interdisciplinary intersection, while the latter details the theoretical and methodological caveats and benefits to be garnered from other interdisciplinary intersections. The result is a vision of postcolonial biblical criticism as complex and conflicted as well as diverse and hybrid. In retrospect, this is perhaps the sort of volume that should precede all work in a new line of interpretation, clearing the critical space necessary for such work to be undertaken within a discipline, but that tends rather to follow such work, pausing early on to cast a critical glance backward and forward, analyzing past trajectories and envisioning future directions. In any case, it is our hope that its appearance at this point—as the postcolonial problematic, barely ten years after its emergence, continues to have ever greater impact on biblical criticism—proves of value, both by way of theory and practice, to its future configuration, development, and expansion.

Bibliography

The Bible and Culture Collective
 1995 *The Postmodern Bible* (New Haven: Yale University Press).
Boer, Roland
 2001a *Last Stop Before Antarctica: The Bible and Postcolonialism in Australia* (The Bible and Postcolonialism, 6; Sheffield: Sheffield Academic Press).
Boer, Roland (ed.)
 2001b *A Vanishing Mediator? The Presence/Absence of the Bible in Postcolonialism* (*Semeia* 88; Atlanta: Society of Biblical Literature).
Carter, Warren
 2001 *Matthew and Empire: Initial Explorations* (Harrisburg: Trinity Press International).
Donaldson, Laura E.
 1992 *Decolonizing Feminisms: Race, Gender, and Empire-Building* (Chapel Hill: University of North Carolina Press).
 1996b 'Postcolonialism and Biblical Reading: An Introduction', in Donaldson 1996a: 1–14.
Donaldson, Laura E. (ed.)
 1996a *Postcolonialism and Scriptural Reading* (*Semeia* 75; Atlanta: Scholars Press).
Dube, Musa W.
 2000 *Postcolonial Feminist Interpretation of the Bible* (St. Louis: Chalice Press).
Dube, Musa W., and Jeffrey L. Staley (eds.)
 2002 *John and Postcolonialism: Travel, Space and Power* (The Bible and Postcolonialism, 7; Sheffield: Sheffield Academic Press).
Elliott, Neil
 1994 *Liberating Paul: The Justice of God and the Politics of the Apostle* (Maryknoll: Orbis Books).
Exum, J. Cheryl and Moore, Stephen D.,
 1998a 'Biblical Studies/Cultural Studies', in Exum and Moore 1998: 19–45.
Exum, J. Cheryl and Moore, Stephen D (eds.)
 1998b *Biblical Studies/Cultural Studies* (The Third Sheffield Colloquium; *Journal for the Study of the Old Testament*, Supplement Series 266; Gender, Culture, Theory, 7; Sheffield: Sheffield Academic Press).
Gallagher, Susan VanZanten (ed.)
 1994 *Postcolonial Literature and the Biblical Call for Justice* (Jackson: University Press of Mississippi).
Horsley, Richard A.
 2001 *Hearing the Whole Story: The Politics of Plot in Mark's Gospel* (Louisville: Westminster John Knox Press).
 2002 *Jesus and Empire: The Kingdom of God and the New World Disorder* (Minneapolis: Fortress Press).

Horsley, Richard A. (ed.)
1997   *Paul and Empire: Religion and Power in Roman Imperial Society* (Harrisburg: Trinity Press International).
2000   *Paul and Politics: Ekklesia, Israel, Imperium, Interpretation: Essays in Honor of Krister Stendahl* (Harrisburg: Trinity Press International).

Horsley, Richard A., and Neil Asher Silberman
1997   *The Message and the Kingdom: How Jesus and Paul Ignited a Revolution and Transformed the Ancient World* (New York: Grossett/Putnam).

Howard-Brook, Wes, and Anthony Gwyther
1999   *Unveiling Empire: Reading Revelation Then and Now* (Bible and Liberation Series; Maryknoll: Orbis Books).

Lee, Archie C.C.
1999   'Returning to China: Biblical Interpretation in Postcolonial Hong Kong', *Biblical Interpretation* 7: 156–73.

Liew, Tat-siong Benny
1999   *Politics of Parousia: Reading Mark Inter(con)textually* (Biblical Interpretation Series, 42; Leiden: Brill).

Moore, Stephen D.
2000   'Colonialism/Postcolonialism', in A.K.M. Adam (ed.), *A Handbook of Postmodern Biblical Interpretation* (St. Louis: Chalice Press): 182–88.

Moore, Stephen D. (ed.)
1998   *In Search of the Present: The Bible through Cultural Studies* (*Semeia* 82; Atlanta: Scholars Press, 1998).

Prior, Michael
1995   *Jesus the Liberator: Nazareth Liberation Theology (Luke 4:16-30)* (The Biblical Seminar, 26; Sheffield: Sheffield Academic Press).
1997   *The Bible and Colonialism: A Moral Critique* (The Biblical Seminar, 48; Sheffield: Sheffield Academic Press).

Runions, Erin
2001   *Changing Subjects: Gender, Nation and Future in Micah* (Playing the Texts, 7; Sheffield: Sheffield Academic Press).

Segovia, Fernando F.
1995a   'Cultural Studies and Contemporary Biblical Criticism: Ideological Criticism as Mode of Discourse', in Segovia and Tolbert 1995b: 1–17.
1995b   'Toward Intercultural Criticism: A Reading Strategy from the Diaspora', in Segovia and Tolbert 1995b: 303–30.
2000a   *Decolonizing Biblical Studies: A View from the Margins* (Maryknoll: Orbis Books).

Segovia, Fernando F. (ed.)
2000b   *Interpreting Beyond Borders* (The Bible and Postcolonialism, 3; Sheffield: Sheffield Academic Press).

Segovia, Fernando F., and Mary Ann Tolbert (eds.)
      1995a   *Reading from This Place*: Vol. 1, *Social Location and Biblical Interpretation in the United States* (Minneapolis: Fortress Press).
      1995b   *Reading from This Place*: Vol. 2, *Social Location and Biblical Interpretation in Global Perspective* (Minneapolis: Fortress Press).
Sugirtharajah, R.S.
      1998a   *Asian Biblical Hermeneutics and Postcolonialism: Contesting the Interpretations* (Maryknoll: Orbis Books; Sheffield: Sheffield Academic Press).
      2001   *The Bible and the Third World: Precolonial, Colonial and Postcolonial Encounters* (Cambridge: Cambridge University Press).
      2002   *Postcolonial Criticism and Biblical Interpretation* (Oxford: Oxford University Press).
      2003   *Postcolonial Reconfigurations: An Alternative Way of Reading the Bible and Doing Theology* (St. Louis: Chalice Press).
Sugirtharajah, R.S. (ed.)
      1991   *Voices from the Margin: Interpreting the Bible in the Third World* (Maryknoll: Orbis Books).
      1998b   *The Postcolonial Bible* (The Bible and Postcolonialism, 1; Sheffield: Sheffield Academic Press).
      1999a   *Postcolonial Perspectives on the New Testament and Its Interpretation*, Special Issue, *Journal for the Study of the New Testament* 73.
      1999b   *Vernacular Hermeneutics* (The Bible and Postcolonialism, 2; Sheffield: Sheffield Academic Press).
Wan, Sze-kar
      2000   'Collection for the Saints as Anticolonial Act: Implications of Paul's Ethnic Reconstruction', in Horsley 2000: 191–215.

Mapping the Postcolonial Optic in Biblical Criticism: Meaning and Scope

Fernando F. Segovia

I have argued for a confluence of Biblical Studies and Postcolonial Studies. This I have done from within the paradigm of cultural studies in biblical criticism, with its distinctively ideological mode of discourse.[1] By this I mean that type of discourse that foregrounds and theorizes a relationship or set of relationships involving domination and subordination. In so doing, therefore, I argue no more and no less than for a confluence of academic formations and critical discourses similar to those already at work between Biblical Studies and such other fields as Feminist Studies, Third World Studies, Minority Studies, Gay and Lesbian Studies. In effect, just as feminist criticism foregrounds the question of gender, liberation criticism that of class, minority criticism that of ethnicity–race, and queer criticism that of sexual orientation, so, I would argue, does postcolonial criticism highlight the question of geopolitics— the realm of the political at the translocal or global level, with specific reference to the phenomenon of imperial–colonial formations.[2] Post-colonial criticism highlights, therefore, the relationship between center and periphery, metropolis and margins—in effect, the imperial and the colonial.

What is the purpose behind such confluence? This is a question that can be approached from either critical formation. I do so here from the point of view of Biblical Studies. It could be done just as well from the perspective of Postcolonial Studies, although in point of fact, as I shall note in the conclusion, religion has not featured prominently in such analysis. My option for Biblical Studies as entrée simply reflects the path of my own journey to this discussion. As a discipline, Biblical Studies constitutes a fundamental component of Christian Studies or the academic study of Christianity, alongside such other components as Historical Studies, Theological Studies, Moral Studies, and Practical Studies. Its

---

1. See Segovia 2000: 119–32 (Ch. 5: 'Biblical Criticism and Postcolonial Studies: Toward a Postcolonial Optic') and 133–42 (Ch. 6: 'Notes toward Refining the Postcolonial Optic').

2. To be sure, as soon as such a statement of focus is made, it has to be taken back. Feminist criticism does a great deal more than address the question of gender, and the same applies, *mutatis mutandis*, to liberation, minority, queer, and postcolonial criticism. Nevertheless, the statement, deficient as it evidently is, proves useful as a first charting of the terrain within ideological discourse and criticism.

focus is on the foundations and beginnings of Christianity.[3] As a field of studies, in turn, Christian Studies represents a fundamental component of Religious Studies or the academic study of religion, alongside other such components as, say, Buddhist Studies, Islamic Studies, or African Religions Studies. The focus of Religious Studies, as I have come to understand it, is on constructions of the other-world (the world[s] of gods and spirits), the this-world (the world of nature and humanity), and the relationship between these worlds offered in the different religious traditions. Consequently, Christian Studies analyzes such constructions within the Christian tradition as a whole, while Biblical Studies does so in terms of the 'biblical' texts, which I see as comprehending both the canonical and the extra-canonical literature—the literature of ancient Israel and the literature of early Christianity.

In bringing Biblical Studies and Postcolonial Studies together, therefore, the purpose is to analyze how the imperial–colonial phenomenon bears on such study. This it does, I would argue, in three ways. An initial word of clarification is in order. To begin with, I see Biblical Studies as involving the analysis of not only the texts of antiquity but also the interpretation of such texts and the interpreters behind such interpretations—the remains, the representations, and the artificers of antiquity. In addition, I see all three such dimensions of the discipline as involving imperial–colonial frameworks: the production of the texts—the world of antiquity, the world of the Near East and the Mediterranean Basin; the reception of the texts by way of the history of interpretation and its interpreters in the West—the world of modernity, the world of Western expansionism and hegemony; the reception of the texts by way of the recent expansion of interpretation and interpreters on a global scale—the world of postmodernity, the world of postcolonialism and neocolonialism. Consequently, as I see it, postcolonial criticism seeks to analyze how the imperial–colonial phenomenon bears on constructions of the other-world, the this-world, and their relationship as advanced in the texts themselves, as construed in the established tradition of readings and readers in the West, and as offered in the contemporary production of readings and readers in the world at large.

How is this confluence to be carried out? For postcolonial criticism to proceed in a well-grounded and well-informed fashion, it is imperative to

---

3. Clearly, I speak here from the point of view of the Christian tradition, both culturally and ideologically. For the tradition, the Bible consists of two bodies of work, traditionally characterized as the 'Old Testament' and the 'New Testament', involving, respectively, the canonical literature of ancient Judaism (defined in different ways by different churches) and the canonical literature of early Christianity (accepted by all churches). Within the tradition, therefore, the conception and exercise of Biblical Studies involves both bodies of work or 'testaments'.

have a solid grasp on the object and parameters of Postcolonial Studies. No more and no less would be asked of anyone who would bring Feminist, Liberation, Minority, or Gay and Lesbian Studies to bear on Biblical Studies. This, however, is a task easier said than done. This is a field of studies that is by no means monolithic but rather highly diverse and conflicted, so that even the definition of the term 'postcolonial' emerges as not at all unproblematic. In this regard, to be sure, the postcolonial optic in biblical criticism proves no different from any other, whether that of gender, class, ethnicity–race, or sexual orientation—these too are all highly diverse and highly conflicted formations and discourses. As such, the adoption of a postcolonial optic calls for no more and no less than the same kind of critical interaction—rigorous and sophisticated—exercised in previous and ongoing incorporations of such other optics into Biblical Studies.

In bringing the optic of geopolitics, of the imperial and the colonial, to bear on biblical criticism, therefore, it is essential to come to terms with the meaning and scope of 'postcolonial' analysis. This I propose to do by way of a review of the literature, with two specific questions in mind: first, what is understood by 'postcolonial' criticism? Second, what is the reach envisioned for such criticism? This review I shall conduct in terms of two different genres: on the one hand, overviews of the field taken from general introductions to critical movements; on the other, mappings of the field taken from detailed introductions to the field as such. By way of transition, I shall look at a recent manual of postcolonial studies—a general introduction to the field. Needless to say, given the scope of the literature in question, the proposed review is representative rather than comprehensive in nature. My aim is not to offer a definitive terminology and conceptual apparatus for all to follow but rather to attain a measure of clarity and consistency, a functional definition, in my own appeal to and use of the field. To put it in other words, by analyzing how 'postcolonial' analysis has been defined and circumscribed in the literature, it is my intention to arrive at a definition and circumscription of my own.

Overviews: Postcolonial Studies as Critical Movement

With the decline of traditional historicism, the rise of formalism, and the more recent and still ongoing explosion of reading strategies and theoretical movements in literary studies, a new genre of literature has gradually come into being. I am referring to the phenomenon of introductory volumes, encompassing both the concise manual form and the expansive encyclopedic form, to the broad spectrum of methods and theories on the critical scene. Sometimes these volumes focus on basic terminology and concepts; sometimes on major currents and figures; and sometimes on both. Such volumes I have always found most informative and most useful and they have become indispensable to the contemporary critical scene. Rather surprisingly, however, not all such introductions contain entries on Postcolonial Studies;[4] some do, however, and I shall deal with these in chronological order.

The Johns Hopkins Guide to Literature & Criticism (1995)[5]
This first example, authored by Georg M. Gugelberger and best described as midway between the concise manual form and the extended encyclopedic form, begins by situating what the author calls 'Postcolonial Cultural Studies' (PCS) within the academy as a variant, a 'major intervention' (p. 581), within a much wider revisionist project at work since the 1960s. Thus, PCS—sometimes used as such; sometimes with the adjective 'cultural' in parentheses; and sometimes without the adjective at all—is presented as a counterdiscourse alongside such others as Cultural Studies, Women's Studies, Chicano Studies, African-American Studies, Gender Studies, and Ethnic Studies. Ultimately, however, PCS emerges as more than just another variant or counterdiscourse, indeed as a sort of umbrella counterdiscourse, gathering unto itself the concerns and interests of the revisionist project as a whole.

Its trajectory—actually described in terms of 'colonialist' and 'post-colonial' studies, with no specific difference drawn between such terms—is unfolded as follows: the 1950s witness the beginning of the new project, 'colonialist' discourse;[6] the 1960s give way to major developments in the critical formulation of its problematic; the 1970s record an increase in 'colonialist' studies, including what is characterized as the central text in 'postcolonial' studies, Edward Said's *Orientalism* (1978); and the 1980s establish the centrality of the 'colonialist' debate with its twofold focus on the impact of imperialism on the colonies and the reaction of the former colonies by way of corrective writing. Writing in the early 1990s, therefore, Gugelberger approaches PCS as a firmly entrenched academic formation and critical discourse, having a well-established intellectual history and a

4. See, for example: Gray 1985; Peck and Coyle 1985; Sarup 1989; Selden 1989; Baldick 1990; Stevens and Stewart 1992; Storey 1993.
5. Gugelberger 1995: 581–84.
6. In the 1950s, Gugelberger argues (p. 581), a major encounter takes place between two cultural projects: an ascendant modernist agenda and a nascent colonialist problematic. In effect, just as the validation of the modernist agenda is about to become institutionalized, a major shift begins to take place as the result of a combination of cultural and political events outside the West, leading to the irruption of the colonialist problematic. In the wake of this encounter, certain fundamental connections come to the surface: on the one hand, the link between colonialism, modernism, and structuralism is well established; on the other hand, the link between the postcolonial, the postmodern, and the poststructural—characterized as far more problematic in nature—is foregrounded.

well-defined ideological slant and forming part of an extensive network of similarly revisionist projects. This postcolonial project he summarizes as follows: 'Postcolonial writing, then, is the slow, painful, and highly complex means of fighting one's way into European-made history, in other words, a process of dialogue and necessary correction' (p. 582). For Gugelberger, therefore, PCS represents by and large a literary project— writing that is non-European in origin, oppositional in kind, dialogical and corrective in mode. This summary is further developed as follows.

To begin with, the specific designation of the project is explained. The adjective 'postcolonial'—sometimes hyphenated; sometimes not—is said to emerge in gradual fashion out of ongoing critical discussions in countries of the British Commonwealth[7] and is directly attributed to the 'postist' world of the 1960s: post-industrialism; poststructuralism; postmodernism; post-Marxism; post-feminism. Thus, given the nomenclature fully in vogue by the 1980s, what first appeared under the rubric of Commonwealth Literature or Studies eventually shifted to the use of the more political term 'colonial' and took on the ubiquitous use of 'post' as prefix, to yield the now familiar 'postcolonial'. In time, this new designation began to encompass and replace what had, until then, been pursued under the category of Third World Literature or Studies. In the process, the project became, as Gugelberger puts it, a further 'tempest' in the new Calibanic world of postism (p. 581).

In addition, the distinctive élan of the project is unpacked as well, in cumulative though unsystematic fashion. First, Gugelberger expands on its non-European origins by emphasizing the expansionist and oppressive European foundations behind such origins. Thus, he declares, PCS involves 'writing and reading practices grounded in colonial experience outside of Europe but as a consequence of European expansion and exploitation of "other" worlds' (p. 582). Second, he highlights its oppositional character, its sense of struggle, and its mode of dialogue and correction. Such studies, he explains, are 'constituted in counter-discursive practices' (p. 582).[8] Third, Gugelberger further expands on its

---

7. Its first use is attributed to the New Zealand critic, Simon During (1985). Subsequently, after appearing in a number of journal articles since the mid-1980s, including a further piece by During himself (1987), the term begins to be used as a full title in the late 1980s and early 1990s: Ashcroft, Griffiths, and Tiffin 1989; Spivak 1990; Adam and Tiffin 1991.

8. As such, Postcolonial Studies are directly related to a broad variety of other counterdiscourses, which one can readily group around three foci: (a) internal colonization, involving the repression of minority groups, such as Minority Studies or Subaltern Studies; (b) patriarchal colonization, involving the repression of women, with reference to both Western women and non-Western women; (c) political colonization, involving the repression of nations or groups of nations, such as Third World Studies, Resistance Literature, Response Literature, Othering Discourse, and Colonialist Discourse.

non-European impulse by pointing to the project's inversion of the existing relationship between numbers and influence. PCS, he argues, drives home the point that 'minority' cultures are actually 'majority' cultures and that 'hegemonized' Western Studies have been 'unduly overprivileged for political reasons' (p. 582). Finally, he further expands as well on its oppositional character by identifying the ultimate goal behind the dialogue and correction in question. Such studies, he declares, aim to push the 'margin' to the 'center' of discourse (p. 582).

In the end, Gugelberger claims, PCS should be seen not as a discipline but as a problematic—'an abstract combination of all the problems inherent in the newly emerging fields' (p. 582). It is not a discipline since it has no definable core; as such, it cannot be disassociated from previous disciplines. It is a problematic because it questions the problems inherent in all disciplines; as such, it is by nature interdisciplinary. In effect, PCS views all disciplines as implicated in the process of colonization. Consequently, PCS studies the totality of 'texts'—in the broadest sense of the term, with literary texts as a most important component thereof—involved in such a process, both the hegemonic texts and the revisionary texts. In so doing, PCS focuses on the ideological dimension of texts rather than the aesthetic; it does not jettison the artistic component altogether, but it does link it to the political. For Gugelberger, PCS represents the ideal, not the practice, of the comparative literature movement, insofar as it seeks to examine texts across both center and margin rather than confining itself—'a deliberate and almost desperate clinging to Eurocentric values, canons, cultures, and languages' (p. 582)—to texts from across the center.

Critical Summary Gugelberger does a fine job of situating Postcolonial Studies within the cultural and social context of the twentieth century. PCS emerges as a further but different counterdiscourse within a broad revisionist project at work since mid-century—not a specific discipline as such but an encompassing problematic. Its meaning and scope are clear. PCS includes within its compass all texts produced in the process of colonization, both from center and margin; these it proceeds to analyze from a marginal perspective by way of dialogue and correction. It is thus a mostly literary enterprise, with a sharp oppositional edge to it. PCS confines itself to the study of texts produced in the process of Western colonization, with no consideration given to the possibility of other cultural or historical applications.[9]

---

9. Critical comments: (A) I find his conceptualization and formulation of the project much too ambiguous. This is due to his concomitant understanding of it as both a counterdiscourse and a problematic. On the one hand, it ranks beside any number of similarly revisionist projects at work, with a clear 'disciplinary' history of its own from the 1950s through the 1990s. On the other hand, it does so by raising a problematic that is inherent in all

Columbia Dictionary of Modern Literary and Cultural Criticism (1995)[10]
The second example, of unknown authorship and belonging to the succinct manual form, makes a basic distinction, primarily historical in character, between 'colonialism' and 'postcolonialism'. While colonialism signifies the direct political control of one country or society by another, understood in terms of historical episodes, postcolonialism stands for a historical phase undergone by many countries after the decline of the European empires in the middle of the twentieth century.[11] This distinction is then applied to the literary production of the postcolonial period. In effect, with the overthrow of the colonial order, two types of literature come to the fore: on one side, writings that analyze the colonial experience from the perspective of indigenous peoples; on the other, writings that deal with life in a postcolonial state, its conflicts and contradictions as well as its advantages and sense of liberation.[12] From this point of view, therefore,

---

other such projects, so that it becomes an abstraction of such problems. I would argue instead for a greater sense of specificity in the face of these other projects, similarly counterdiscursive and revisionist. Indeed, this is a specificity that Gugelberger himself grants but occludes through his unnecessary distinction between a 'discipline' and a 'problematic'. Approached in this way, Postcolonial Studies would bring to the revisionist project a specific problematic of its own, which does affect all others but is also affected by all others in turn. This problematic has to do with the relationship between center and margins. One may speak of it, therefore, as a field of studies. (B) I also find his definition of the project, its meaning, too restrictive and too loose. Postcolonial Studies should examine not only the cultural production but also the material matrix. It should be literary as well as social, having within its purview texts from across the disciplines as well as the different dimensions of human society. Moreover, analysis of cultural production should extend beyond the strictly textual to cover all other components as well—the pictorial, the musical, and so forth. Postcolonial Studies should provide, especially when invoked, at least a working conception of what is meant by such terms as imperialism and colonialism. (C) I further find his envisioned reach of the project, its scope, much too limited. Postcolonial Studies should actively entertain the study of colonialism in transhistorical and transcultural perspective.

10.   Childers and Hentzi 1995. The manual has entries on 'Colonialism', 'Postcolonialism', 'Third-World Criticism', 'Subalterns', and 'Subaltern Studies'. The authors of these entries are not identified.

11.   The distinction as formulated, however, is deeply flawed, since it bypasses altogether the imperial and colonial experience of the whole of Latin America: the historical phenomenon of postcolonialism begins with the end of the eighteenth century (Haiti), continues through the nineteenth century, and concludes with the twentieth century (Cuba), as wars of liberation are waged against France, Portugal, and Spain. In the end, within Latin America—francophone, lusophone, and hispanophone America—only Puerto Rico and a number of other Caribbean islands remain under the control of imperial powers, the United States and France, respectively.

12.   The *Dictionary* makes no reference to 'imperialism' except for a partial argument against the Marxist position: the view that colonialism should be seen as the product of a necessary imperialist stage in the development of advanced capitalist countries (involving the exportation of capital and the search for new markets among less developed societies) has met only with 'limited success'.

one may speak, by extension, of Colonial Studies as well as Postcolonial Studies, both arising in the postcolonial world of the second half of the century.

Besides this primary distinction, the *Dictionary* also introduces the rubric of 'Third World Criticism', defined as criticism involving the cultural output of a Third World country, criticism written by residents of that country, or criticism involving Third World cultures in general. Theoretically, this category is more extensive than that of postcolonial criticism, since Third World countries are defined as those that have one or more of six characteristics in common, of which one is emergence from colonial rule.[13] In practice, however, most postcolonial countries qualify as Third World countries and vice versa. Consequently, Postcolonial Studies and Third World Criticism may be regarded as largely synonymous categories in this view. Lastly, the *Dictionary* further introduces the category of 'subalterns'—adapted from the terminology of the British military, where it refers to commissioned officers below the rank of captain—which is said to have a twofold application: first, as a catch-all designation for members of subordinated populations—the colonized, women, blacks, the working class; second, and most often, with reference to those oppressed by British colonialism and by the upheavals of the postcolonial period. Strictly speaking, therefore, this rubric can only be seen as synonymous with 'postcolonial' in its second meaning, and even then with a seeming bias toward the British experience.[14]

Critical Summary The *Dictionary* follows Gugelberger in characterizing Postcolonial Studies as a literary enterprise by and large, while narrowing the definition of the term 'postcolonial'. With regard to meaning, Postcolonial Studies signifies literature written in the historical postcolonial period and from the perspective of the colonized. Such literature encompasses life in both the colonial and the postcolonial world. With regard to scope, Postcolonial Studies would be restricted not only to the experience of Western colonization but also to the final stage of this process.[15]

---

13. The other five include economic factors ('undeveloped' economy vis-à-vis capitalist and socialist countries; relatively small natural resources or low agricultural production; relatively low levels of industrialization) as well as political considerations (turbulent political instability; refusal to form alliances with either the capitalist or the socialist block).

14. 'Subaltern Studies', in turn, is described as having a twofold application: in general, it refers to the academic study of the lives and writings of subalterns; in particular, it is associated with a circle of Indian intellectuals and their journal based in New Delhi. This latter group is represented as engaged in the politicization of the colonized: bringing about political change through alterations in consciousness and culture and thus pushing issues of postcolonialism to the forefront of critical and theoretical discussions in the West.

15. Critical comments: (A) I would argue for a broader understanding of the term 'postcolonial', in which the historical dimension represents but one aspect of the discussion.

Critical Terms for Literary Study (1995)[16]

A third example, from the pen of Seamus Deane and of the expansive encyclopedic variety, is actually a double entry on 'imperialism' and 'nationalism'. Such juxtaposition of concepts is not uncommon in the critical literature, given the nationalist agenda at the heart of anti-imperial movements of liberation. In fact, Deane subscribes to the commonly held view of nationalism as 'a continuation of imperialism by other means' (p. 360), given its replication of those discourses that had been used in its repression and against which it had struggled. The piece deals, therefore, with variations of the same phenomenon. It is not an easy piece: its line of argumentation, full of sharp insights throughout, proves, in structure as well as in formulation, rather convoluted and elusive. I seem to discern a threefold movement at work: first, a discussion of imperialism, with a focus on the work of Joseph Conrad; second, an analysis of postcolonial discourse in the light of postmodernism and decolonization; finally, a discussion of nationalism, with a focus on Irish literature by way of William B. Yeats and James Joyce. For Deane, material matrix and literary production clearly belong together.

In the beginning discussion on imperialism, Deane provides a twofold definition applicable to all of its variations: an expansionist economic system, taken as grounded in universal human nature, as well as a magnificent cultural system, viewed as either a precondition for or a result of the economic system in place. Two groups of variations are mentioned. First, the imperial formations of the West—indeed, imperialism is described as a 'peculiarly Western form of domination' (p. 354), extending from the sixteenth through the twentieth centuries. Such formations include: Portugal, Spain, the Netherlands, Russia/the Soviet Union, France, Great Britain, and the United States. Second, non-Western imperial formations—characterized as exceptions to the rule in modern times. Two are mentioned: the Japanese Empire and the Ottoman Empire. The discussion, however, centers exclusively on the West. Most interesting in this regard is the inclusion of the Soviet Union among the Western formations, signified by a slash as a continuation of Russia. Moreover, both capitalism and communism are identified as the economic systems at work in the West—the latter obviously as the core of the Soviet Empire; the former as the core of all other Western empires. For Deane, therefore, the ideological opponents of the Cold War, 'East' and 'West', represent

(B) I would also argue for a view of the postcolonial that involves both material matrix and cultural production. (C) I would argue as well for a consideration of the postcolonial as encompassing a transhistorical and cross-cultural perspective.

16. Deane 1995. Interestingly enough, in the first edition of this 'introduction to the work of literary theory' (1990), there was no entry on Postcolonial Studies; this piece was added for the second edition.

but different facets of the same Western imperial tradition. The discussion, however, centers exclusively on the capitalist West.

This beginning discussion posits an important distinction, temporal as well as structural, between 'imperialism' and 'colonialism'. Temporally, colonialism precedes imperialism, with the end of the nineteenth century in general and the 'scramble for Africa' unleashed by the Berlin Conference of 1885 in particular as a turning point in this regard. Colonialism stands, therefore, for the rise of empire—an 'early, amateur' form of imperialism (p. 355), while imperialism signifies its fullest expression—what comes to be called the 'New Imperialism'. Structurally, imperialism transforms colonialism. Whereas colonialism proceeds in a 'ramshackle, personal' way (p. 355), imperialism develops a highly coherent organizational form as well as a highly defined missionary project to the world.[17] In all formations, imperialism proves quite flexible in internal structures and quite global in ambitions and range. Consequently, imperialism may be said to represent for Deane the modernization and globalization of colonialism. The process proved successful on two counts: the enormous migration of Europeans over the course of the nineteenth century, leading to the establishment of neo-Europes across the globe; the attendant rationale for the defeat and expropriation, the enslavement and extermination, of non-Europeans across the globe, on the grounds of historical destiny and racial superiority.[18]

The ensuing discussion on postcolonial discourse—seemingly used interchangeably with the terms 'postcolonialism' and 'postcoloniality'— scrutinizes its relationship to both postmodern theory and the imperial enterprise, tying it much more closely to the former than to the latter. The discussion revolves around the Western representation of Self and Other at work in imperialism. Such representations advanced, most powerfully as well as most effectively, a construction of the West as a highly developed and articulated cultural formation, a site of 'propriety and order', alongside a view of the non-West as a highly primitive and amorphous cultural formation, a site of 'chaos and disorder' (p. 359). On the basis of

17.   Both are marked, Deane argues (p. 354), by economic rapacity, disguised in different ways by their respective literary, historical, and political discourses: (a) colonialism yields a tale of adventure, driven by an ethic of personal heroism set within the context of a specific national–religious formation; (b) imperialism gives way to a crusade for civilization and development, involving bureaucracies, technologies, and controls.

18.   Such justification reveals a twofold theoretical foundation: (a) a Hegelian philosophy of history, whereby the nations of Europe are represented as in charge of bringing human history to completion, with all others as having already fulfilled their historical destinies; (b) a neo-Darwinian view of racial evolution, whereby the nations of Europe are represented as the bearers of Progress, signified by technological advance, in the path toward Civilization, signified by development and modernization.

such binary constructions, imperialism justified and promoted the idea of a common destiny on the part of the West: the spread of a universal civilization in the face of non-Western barbarism.[19] In so doing, imperialism brought together the discourse of Darwinism, with its vision of natural selection and survival, and the discourse of humanism, with its vision of enlightened ideals. In so doing, however, imperialism also engaged in systematic and sustained devastation of the Other across the globe.

For Deane, postcolonial discourse has focused too much on the question of representation and not enough on the record of devastation. It has turned for grounding to postmodern theory, with deconstruction as primary signifier, rather than to historical experience. Consequently, it has been marked by a playful sense of pleasure in the ultimate indeterminacy of discourse, based on the nature of language, rather than by a tragic sense of catastrophe, based on the violence and exploitation of imperialism. The result has been overriding concern with representation of the Other as inevitable misrepresentation, yielding a celebration of otherness that is essentially depoliticized, rather than with representation of the crimes of imperialism, bypassing thereby the cultural power and political purposes of representation. To be sure, postmodern theory does find its historical bearings in decolonization, insofar as it exposes and disturbs, in its celebration of otherness, the repressions of Western representation. However, postmodern theory does not constitute the historical companion of decolonization, insofar as it identifies language with power or sees language as the effect of power and insofar as it leaves no space for representation on the part of the repressed. For Deane, therefore, postmodern theory—and hence postcolonial discourse—emerges as a ruse of power, a contemporary form of Western liberalism, radical in its openness to otherness but Western in its gaze on otherness.

In the concluding discussion on nationalism, Deane further challenges postcolonial discourse. As stated earlier, he follows the standard critique of nationalism as bringing about, upon initial rejection, the ultimate reinscription of imperialism. This it does in two ways: by appealing to the categories of empire (race; essence; destiny; language; history) for a definition of its own

---

19. At the heart of such a sense of destiny lies, Deane notes (p. 359), a profound contradiction: the definition and dissemination of a universal civilization along highly specific national lines. For the British Empire, civilization involved a combined discourse of gentlemanly behavior and Christianizing mission; for the French Empire, the offer of French culture, in keeping with the ideals of the French Revolution; for the American Empire, a combined discourse of moral and material improvement. In each and every case, therefore, a particular vision of national identity and national purpose is turned into a general mission for humanity. Such concretization of universalism is due, as the discussion on nationalism makes clear, to the influence of nationalism on colonialism and imperialism in Europe.

presence and identity; on the other hand, by adopting the requirements of empire (modernization; development; class and gender divisions) for its own definition of civilization. The result is a situation involving a claim to cultural independence alongside economic subservience. Nationalism, Deane argues, begins not in Europe but in South America. The great revolutions of the late eighteenth century and early nineteenth century lead to political independence from the Spanish Empire by 1825; in their wake, however, a huge influx of capital from Europe yields the grip of economic domination behind the appearance of cultural independence. Then, nationalism comes to Europe in the course of the nineteenth century, as a result of which imperialism takes on distinctive national hues behind a common core of capitalism.[20] Finally, from the middle of the twentieth century, nationalism drives the movements of liberation in the other colonial possessions of Europe, resulting in the same bifurcated reality—witnessed more than a century earlier in South America—of tight economic subservience side by side with alleged cultural independence.[21] Imperialism and nationalism are thus quite closely related, influencing one another in various and complex ways. Yet, postcolonial discourse, in its postmodernist and deconstructive celebration of otherness, increasingly bypasses not only the global reality of economic control, 'unshaken, even extended' (p. 368), but also the question of power and culture.

Critical Summary Deane would agree with both the *Dictionary* and Gugelberger in viewing Postcolonial Studies as an essentially literary enterprise, though with a twist, and side with the *Dictionary* in opting for a wide definition of the postcolonial. In terms of meaning, Deane expresses fundamental disagreement with the literary turn in Postcolonial Studies, due to its postmodernist orientation. Such studies must include, he argues, analysis of historical experience and reality, both with regard to the record of imperialism and the nature of nationalism. In terms of scope, the

---

20.   In both cases, Deane points out, the development is structurally the same: leadership by bourgeois elites; declaration of a cultural–national independence; and failure to release the proletariat from poverty. In Europe, however, nationalism and imperialism meet, for the first time, their 'true international or transnational Other' (p. 362)—socialism, with its broader vision of humanity and its call for liberation from an unjust economic system. In this respect, although not pursued as such, communism can only represent a betrayal of socialism, given the designation of the Soviet Union as an imperial formation and its economic system as the basis for such a formation.

21.   Such national formations become, Deane argues, 'caricatures of the unawakened communal consciousness they replace': a non-intellectual subproletariat that represented the national consciousness is replaced by an intellectual proletariat, 'with bourgeois pretensions', that claims to represent national consciousness (p. 361). In the name of the national, moreover, such formations engage in various forms of reactions, reinscribing thereby the repression suffered at the hands of imperialism.

postcolonial, while arising out of the process of decolonization beginning in the mid-twentieth century, would certainly encompass the study of the material matrix and literary production of 'imperialism' properly defined and its aftermath. It is not clear whether it would also cover the period of 'colonialism' as well. If so, then its compass would extend to the early, non-formal imperial formations of the West; if not, then it would be restricted to the later, formal formations. In any case, the emphasis is clearly on the former, given the strict definition of 'imperialism' as the transformation of colonialism in Europe at the end of the nineteenth century.[22]

A Dictionary of Cultural and Critical Theory (1996)[23]
The final example, by Aparajita Sagar and of the expansive encyclopedic type, begins by focusing on the concept of 'Postcolonial Studies' as such and then uses this initial vision of the field as springboard for a discussion of a variety of discourses, from both the Third World and the West, that precede it in time but that become an integral part of its own problematic as well.[24] In so doing, the entry provides a concise overview of the field—its meaning and scope; its background and influences; its questions and debates. At the same time, however, the entry also circumscribes the field in very specific and important ways, so that the resultant overview is not as comprehensive as the title would seem to indicate. I see a threefold development at work in the discussion. Sagar begins by defining and mapping the field. She then turns to three discourses operative in the Third World—Pan-Nationalism; Nationalism; Diaspora—and shows how such discourses enter into and affect Postcolonial Studies. Common to all, she concludes, is the fundamental question of identity. Finally, she deals with

22. Critical comments: (A) I would affirm the inclusion of material matrix alongside literary production within the purview of Postcolonial Studies, though I would argue for a consideration of the whole of cultural production, not just its literary output. (B) I would argue for a different definition of colonialism and imperialism, going beyond its historical (sequence) and structural (transformation) development in the West. Properly speaking, given the definition, the term 'empire' could only be bestowed on those formations at work in the West after the end of the nineteenth century—not before and not elsewhere. (C) I would insist on an explicit consideration of Postcolonial Studies as a transhistorical and cross-cultural phenomenon. Here such an expansion in realm of vision is implicitly granted by the designation of two imperial formations outside the West, the Japanese and the Ottoman. (D) I would argue, within the Western imperial phenomenon, for inclusion of the experience and reality of the Americas within the optic of Postcolonial Studies. Far too often such studies are limited to the twentieth century and hence limited to the worlds of Africa and the Near East as well as Asia and the Pacific.

23. Sagar 1996.

24. The reference to Postcolonial Studies as a 'field' is not Sagar's but mine. She herself uses this category or 'rubric' throughout, invariably with verb forms in the third person singular. She does use the term 'formation' in this regard, as a 'study' that encompasses a host of 'academic disciplines', but only once (p. 423).

three theories at work in the West—Marxism; Psychoanalysis; Decon-struction—and describes their influence on and use by Postcolonial Studies. Throughout, Sagar foregrounds the critiques brought to all such discourses by Feminist Studies as well as Subaltern Studies.

The initial configuration of the field is carried out in two steps: first, by delimiting the parameters of the field to be covered; second, by refining the field as outlined by way of challenges and responses.

To begin with, an overall description of the field, its meaning and scope, is provided. At its broadest, Postcolonial Studies would include the study of 'all the effects of European colonization in the majority of the cultures of the world' and hence would encompass all academic disciplines across the globe (p. 423). Such a vast undertaking, Sagar argues, can only be deemed doable and coherent from a highly removed vantage point, such as that of the Western academy. For her own purposes, however, Postcolonial Studies will be pursued in terms of anglophone 'postcolonial cultural studies' as pursued in the Western academy, though with due attention to their development in the Third World.[25] Clear boundaries are imposed thereby on the definition and mapping of the field. The first of these, materially crucial, is implicit. The base description of Postcolonial Studies limits the field to a concern with Europe, its process of 'colonization'—a concept in itself not defined—and the effects of such colonization. Any concern with colonization prior to or outside of Europe is, by definition, excluded from consideration. This restriction remains unexplained. Two others, procedurally significant, are explicit. Given its anglophone orientation, the discussion will focus on the process and effects of colonization on the part of England; given the emphasis on culture, the discussion will address cultural studies as practiced in the Western academy. All other processes of Western colonization, from the early imperial formations of Spain and Portugal to the latest formation of the United States, as well as all other fields of study are excluded as a result. A rationale for this twofold restriction is given: the vastness of the field as a whole. In retrospect, therefore, the entry would have been better entitled along the lines of 'postcolonial cultural studies (anglophone)'.

Yet, circumscribed as it is, such a description, Sagar explains, has proved difficult. Consequently, further refinement of the meaning and scope of the field as outlined is provided through a series of challenges and responses.

Four fundamental objections are summarized. First, with regard to the use of the prefix 'post' in the conception of the field. Colonialism, critics

---

25.   Sagar provides no definition of cultural studies but refers the reader instead to the corresponding entry in the *Dictionary* (Green 1996). This entry begins with a definition: 'A diverse body of work from different locations concerned with the critical analysis of cultural forms and processes in contemporary and near-contemporary societies' (Green: 124).

counteract, is by no means defunct, as the term would imply: the process of decolonization did not put an end to the system of colonial exploitation. Second, with respect to the erasure of difference in the constitution of the field. Critics see homogenization at work across the board: within the Third World, between the nations and cultures of Africa, Asia, and the Caribbean; between the Third World and internal colonization within Europe; within the Third World, between nations with large indigenous populations and settler colonies with minority indigenous populations. Third, with respect to the referential framework used for the deployment of the field. Two variations are named. On the one hand, critics point out that the nations of the Third World are analyzed thereby in terms of their relationship to imperialism rather than in their own terms or in relation to one another. On the other hand, critics observe that cultural practices in the Third World that arise under colonialism but that are not directly related to it as such are examined thereby, inappropriately, in terms of such a context. Finally, with regard to the defining role of culture in the delineation of the field. Such emphasis, critics claim, passes over the system of exploitation of imperialism as well as its continuing grip in the world.

To each objection but one, the last, Sagar offers a counter-response. To begin with, as a means of conceiving the field, the prefix 'post' proves appropriate because of its ambiguity. The temporal reference may be seen as pointing not to the end of colonialism, and thus understood in terms of decolonization, but to its launching, and hence along the lines of 'from the beginning of colonialism' (p. 424). The result would be inclusion within its purview, beyond the attainment of formal political independence, of the process of neocolonization through economic subservience to Western capitalism. Similarly, for a proper constitution of the field, its structural grounding on the principle of difference should be recalled and activated. Consequently, it is imperative for the field to be keenly aware of and responsive to the enormous variety of postcolonial formations. In this regard, both a priori coincidence and a priori discontinuity are to be discarded as working principles. Lastly, as organizing principle for the deployment of the field, the referential framework invoked should not be seen as determinative. From the point of view of the critical analysis of nations, orientation to the imperial centers should be seen as descriptive rather than prescriptive: the focus on imperialism—a concept also left undefined—by no means rules out critical reflection on either internal concerns or relations to other nations of the Third World. From the point of view of the critical study of cultural practices, orientation to the colonial framework should be viewed in terms of the larger political context: such practices, whether directly related to it or not, were produced within it.

Sagar's position is beyond doubt. The field as outlined, presently in the process of 'rapid institutionalization' (p. 424), constitutes a valid and productive undertaking, provided that certain caveats are observed: first, the field must take into account the phenomenon of colonialism as a whole; second, differences in postcolonial formations must be acknowledged and theorized; third, the reference of nations to imperialism must be pursued in view of the homogenizing tendencies of imperial control and of cultural practices to colonialism approached in sophisticated and rigorous fashion. It is not clear, however, whether for Sagar the same judgment would apply to Postcolonial Studies widely conceived. Once such a view of the field at its broadest is laid out, it is never discussed again.

Two comments are in order. The first has to do with the failure to address the final objection—lack of attention in Postcolonial Studies to the system of exploitation, both past and ongoing. Given the circumscription of the field in terms of cultural studies as pursued in Western academic circles, such omission is understandable and inevitable. It is curious, nonetheless, that this particular objection is simply passed over. The second concerns the question of difference and its articulation within the piece itself. In response to the second objection, the specter of homogenization, Sagar points to the grounding of the field on the principle of difference. Such difference, she adds, must not be confined to issues of nation-states and national origins but must include as well questions of class, gender, race, ethnicity, and sexual orientation. That is the reason why such critique is deployed throughout, especially from the perspective of gender and subordination (feminism and subalternity), on all discourses finding their way into Postcolonial Studies.

This critique is deemed fundamental and imperative. For Sagar, at the core of Postcolonial Studies lies, as its constitutive principle of difference makes clear, 'the resistant reading of power' (p. 426). From the first, postcolonial discourse has been oppositional in nature—highly attentive to the ways in which language and culture are produced and hence engaged in the theorizing of both culture and language. Its object has been the 'colonial, neocolonial, patriarchal, discursive, and material manifestations' of power, in all of their complexity; its aim, to 'unsettle its epistemology, its claims to truth, and its strategies of representation' (p. 426). At present, this oppositional impulse can only be preserved, given ongoing institutionalization, if the various caveats listed above are taken to heart, but also, and above all, if the principle of difference is duly expanded—if difference is foregrounded and appropriated beyond the realm of the national. The result is a far more complex vision of the field, as a variety of other discourses, highly oppositional as well, are brought to bear upon it in sustained and systematic fashion.

Critical Summary Sagar follows, though not in unqualified fashion, what Deane characterizes as the literary turn in Postcolonial Studies and thus sides with both Gugelberger and the *Dictionary*. Sagar also follows, along the lines of Gugelberger and Deane, a rather restricted view of the postcolonial reach. With regard to meaning, Sagar adopts both a theoretical and a practical position: in theory, all the effects of colonization are regarded as within the purview of the field; in practice, cultural studies becomes the exclusive focus of inquiry. Thus, while in principle open to the analysis of historical experience and reality, Sagar chooses a different path. With regard to scope, Sagar limits herself to European colonization, with that of England as the exclusive focus of inquiry.[26]

From General Overviews to Detailed Mappings: Transition

As a transition from general introductions to critical movements to detailed introductions of the field, I should like to consider what could be regarded as a mixed genre—a general introduction to the field, bringing together, in manual rather than encyclopedic fashion, a list of entries, involving central concepts as well as critical movements, and a delimiting focus on 'Postcolonial Studies'. This volume, *Key Concepts in Post-Colonial Studies*, marked the third collaboration on the part of three Australian critics—Bill Ashcroft, Gareth Griffiths, and Helen Tiffin.[27] While the volume contains an entry on 'Post-colonialism/Postcolonialism' as such, in which the field as a whole is approached and which I shall thus use as main point of reference, a number of other entries prove helpful in this regard as well.[28] The value of the volume is to present in condensed form what prove to be rather complex discussions.

The exposition of term and field proceeds in three stages: first, a definition is provided by way of historical development; then, various areas

---

26. I would offer the following observations. (A) I would support and stress the theoretical definition of Postcolonial Studies as encompassing cultural production as well as material matrix. The omission of this latter dimension from consideration strikes me as much too swift and in need of a more substantial rationale. (B) I would argue for a definition, howsoever inchoate, of the concepts of 'colonization' and 'imperialism'. Both are invoked without explanation. (C) I would further argue for an explicit consideration of the postcolonial as a transcultural and transhistorical phenomenon. At the very least, a rationale is in order for the delimitation of the postcolonial optic to Europe. (D) I would heartily support the need to discuss how other discourses interact with the postcolonial. In this regard I found most to the point the foregrounding of the principle of difference as fundamental to the field and the imperative expansion of this principle through the incorporation of other angles of difference, such as race and class, gender and sexual orientation.

27. Ashcroft, Griffiths, and Tiffin 1998. For their other collaborative efforts, see: as co-authors, Ashcroft, Griffiths, and Tiffin 1989; as co-editors, Ashcroft, Griffiths, and Tiffin 1995.

28. Ashcroft, Griffiths, and Tiffin 1998: 186–92. The other entries, in terms of importance, are as follows: 'Colonialism' (pp. 45–51), 'Imperialism' (pp. 122–27), 'Neo-colonialism' (pp. 162–63); then, 'Colonial Discourse' (pp. 41–43) and 'Post-colonial Reading' (pp. 192–93); finally, 'Globalization' (pp. 110–11) and 'World Systems Theory' (pp. 238–41).

of critical discussion related to this process are invoked and analyzed; finally, a working definition is advanced in the light of such discussions.

Definition

To begin with, a definition is given and amplified in terms of three sequential stages of academic usage. The definition proper is brief—the term, the term is said to deal with 'the effects of colonization on cultures and societies' (p. 186)—but not entirely helpful, since the term 'colonization' remains undefined. For this one must resort to the entries, closely related, on 'colonialism' and 'imperialism'. Both take Edward Said's definitions in *Culture and Imperialism* (1993) as a useful point of departure: 'imperialism' stands for the practice, theory, and attitudes of a dominating center over a distant territory, while 'colonialism' represents the implantation of settlements on distant territory, invariably a consequence of imperialism. Both also go beyond it.

To be sure, imperialism and colonialism are described as long-standing historical frameworks. Thus, imperialism, broadly defined as 'the formation of an empire' (p. 122), is said to take place whenever any nation extends its domination over other nations, and hence advanced as a constant in history. Here Rome emerges as the foundational model for subsequent imperial formations and its concept of the *imperium populi Romani*, describing its control over the Mediterranean Basin, as the foundational pattern for subsequent imperial practices. This *imperium*, regardless of interpretation, was 'the creation and instrument of a self-perpetuating oligarchy'—a fundamental factor in modern imperialism.[29] Similarly, colonialism, broadly defined in terms of 'colonial settlements' (p. 46) or 'overseas colonies' (p. 123), is portrayed as an aspect of many earlier civilizations, hence a recurring phenomenon in history as well. Throughout, moreover, relations between center and colonies are conceived in terms of a central *imperium* and a periphery of 'provincial, marginal and barbarian cultures' (p. 46).

At the same time, both imperialism and colonialism are said to undergo fundamental transformation in their Western incarnation. As a result, both terms are invariably used with reference to this particular historical formation, especially in terms of its climactic stage, what is often characterized as the period of 'classical imperialism'. This Western formation is described as long-lasting and far-reaching: its origins are traced to post-Renaissance Europe, thus yielding a framework five

29. Two different interpretations of the concept of the *imperium populi Romani* are outlined: the republican version, espoused by Marcus Tullius Cicero, where power was said to reside in the people and to be bestowed by the people on its magistrates abroad; and the monarchical version, pushed by Caesar Augustus, where power was claimed as invested in the *imperator*, to whom all the people must show allegiance.

hundred years in the making; its scope is depicted as global, involving the Europeanization of the entire world through the diaspora of countless ordinary Europeans over the centuries in question. In the course of this long trajectory and expanding reach, imperialism and colonialism take on highly distinctive characteristics in the West.

On the one hand, imperialism becomes implicated in the development of capitalism—from mercantilism, to industrialism, to globalism; in the process, it is further affected by a number of other emerging forces as well—nationalist sentiment, population transplantation, and cultural superiority. Three major stages are distinguished in this regard.[30] The first, the Age of Discovery (fifteenth and sixteenth centuries), marks the beginning of European expansionism and mercantilism. The second, the Age of Mercantilism (seventeenth and eighteenth centuries), represents the consolidation of mercantilism and expansionism through nationalism: the competitive acquisition of wealth among nation-states and the promotion of the economic and political interests of the nation-state.[31] The third, the Age of Imperialism (nineteenth and twentieth centuries)—within which the period of 'classical imperialism' is located (1880s to 1910s)—stands for aggressive expansionism on the part of the modern industrial powers for a variety of political, cultural, and economic reasons.[32] Such militant expansionism comes to an end with the First World War and begins to be reversed after the Second World War. In the second half of the

30. I would note that neither the overall process nor the differentiation of each stage is as precise as one would wish. Both the whole and its constitutive elements remain far too skeletal in composition.

31. Such consolidation, traced symbolically to Oliver Cromwell's Navigation Act of 1651, is pursued through such measures as the imposition of tariffs in order to discourage imports and the offer of bounties and rebates for the purpose of encouraging exports. Its basic principle involved a twofold component: a belief that the wealth of the world was fixed and the resultant conviction that gain on the part of any one nation represented loss on the part of other nations. From this point of view, the acquisition of colonies was viewed as a way of depriving competing nation-states of wealth, real or potential.

32. The emergence of aggressive capitalism is tied directly to the industrial transformation of Europe (1750–1850), beginning with the British Isles. To begin with, Great Britain, already in possession of a colonial empire and with control of the seas by the early nineteenth century, undergoes a period of enormous expansion in productive capacity, eventually becoming a factory to the world, exporting its excess goods throughout under the doctrine of free trade. During this period, colonial annexations are, at first, replaced by economic penetration. By the 1880s, however, the stagnation of capital leads to an openly imperialist movement, symbolically tied to the Berlin Conference and the Scramble for Africa of 1885, involving not only economics (erection of a protective tariff wall around the empire) but also politics (territorial expansionism) and culture (discursive hegemony). This period of 'classical imperialism' comes to an end in the 1910s, symbolically associated with the outbreak of the First World War in 1914. Subsequently, capitalism endures in the remainder of the twentieth century by transmogrifying itself into internationalism and globalism.

twentieth century, therefore, imperialism, in keeping with its ability to change centers and adapt itself to an ever-shifting world situation of power, develops into globalism—'the supra-national operations of economics, communications and culture' (p. 112).

On the other hand, colonialism becomes implicated in the modern capitalist system of economic exchange. Thus, colonies are regarded and organized as suppliers of raw materials for the economies of the colonizing powers. Moreover, relations between colonizers and colonized are cast in terms of a rigid hierarchical difference (economic, cultural, or social), yielding highly unfair and highly resistant exchanges. Such hierarchies and exchanges further involve issues of race, gender, and class throughout the different colonies. As a formal phenomenon, colonialism comes to an end in the mid-twentieth century, with the struggles for liberation of the 1940s through the 1960s; in the post-independence period and through the rest of the century, it continues, however, as neocolonialism, signifying 'any and all forms of control over the ex-colonies' (p. 163) by the former colonial powers or the new superpowers.

To recapitulate: while imperialism and colonialism constitute long-standing and recurring historical phenomena, such terms convey the unique characteristics developed in the Western formation, temporally and spatially circumscribed as they are. It is against the background of such understandings of imperialism and colonialism, therefore, that the definition of post-/postcolonialism cited earlier—'the effects of colonization on cultures and societies'—is put forward. However, since the understanding of the 'effects' in question has varied in academic discourse, a threefold sequential development is posited: first, from the 1940s through the 1970s, the term is understood in chronological terms, used by historians to refer to the post-independence period following upon the Second World War. Subsequently, beginning in the late 1970s, a cultural understanding of the term ensues among literary critics. At first, and without recourse to the rubric as such, critics like Edward Said, Gayatri Chakravorty Spivak, and Homi Bhabha proceed to analyze, in various ways, the power of representation present in colonialist discourse and its effects on metropolis and colonies alike. Such focus comes to be known as colonial discourse theory. Later on, the rubric itself is employed, in hyphenated fashion, by critics from countries of the English Common-wealth with reference to cultural interactions in literary circles of colonial societies. This the authors describe as an attempt to politicize the concerns of fields like Commonwealth Literature and New Literatures in English, at work since the 1960s. More recently, the term has been employed, mostly without the hyphen, by a variety of academics to signify the political, linguistic, and cultural experience of the former colonies of Europe.

Areas of Critical Discussion

As the process of definition readily attests, both term and field are characterized as 'a potential site of disciplinary and interpretive contestation' from the start (p. 186). Such contestation is approached from three different angles: the deployment and function of the hyphen; the meaning of the prefix 'post'; and the danger of homogenization. While the latter two discussions are common in the literature, as already observed elsewhere, the other surfaces here for the first time, not surprisingly, given its portrayal as *passé* at this point.

First, many critics came to insist on the hyphen in direct response to the development of colonial discourse theory. They saw such theory, given the strong influence of poststructuralism on its major proponents, as focusing on the discursive power of colonialism to the detriment of its material effects. The hyphen was thus proposed as a signifying solution in this regard: the unhyphenated 'postcolonial' would refer to colonial discourse theory, while the hyphenated 'post-colonial' would stand for the field as a whole, of which colonial discourse theory would represent but one component. This critical discussion, the authors note, has largely come to an end. Nowadays, both spellings may still be invoked, but the distinction itself has given way. Both forms represent but variations of the same rubric, each comprehending the same and broad variety of areas of study—the discursive operations of empire, to be sure, but also the territorial conquests of Europe; the various institutions of European colonialisms; subject construction in colonial discourse and the resistance of such subjects; the various responses to such incursions and their contemporary colonial legacies in both pre- and post-independence nations and societies. Moreover, the initial focus on the cultural production of such nations and societies has been replaced by critical analyses of all sorts—historical; political; sociological; economic—as the different disciplines take up the global effects of European imperialism.

Second, debate concerning the force of the prefix 'post' has gone way beyond a straightforward understanding of it, as used by historians of the post-Second World War era and still encountered occasionally today, as a temporal designation for the period following the end of colonialism. Critics have gone in different directions in this regard, with four main areas of concern in evidence: chronological expansion in the understanding of postcolonial societies, taking into account relationships between and across the different political periods (precolonial; colonial; postcolonial) in such societies; transhistorical expansion in the study of postcolonial societies, going beyond the customary focus on European colonization; academic expansion in the analysis of the postcolonial phenomenon, now applied to any number of subject positions, professional fields, and critical enterprises;[33] and conceptual expansion in the understanding of post-colonial literature, keeping apart a focus on the scope and nature of anti-colonial resistance in writing (a project involving a social force and the various resistances to it) and a focus on the literary character of Third and Fourth World cultural groups (a project involving the comparative study of nations and cultures). Given the nature of the discussion, the authors foresee no resolution in this regard, only continuing debate.

Third, from the beginning, but also sharpened by the discussion regarding transhistorical expansion, critics have raised the specter of homogenization in postcolonial studies. The rubric, they charge, brings together far too much and too disparate material within its optic—too many colonial encounters and postcolonial situations, each unique in its own way—leading to the emergence of a model in which general principles are underlined and specific differences are elided. Following Robert C. Young (1995), the authors argue strongly for a *via media* in this regard: particular historical locations and the general discourse of colonialism need to be brought together, so that both similarities and differences among the multiplicity of colonial encounters and postcolonial situations are observed and theorized. Thus, neither the option of an abstract discourse removed from precise historical conditions and material realities nor the option of localized material inquiry without a broader discursive framework is acceptable. In fact, they point out, recent work in the field reveals 'signs of a fruitful and complementary relationship' between a variety of approaches (p. 190).

Working Definition
The end result of this critical overview amounts to a revisiting and reviewing of the question of definition, leading not so much to a reformulation of the initial definition, properly corrected and amplified, but to a reconceptualization of it, and ultimately of any other definition advanced, in the light of the nuances and complexities generated by the critical discussion. Thus, at one moment and with respect to a specific distinction, the authors argue, 'Clearly any definition of post-colonialism needs to include a consideration of this wider set of local and specific

33. This academic expansion is described through the eyes of Stephen Slemon (1994): (a) a way of ordering the critique of totalizing forms of Western historicism; (b) a portmanteau term for a retooled notion of 'class'; (c) a subset of postmodernism and poststructuralism as well as the condition from which these two structures of cultural logic and critique emerge; (d) the condition for a nativist longing in post-independence national groupings; (e) a cultural marking of non-residency for a Third World intellectual cadre; (f) the inevitable underside of a fractured and ambivalent discourse of colonialist power; (g) an oppositional form of 'reading practice'; (h) a category of 'literary' activity springing from a new and welcome political energy within what used to be called 'Commonwealth' literary studies.

ongoing concerns and practices', and then add, 'It is unlikely that these debates will be easily resolved' (p. 189). What is true of this particular distinction is ultimately true of all others as well. Any definition, such as their own, must include a sense of not only the critical considerations but also the critical positions at work. Their own definition should be seen therefore as a working definition, with the following specifications in mind:

— As the title chosen for the entry itself indicates, 'post-/postcolonialism', no significance whatever is attached to the presence or absence of the hyphen in the rubric. Whether invoked or not, both term and field are seen as properly encompassing a broad range of objects of analysis, lines of inquiry, and fields of study.

— The force of the prefix 'post' emerges as expansive, so that its use in the rubric becomes correspondingly multivalent. Both term and field are viewed, therefore, as properly involving a wide variety of areas of concern. Only one such expansion, the transhistorical, appears to be called into question: at the present time, it is argued, both term and field remain grounded in the Western formation of imperialism and colonialism. It is not entirely clear, however, whether such circumscription is presented simply as a matter of fact or as an ongoing desideratum.

— As it stands, there is no 'inherent or inevitable' reason (p. 190) why the rubric should signal homogenization—a reductionist surrender of location and materiality to principle and theory. Both term and field are seen, rather, as requiring a proper balance between a particular focus on historical conditions and an abstract focus on general discourse. Only then can the unique as well as the comparative character of colonialism be kept duly in view, for the benefit of both, so that both unconnected localized analyses and ungrounded simplistic generalizations are avoided in the process.

Critical Summary In terms of meaning, Ashcroft, Griffiths, and Tiffin opt for a wide view of Postcolonial Studies: beyond the literary and the cultural, toward any number of disciplines, any number of approaches, and any number of interests. On this score, they stand with Deane and in opposition to Gugelberger and the *Dictionary* (in theory) and Sagar (in practice). In terms of reach, the stance taken proves ultimately ambiguous. While presenting imperialism and colonialism as transhistorical and transcultural phenomena, they point to a fundamental grounding of the field in the conditions, practices, and effects of the Western formation, given the transformation of these phenomena within their Western framework. Whether such grounding is deemed descriptive or prescriptive, however, is unclear. In any case, on this point they end up siding with Sagar, Deane, the *Dictionary*, and Gugelberger.[34]

Mappings: Postcolonial Studies as Field

In the 1990s, with the rapid growth of Postcolonial Studies and the vertiginous proliferation of scholarship, more detailed mappings of the field began to appear in the literature. While such mappings do entertain at times the relationship of Postcolonial Studies to other critical movements, their focus remains steadily on the field as such—its origins and influences; its trajectories and proponents; its debates and discussions; its challenges and future. These mappings have taken different forms, ranging from the concise to the substantial and from the specific to the comprehensive. Some have appeared as introductions to general readers in the field, which bring together extracts from a variety of authors on a variety of topics.[35] Others serve as editorial introductions to collections of essays on particular aspects or dimensions of the field, usually placing such dimensions or aspects against the background of the field as a whole.[36] Several function as introductions to monographs on specific areas or concerns in the field, usually in the form of first chapters that take a look at the concern or area in question in light of the field.[37] Lastly, a number appear as volume-size introductions to the field, with overviews of its different constitutive components.[38] In what follows I limit myself to this last category—the full-fledged, general introduction. I do so not only as a way of keeping the task at hand within manageable bounds but also because the explanatory and

34. The following comments are in order: (A) I fully endorse the wide definition of Postcolonial Studies adopted, which encompasses both material matrix and cultural production. (B) I find the definitions of 'imperialism' and 'colonialism' as too limited, given their grounding in those of Edward Said (exercise of power; acquisition of territory). (C) I would push for a broader consideration of both phenomena outside the Western formation: the distinctive characteristics of the latter should not prevent inquiry into other historical and cultural formations.

35. See, e.g., Williams and Chrisman 1994; Ashcroft, Griffiths, and Tiffin 1995, which contains not only a general introduction to the volume (pp. 1–4) but also individual introductions to its fourteen divisions, each devoted to a different major area or concern of the field; Moore-Gilbert, Stanton, and Maley 1997.

36. See, e.g., Barker, Hulme, and Iversen 1994; Sprinker 1995; Prakash 1995.

37. See, e.g., Spurr 1993; Boehmer 1995: 1–11 ('Introduction'); Young 2001: 1–11 ('Colonialism and the Politics of Postcolonial Critique') and 12–69 ('Basic Concepts').

38. In addition to those to be examined, the following should be mentioned as well: Childs and Williams 1997: 1–25 ('Points of Departure'); Moore-Gilbert 1997: 5–33 (Ch. 1: 'Postcolonial Criticism or Postcolonial Theory?'); Quayson 2000: 1–22 ('Introduction: *Postcolonializing*').

pedagogical tenor of these volumes proves eminently suitable for my purposes. Among those available, furthermore, I have chosen those that foreground the question of circumscription in particularly effective fashion.

Leela Gandhi: *Postcolonial Theory* (1998)[39]
In her Preface to the volume, Gandhi sets forth, explicitly and from the start, its rationale and objective. In the last ten years (a reference to the late 1980s and the 1990s, given the date of publication), she points out, postcolonialism has become a major critical discourse—alongside such others as poststructuralism, psychoanalysis, and feminism—in academic circles, giving rise to an enormous body of work, quite diverse as well as quite interdisciplinary in nature. At the same time, she notes, the term itself remains 'diffuse and nebulous', without 'an "originary moment" or coherent methodology', unlike, for example, deconstruction or Marxism (p. viii). The volume is conceived, therefore, as an attempt 'to "name" colonialism' (p. viii). This it sets out to do in twofold fashion: first, by tracing its intellectual and cultural background; second, by laying out its major concerns and themes.[40] In the first and last chapters, Gandhi pursues the question of 'naming' as such: while the introduction ('After Colonialism') takes up questions of definition and circumscription, the conclusion ('Postcolonial Theory') focuses on difficulties and criticisms.

Naming Postcolonialism The introduction proves most insightful with respect to the overall orientation and tenor of the volume. Three issues in particular should be noted: the origins and élan of postcolonialism; the formal distinction between postcolonialism and postcoloniality; and the psychoanalytic interpretation of postcolonialism.

To begin with, Gandhi describes the origins of postcolonialism by turning to the discussion on 'subalternity', which, as pointed out earlier, began in the Indian subcontinent with a collective of Indian intellectuals known as the Subaltern Studies Group and its work on subordination in South Asian Studies. This project she invokes not so much as a direct historical context for its emergence but rather as a general intellectual climate for its élan, insofar as the concept of subalternity is relevant to any discourse concerned with relationships of domination and subordination,

---

39. Gandhi 1998.
40. The first part consists of Chs. 2 and 3, which provide an intellectual history of the discourse as well as an account of its location within the new humanities, respectively. The second part is carried out in Chs. 4 through 8, which deal, sequentially, with colonial discourse, feminism, nationalism, postnationalism or globalization, and literature.

such as postcolonialism. Two particular moments in the discussion are distinguished. Beginning in the early 1980s, the Group undertook an analysis of subordination, in all of its various expressions and fully attentive to all of its complex ramifications, in South Asian society. In so doing, they sought to allow the people to surface in 'the jealous pages of elitist historiography' (p. 2), speaking for and giving voice thereby to the oppressed. In the wake of this project, Gayatri Spivak raised her well-known question and challenge regarding the representation and representability of the oppressed, Who can speak for the subaltern? (Spivak 1985). In contrast to Spivak herself, Gandhi points out, who answered her own question with a strong negative, postcolonialism responds with 'the greatest enthusiasm' to such a question (p. 2), as it turns to the condition of subalternity in the Third World.

So much so, in effect, that the result becomes 'a confusing and often unpleasant babel of subaltern voices' (p. 3), making it exceedingly difficult to make sense of the many competing and discordant perspectives and theories coming together under the one rubric. Most salient in this regard, Gandhi points out, is the cleft between Marxism and poststructuralism, between a 'politics of structure and totality' and a 'politics of the fragment', with the former charging that postcolonialism lacks the necessary wherewithal to mount a proper structural critique and the latter claiming that postcolonialism stands in danger of becoming another totalizing grand narrative (p. 167). Given such utter lack of consensus, Gandhi opts for a formal distinction between 'postcoloniality' and 'postcolonialism'—between the particular historical condition addressed (the aftermath of colonization) and the theoretical engagement with such a condition (the postcolonial remembering). This distinction, she argues, not only serves to clarify the relationship between the material and theoretical dimensions of the field but also allows for an evaluation of theoretical engagement in light of its ability to comprehend a highly complex historical condition. Thereby, a sense of order as well as a sense of critique are introduced into an otherwise chaotic and unmanageable rubric and field—a way out of 'babel'.

Within this proposed interpretive framework, the relationship between postcoloniality and postcolonialism is cast in psychoanalytic terms: in the wake of decolonization, the postcolonial condition is depicted as tending toward repression, while postcolonial engagement is portrayed as an imperative process of therapeutic anamnesis. Postcoloniality emerges as highly ambivalent: at once, a moment of great rejoicing and profound anxiety, marked by the creative possibilities of a radical departure from the colonial past, a new beginning, yet haunted by the enduring weight of that past and the possibility of failure, a derivative reality. The contradictions at work in such a historical condition, Gandhi notes, often lead to a desire to forget the colonial past—a 'will-to-forget' involving the repression of the 'uncomfortable realities of the colonial encounter' and the 'painful memories of colonial subordination' (p. 4). Yet, repression does not signify emancipation. The colonial past is a highly ambivalent period in which contestation and resistance go hand in hand with complicity and seduction. For Gandhi, therefore, postcolonialism—as 'a disciplinary project devoted to the academic task of revisiting, remembering, and interrogating the colonial past' (p. 4)—emerges as the way to retrieve the full ambivalence of this colonial past and hence a means for therapeutic remembering, 'a complex project of historical and psychological "recovery"' (p. 8). Only then, can postcolonial subjects learn to live with a divided past and proceed into the future with a measure of self-understanding, beyond the demand for a radical beginning and the burden of a derivative reality.

As a transition to the next section, I would note that Gandhi advances this framework of postcoloniality as condition and postcolonialism as theory against the background of other attempts to deal with difficulties and criticisms of the field. On the one hand, she refers to the question of hyphenation and its signifying force in the rubric ('post-/postcolonialism'): while some argue for its presence as a distinctive temporal marker, whereby the 'post' signals what comes after the end of colonialism, others prefer omission to convey an extended temporal designation, so that the 'post' stands for the onset of colonialism. On the other hand, she mentions the issue of nomenclature: some opt for 'postcoloniality', or 'the postcolonial', as a more existential term, in reaction to 'postcolonialism', identified with the academic discussion. While Gandhi does not pursue either discussion, her stance is nonetheless clear: both rubrics are in order and useful; both also deal with the colonial past and the colonial aftermath.

Evaluating Postcolonialism Beyond these issues of hyphenation and nomenclature, briefly raised and just as briefly dismissed, the conclusion turns to two other problematic areas whose impact Gandhi clearly perceives as far more substantial and significant. Both have to do with the danger of homogenization.

The first area involves generalization in application: a view of colonialism as the fundamental category of experience for a large segment of humanity across the globe, without proper attention to and analysis of the differences among them, not only *across* but also *within* societies and cultures, so that differences, whether in the experience of colonialism and anti-colonialism or in such other categories as gender and class, remain entirely overlooked and untheorized. The second area involves generalization in interpretation, encompassing a variety of critical positions. First and foremost, postcolonialism may preserve the privileging of the center through its ordering and analysis of cultures and societies, their histories and concerns, in terms of that center, given the continued use of colonialism as point of reference and its deployment as a comprehensive chronological framework via the employment of the prefixes 'pre' and 'post'. Postcolonialism may also fall prey to a number of other temptations: forcing the 'contingent and random' diversity of the colonial encounter into a universal relationship of coercion and resistance (p. 171), passing over the full archive of colonial history and downplaying in particular the consent of the colonized in colonialism; claiming 'cognitive mastery' over history (p. 173), risking the charge of depoliticization and taking away critical self-consciousness from those in the colonial past; viewing itself as the end result of a process of 'progress and perfectability' (p. 174), ignoring thereby both the problems of neocolonialism and the sharp divisions between societies and cultures; and interpreting the postcolonial moment as a cultural compromise between 'colonial structures and indigenous processes' (p. 175), succumbing to the hierarchical language of the center involving imperial culture and native experience.

With regard to universalizing application, Gandhi specifically calls into question the erasure of difference between settler colonies, such as Canada and Australia, and native colonies as well as claims to postcoloniality on the part of previously colonized countries, such as India, without regard for their own internal histories of subordination.[41] Any such eliding of differences, external or internal, she argues, renders postcolonialism a flawed enterprise, morally as well as politically, in its proposed analysis of domination and subordination. With regard to universalizing interpretation, Gandhi simply responds that postcolonialism need not engage in repetition or amnesia but can also provide, when properly conceptualized and formulated along the lines proposed, a 'way through and therefore out of the historical imbalances and cultural inequalities' of the colonial encounter (p. 176). Conceived as such, postcolonialism becomes an effective ethical paradigm, eminently suitable for a systematic critique of institutional domination and subordination. In sum, as critical discourse,

---

41. For the first type of homogenization, Gandhi (pp. 168–70) has in mind the project that shifted the approach to literatures from previously colonized countries from the category of 'Commonwealth literature' to that of 'postcolonial literatures' with its view of the latter as actively engaged in challenging the center and its language, 'writing back to the centre'. For a key text in this regard, see Ashcroft, Griffiths, and Tiffin 1989. In the process, all postcolonial literatures are regarded and interpreted in the same fashion, erasing differences between the countries and areas involved, including what for Gandhi remains a 'fundamental incommensurability' (p. 170) between the settler colonies and the native colonies that endured the full brunt of the colonial enterprise. No particular individual or volume is invoked for the second type of homogenization.

postcolonialism must incorporate difference at the heart of both the historical condition and the theoretical engagement; the proposed vision of it as therapeutic anamnesis is meant to do precisely this.

Critical Summary Given the adopted distinction between postcoloniality and postcolonialism, Gandhi follows a broad definition of the field: the complexity of the postcolonial condition is emphasized and the adequacy of postcolonial engagement is predicated on its ability to encompass and conceptualize such complexity. On the issue of meaning, therefore, she is clearly on the side of Ashcroft, Griffiths, and Tiffin as well as with Deane. In fact, the distinction is advanced as a deliberate attempt to bring the material and theoretical correlates of the field into close relationship with one another. On the issue of scope, however, Gandhi proves more restrictive. The entire discussion concerning condition and theory is conducted within the framework of European colonialism and its postcolonial aftermath and rereading in the course of the twentieth century. Gandhi stands, therefore, with all those works and authors examined thus far, though by way of silence rather than argumentation; any consideration of colonialism or postcolonialism as transhistorical or transcultural phenomena is simply not mentioned.[42]

Ania Loomba: *Colonialism/Postcolonialism* (1998)[43]
Loomba, like Gandhi, lays out, immediately and straightforwardly, the rationale and objective for her volume in the Introduction. The recent field of Postcolonial Studies has, she argues, generated 'a great deal of excitement' as well as 'confusion and scepticism' (p. xi); as a result, it finds itself both 'fashionable' and 'beleaguered' (p. xii). Dissatisfaction has come from a variety of sources: inside as well as outside the academy; the Western academy as well as Third World academics; academics of a more traditional bent as well as those sympathetic to such studies; established voices as well as beginning students. Such dissatisfaction is wide-ranging:

---

42. Critical comments: (A) While I find myself very much in agreement with the objective of taking social context as well as cultural production into consideration in defining the field, I do not find the proposed distinction between 'postcoloniality' and 'postcolonialism' as the best way to convey such breadth. (B) While I applaud analysis of the 'colonial' within the purview of the 'postcolonial', I would argue for, at the very least, a working definition of the concepts of 'imperialism' and 'colonialism', and hence ultimately of 'postcolonialism' as well. (C) I find the exclusive focus on European colonialism, with a decided bent for the English experience, to be much too confining; a critical consideration of such phenomena as transhistorical and transcultural is very much in order. (D) While I fully espouse the emphasis on difference in the field, I do believe that the psychoanalytic framework within which the entire project has been cast proves much too confining. There is more to theoretical engagement than therapeutic anamnesis.

43. Loomba 1998.

disabling disagreements regarding what the field means and comprises; a forbidding style of formulation and composition; ironic mix of distance from practices in non-Western societies and cultures and intimacy with Western postmodernism. All of this Loomba readily grants: the term, she concludes, has become so 'heterogeneous and diffuse' that it cannot 'satisfactorily describe' its object and parameters of study (p. xii). Taking such dissatisfaction to heart, Loomba sets out to write, following the guiding principles of 'The New Critical Idiom Series' of which it forms a part,[44] an introductory volume that brings out the 'intellectual and political possibilities' of such studies (p. xiii).

This, she readily admits, is a task easier said than done. The field, for one, is profoundly interdisciplinary, involving a great variety of sources and practices, approaches and perspectives. In addition, its intricate mode of expression is partly unavoidable, due to recent developments in the social sciences and in literary studies. Moreover, given the spatial and temporal dimensions of colonialism, any attempt at summarizing or theorizing proves exceedingly difficult. Her proposed approach is twofold. On the negative side, avoidance of hard-and-fast definitions and detailed accounts of colonial histories and ideologies. On the positive side, presentation of important concepts, events, and issues in terms of key debates and scholarship, providing thereby a keen sense of their complexity as well as of their interrelations. The result is a threefold structure: a first chapter situates colonial and postcolonial studies within contemporary intellectual debates; the second pursues the question of colonial and postcolonial identities; the third chapter concentrates on challenges to colonialism. The question of definition and parameters is taken up at the very beginning of the first chapter.

Defining the Terms The process of definition is gradual, beginning with colonialism and imperialism, addressing neocolonialism and neo-imperialism on the way, and then turning to postcolonialism. Its point of departure is the common equation of colonialism and imperialism. The process proceeds by way of opposition to this identification, drawing on Marxist thinking for clarification but ultimately advancing a very different understanding of the concepts in question.

First, colonialism and imperialism are treated together. Following the *Oxford English Dictionary*, colonialism is initially defined as 'the conquest and control of other people's land and goods'; as such, it is said to

---

44. As described at the beginning of the volume (p. ii), the series consists of introductory guides to contemporary critical terminology. Each volume is meant to provide a guide to the use of the term, offer an original and distinctive overview by a leading critic, and relate the term to the larger field of cultural representation. In so doing, each volume is to be ruled by the following norms: clarity, lively debate, and the widest possible range of examples.

represent a 'recurrent and widespread feature of human history' (p. 2). A variety of examples is provided, all curiously described as 'empires': the Roman Empire; the Mongol Empire; the Aztec Empire; the Vijaynagara Empire; the Ottoman Empire; and the European empires of the sixteenth century onwards. At the same time, a fundamental difference is posited between this last formation and the rest. This difference is described from a Marxist perspective: while previous formations were pre-capitalist (exacting tribute, goods, and wealth), European colonialism emerged alongside capitalism (restructuring economies; establishing complex relationships, with human and natural resources flowing in both directions; benefiting from profits).[45] To be sure, European colonialism was not monolithic: strategies and patterns of domination differed widely; however, all variations produced the economic imbalance at the heart of capitalism. Loomba thus speaks of colonialism as 'the midwife that assisted at the birth of European capitalism' (p. 4). Again following the *Oxford English Dictionary*, imperialism is initially defined as 'a political system in which an imperial centre governs colonized countries' (p. 6). Although often equated with capitalist colonialism, imperialism, Loomba notes, also has a long-standing 'pre-capitalist past' (p. 4). A list of examples is given here as well, though much shorter: Imperial Spain and Imperial Russia. Again, a fundamental difference is laid down between recent imperialism and the rest. This difference is also approached from a Marxist perspective: imperialism as the highest stage of capitalism (superabundance of capital as a result of the growth of finance-capitalism; impossibility of investment at home, given limited supply of labor, hence investment in colonies, abundant in resources but lacking in capital; subordination of non-industrialized countries for sustained growth; rivalry between the various empires ultimately leading to its demise). Loomba can thus speak of imperialism as 'the highest stage of colonialism' (p. 6).

Thus defined, imperialism has no need of direct colonial rule, making way for the use of the terms 'neoimperialism' and 'neocolonialism'. Such imperialism constitutes, in effect, a global system, 'an economic system of penetration and control of markets' (p. 6), whereby labor and markets are assured for industry and goods by economic relations of dependency and control. Moreover, while a politically defined imperialism comes to an end with the granting of independence, an economically defined imperialism is not at all affected by such changes.

---

45. This difference, Loomba points out (p. 3), has been explained from any number of perspectives: the much greater distance involved; greater incidence of violence and ruthlessness; better organization; superiority of race. Thus, the Marxist position clearly emerges as the most satisfactory one for her.

Colonialism and imperialism, Loomba concludes, are thus defined in different ways according to their historical mutations. To sum up: first, there is colonialism; then, European colonialism (capitalism); subsequently, imperialism (advanced capitalism); lastly, neo-imperialism (imperialism without colonies). Against this background, then, she advances, rather unexpectedly, a spatial rather than temporal understanding of both terms and relationship: let imperialism, and neo-imperialism, stand for what originates in the center, the place from which power flows—'the process that leads to domination and control'; let colonialism, and neocolonialism, stand for what happens in the margins, the place that is penetrated and controlled—'the result ... of imperial domination' (pp. 6–7). Such revisioning of colonialism and imperialism cannot but affect the understanding of postcolonialism as well.

This understanding is advanced by way of critiques of the concept itself. First, the term has been opposed on the basis of contemporary realities. While the prefix conveys the sense of ideological aftermath, the postcolonial as supplanting the colonial, the inequities of colonial rule endure. Postcolonialism (formal independence) and neocolonialism (economic and/or cultural dependence), it is argued, go hand in hand. Loomba agrees: both formal decolonization and the reinscription of imbalance must be taken into account. Second, opposition has also come on the grounds of historical vagueness. While the prefix conveys the sense of temporal aftermath, the postcolonial as coming after the colonial, the process of decolonization lasts almost two centuries, from the late eighteenth century to the late twentieth century. Colonialism and decolonization, it is pointed out, encompass a broad variety of perspectives. Loomba agrees: the different dynamics in question must be taken into account. The term has been further challenged on the grounds of internal realities. Postcolonialism involves complex internal hierarchies based on profound social and racial differences.

Postcolonialism, it is noted, brings together groups that cannot be characterized in the same way (Creoles; mestizos; natives) as well as groups that remain colonized. Loomba agrees: the internal dynamics of colonialism and postcolonialism must be taken into account. Lastly, challenge has come as well on the basis of subjective disposition. Postcolonialism signifies the contestation of colonialism, its domination and legacies, wherever it should take place. Postcolonialism, it is proposed, presupposes neither the doing away with nor the passing away of colonialism but resistance to it in any number of situations, from anti-colonial struggles to displaced diasporas to globalization critiques. Loomba disagrees: this proposed linking of postcolonialism to subjectivity results not only in a flattening of situations and concerns but also in a shift of focus from locations to individuals; to the contrary, she argues, specific histories and positions must be taken into account.[46]

In the end, and in keeping with her sequence of responses to the various critiques of the term, Loomba advances a broad understanding of postcolonialism as a concept to be used only 'with caution and qualifications' (p. 18). The latter are outlined as follows: on the one hand, the ideologies and practices of colonialism are 'historically, geographically, and culturally variable'; on the other hand, such practices and ideologies do 'have something in common' as well (p. 18). Postcolonial analysis demands, therefore, a fine balance between 'the universals and the particulars in the oppression' of colonized societies (p. 18). For Loomba, therefore, postcolonialism emerges as a process that is at once general, 'with some shared features across the globe', and concrete, not to be 'uprooted from specific locations' (p. 19).

Addressing the Objections In addition to the critiques raised with regard to the force of the term as such, various other objections are identified and addressed: exclusivity of focus; avoidance of material matrix; a penchant for abstraction; scholarly reductionism.

To begin with, postcolonial analysis, it is claimed, ties the societies and cultures in question much too tightly to the history of colonialism, largely ignoring thereby their own realities and experiences not only prior to the advent of the imperial–colonial framework but also alongside the imperial–colonial relationship. Loomba agrees: just as there is a danger in romanticizing the native by downplaying the relationship, by glorifying the precolonial past or the autochthonous culture, as postcolonial theory has often warned, so there is a corresponding danger in submerging the native by absolutizing the relationship, by seeing all in terms of the intervention. The imperial–colonial phenomenon, Loomba argues, cannot and should not be made to account for the whole of such societies and cultures. Similarly, postcolonial analysis, it is pointed out, tends to leave out the language of geopolitical domination and economic exploitation.

46.   For this particular critique, Loomba has Klor de Alva (1995) in mind. For Loomba, Klor de Alva emerges as a typical proponent of the union of postcolonialism and poststructuralism: recourse to poststructuralist historiography to argue on behalf of multiple histories rather than a single history, with extension of the postcolonial category to those under oppression and in opposition both in previously colonized and previously colonizing countries. This identification of postcolonialism with oppositional subjectivity Loomba rejects on two counts: first, borrowing from the Marxist tradition, she argues that the emphasis on multiplicity conceals the workings of global capitalism; second, she adds that the emphasis on contestation excludes many others involved in the same situation. In effect, she claims, a 'too-quick enlargement' of the category (p. 13), such as that proposed by Klor de Alva, turns it into 'a vague condition of people anywhere and everywhere' (p. 17).

Loomba agrees, with a twist: while much work of this type is undertaken, it is often not included in the developing canon of the field. Moreover, postcolonial analysis, it is argued, leans toward generalities instead of specificities, making increasing use of highly abstract argumentation while dispensing with the details of local and concrete situations. Loomba agrees: 'metropolitan' postcolonial theory often presents itself as general in location and scope, without paying sufficient attention to the world at large and the local in that world. Lastly, postcolonial analysis, it is claimed, often turns into a reading of the main proponents of 'metropolitan' theory, with too much attention paid to a handful of authors and their latest publications. Loomba agrees: such is the result of the star system operative in the Western academy, where such voices reside, and of the nature of theory itself, given its tendency toward self-reference. Such a limited and limiting focus, Loomba points out, ultimately works against both scholarly creativity and breadth, preventing critical interaction with such literature as well as expertise in specific societies and cultures.

Loomba's responses to all critiques and objections has a common denominator. There is no question that postcolonial analysis is fraught with dangers and difficulties. Nonetheless, it is a task very much worth pursuing, provided that the fragile balance between the imperial–colonial and the indigenous, the material and the cultural, the universal and the specific, and the theoretical and the practical is keenly observed throughout.

Critical Summary Loomba's insistence on breadth within the field is quite sharp throughout. On almost every point of contention, she comes down on the side of inclusion and nuance. While such an expansive range of concerns and pursuits may, and does, prove disconcerting, making it difficult to get a handle on the conception and exercise of the field, it is nonetheless essential and fruitful for the project as a whole. The impact on definition is considerable: attention is to be paid to both cultural production and material matrix. On this point, Loomba follows Gandhi and all those behind her (Ashcroft, Griffiths, and Tiffin; Deane). The impact on scope is less extensive. In theory, Loomba looks upon colonialism and imperialism as present through history and across cultures. In practice, she isolates the European formations of the nineteenth century and beyond, given her definition of European colonialism as capitalism and of European imperialism as advanced capitalism or neo-imperialism. In so doing, however, she does insist keenly on breadth, on the need to keep the different formations in mind. On this point, while lining up behind all others, she sides most closely with Ashcroft, Griffiths, and Tiffin.[47]

47. Critical comments: (A) While I find the effort to define the various concepts in question laudable, I find the process itself and the resultant definitions rather problematic.

John McLeod: *Beginning Postcolonialism* (2000)[48]
In a brief Introduction, McLeod follows Gandhi and Loomba in setting forth, explicitly and up front, the rationale and objective of the volume. These are conveyed via the goals and parameters of the series, 'Beginnings', in which it appears: works designed 'to give practical help to students beginning to tackle recent developments in English, Literary Studies and Cultural Studies'.[49] This multiple concern with practice, pedagogy, and foundations is evident throughout. The result is a volume that is at once introductory and sophisticated, descriptive and constructive, pointed and detailed.

All new developments and hence all beginnings in such developments, McLeod ventures, represent a mixture of excitement and disorientation, insofar as they bring together the enthusiastic expectation of exploring unknown territory and the unsettling unfamiliarity of any such undertaking. In postcolonialism, McLeod continues, this ambiguity becomes most profound. While it does constitute 'one of the most exciting and challenging fields of study that has emerged in recent years' (p. 1), it also proves 'especially challenging' and 'particularly difficult' (p. 2). There are two reasons for this. First, the range of activities characterized as 'postcolonial' is immense, making it difficult to find a suitable point of departure. Second, the range of critical practices applied to the 'postcolonial' is also immense, making it likewise difficult to decide on any particular approach. The result has been 'discord and conflict' in the field, of such magnitude, in fact, that the term itself has been called into question as 'a meaningful concept' (pp. 2–3). McLeod opts for a middle path.

Sets of definitions are advanced on the grounds of economic theory, only to be bypassed in the end for a spatial understanding that, while attractive, remains singularly unrelated to the preceding discussion. This spatial understanding, moreover, is not carried through to the ensuing definition of postcolonialism. (B) I also find the insistence on openness and inclusion most laudable, especially on behalf of a discourse that is attentive to both general principles and concrete details. (C) With regard to meaning, I can only praise the insistence on both material matrix and cultural production, in all of their diversity, as proper areas of analysis. (D) With regard to scope, I would argue for a more substantial consideration of the imperial–colonial phenomenon as transhistorical and transcultural, especially in light of not only the option for inclusion throughout but also the need for balance between generalities and specificities. The demarcation of the European formations as a set unto themselves seems to go against both of these working principles.

48. McLeod 2000.

49. According to the programmatic statement (p. ii), the series seeks to convey such 'practical help' in three ways: (a) engaging the new developments and fostering similar engagement among students; (b) providing an account of both the history and the context of each development; (c) working out a practice that is informed by and about theory. Toward this purpose, then, each volume is conceived as a combined introduction–contribution to the new development in question, seeking to provide students with a firm but critical foundation for further work and doing so with a premium on first principles and clarity of presentation.

The difficulties of the field are certainly real and cannot be simply bypassed; at the same time, they should not be allowed to prevent postcolonial analysis from going forward. After all, he points out, postcolonialism does have by now a critical history. The concept need not be abandoned, but it must be employed 'self-consciously and productively' (p. 3), and, for this to happen, one must come to terms with this history and its range of meanings. For McLeod, therefore, a 'beginning' in post-colonialism is very much in order. This is a volume that holds together in creative tension the enthusiasm and the unsettlement generated by the field; a volume that places each reaction at the service of the other, fostering excitement by highlighting the variety of sources and approaches embraced by the field and channeling disorientation by stressing the challenge of the field to all assumptions regarding thinking and reading.

To bring this about, McLeod deploys a twofold strategy: first, in terms of approach, he opts for a focus on reading practices; second, in terms of activity, he settles on two sets of literary texts. The textual groupings are identified as follows: on the one hand, 'literatures in English' by authors who come, directly or indirectly, from countries with a history of colonialism; on the other hand, 'older, more familiar literary works' of English literature that seem on the surface unrelated to questions of empire (p. 1). The reading strategies, six in all, are described as major issues in the field: colonial discourses; nationalist representations; the nation in question; rereading and rewriting English literature; feminism; diaspora identities. These are pursued both by way of individual chapters within the volume's central section (Chs. 2 through 6) and across the various chapters, as called for by the discussion. The overall design and contours of the volume are thus clear: a concern with reading and reading activities; a focus on texts of literature; a concentration on literature in English, from both the imperial center and its once-colonized territories.

The aim of this 'beginning', McLeod concludes, is not an attempt at homogenizing, either with respect to the various literatures or the various ways of reading such literatures examined. That is simply impossible, for there is no single postcolonialism. The aim, rather, is precisely to foreground the variety comprehended by the term, for out of such variety 'comes possibility, vitality, challenge' (p. 3). Thus, rather than doing away with the term 'postcolonialism', as its many and sharp difficulties would seem to warrant, McLeod seeks to use it with a 'healthy degree of self-consciousness and suspicion', so that it remains an 'enabling term' (p. 3).[50]

---

50. It is in this context that McLeod takes up the issue of the hyphen (p. 5). Without any account of previous discussion on this matter, the following distinction is advanced: 'post-colonialism' appropriately designates a historical period—what follows upon colonialism, independence, or the end of Empire; 'postcolonialism' refers to representations, reading

Within this 'beginning', questions of meaning and scope are pursued in the first and last chapters, which deal, respectively, with the emergence of the field and its critics.

Defining the Field McLeod begins to work his way toward a definition of 'postcolonialism' by placing it in context: first, historically, against the process of decolonization in the twentieth century; second, intellectually, in the light of major critical developments toward the latter quarter of the century. In both respects, it is the British Empire that informs and guides the inquiry. Historically, the century witnessed a dramatic reduction in the reach of the empire, from control over a vast area of the earth at the beginning of the century to a few remaining colonies in the Caribbean and the South Atlantic by the end of the century. As such, the twentieth century is said to have brought about 'colonial demise' and 'decolonisation for millions of people who were once subject to the authority of the British crown' (p. 6). Yet, McLeod points out, the legacy of empire and colonialism, both material and cultural, is evident across a wide variety of 'domains' (p. 7). Intellectually, within the domain of literature, the latter part of the century witnesses a shift in conceptual framework from 'commonwealth' to 'postcolonialism'. By the end of the century, therefore, postcolonialism stands as both an indisputable historical fact and an established intellectual perspective.

McLeod further zeroes in on the concept by way of 'colonialism', in itself described as a term that 'has taken many different forms and has engendered diverse effects around the world' (p. 7). This term is approached indirectly as well, by way of 'capitalism' and 'imperialism'. First, McLeod follows the thesis of Dennis Judd (1996) that the primary force behind the imperial structure was the desire for enrichment. From the late seventeenth century, he argues, colonialism and capitalism go hand in hand in the West: a commercial project involving the acquisition of foreign markets for Western goods as well as cheap natural resources and human labor from abroad is accompanied by the acquisition and settlement of foreign territories. The result was enrichment for the imperial centers and exploitation for the colonial margins. Second, McLeod follows the thesis of Peter Childs and Patrick Williams (1997) on imperialism as the ideology that upholds the legitimacy of economic and military control of other nations. Since such control, he argues, does not require the settlement of foreign lands, colonialism, with its acquisition and settlement of foreign territories, represents but a variation of this ideology. The result is that,

practices, values—all of which appear across the two historical periods. To avoid confusion in this regard, he further opts for the terms 'once-colonised' or 'with a history of colonialism' instead of 'post-colonial'.

while colonialism has virtually come to an end today, imperialism remains a vibrant force in the world.

In sum, for McLeod, colonialism emerges out of capitalism and represents 'a particular historical manifestation of imperialism, specific to certain times and places' (p. 8). Its distinguishing features are: settlement of territory; exploitation of resources; and the attempt to govern the peoples of the occupied territories.[51] In the wake of decolonization, imperialism does not disappear but rather endures in a different historical manifestation, the economic exploitation of other nations. In light of these various definitions, McLeod goes on to offer a definition of postcolonialism.

Such a definition, he argues, is predicated on two fundamental observations. First, the effects of colonialism on representations, reading practices, and values do not come to an end with the cessation of colonialism: any definition of the postcolonial must take this into consideration. Second, colonialism has not disappeared entirely from the world, either in terms of peoples or of groups within nations: any definition of the postcolonial must take this into consideration as well. A definition of the postcolonial must thus incorporate historical continuity as well as historical change, acknowledging the enduring presence of 'the material realities and modes of representation common to colonialism' in the world, while recognizing that 'important ... changes' have taken place and affirming 'the promise, the possibility, and the continuing necessity of change' (p. 33). The resulting definition, formulated solely in terms of the realm of literature, is advanced as an 'umbrella-term' (p. 33). With respect to content, three areas of reading are outlined: texts produced in formerly colonized countries; texts produced in the diasporas of the formerly colonized countries; texts produced in the former imperial centers. With respect to approach, the reading envisioned is described: it should foreground contestation and, as such, demands a radical reconceptualization of traditional methods and models. Several caveats accompany this definition. To begin with, the three areas of reading cannot be brought together under the banner of a single and unified postcolonialism. Further, each area is characterized by diversity and heterogeneity. Lastly, while postcolonialism aims at contestation, it may not always prove successful in attaining this objective.

Anticipating the Objections This definition of postcolonialism is advanced in full knowledge of the various critiques lodged over time against both concept and field. These objections McLeod divides into two major categories: those revolving around its connection to Commonwealth

---

51. This definition McLeod borrows from Boehmer 1995.

Literature, regarded as much too close; those centering on its oppositional stance, regarded as much too compromised.

Within the first category, two particular objections are noted, both involving the charge of homogenization. The first is that postcolonialism basically follows the geographical divisions of Commonwealth Literature, thereby not only favoring Great Britain as point of reference but also engaging in a selective use of countries.[52] This critique McLeod counters directly. In recent times, he points out, postcolonialism has extended its reach beyond the traditional boundaries of the Commonwealth, now looking to Ireland as well as Scotland and Wales, and even beyond the Commonwealth as such, by drawing on a variety of other colonial contexts. While for him there is much to be said for such expansion, a note of caution is nonetheless introduced: expansion may lead to detachment from geographical and historical referents and hence, ultimately, to a theory without proper attention to specifics. The second objection, which builds on the first, is that postcolonialism disregards history and, as a result, tramples over critical differences both within and between nations. This critique McLeod directly counters as well. Homogenization, he argues, is by no means inevitable; in fact, the ideal is to engage in comparative analysis, while paying attention to the different national and cultural contexts.

Within the second category, five different objections are cited, all raising the specter of a hidden neocolonialism at work in postcolonialism: indebtedness to Western theory; creation of an academic ghetto; option for anti-foundationalism; the problematic of temporality; relationship to global capitalism.

First, because of its thorough dependence on Western theory, postcolonialism has been portrayed as unable to deal adequately with

---

52. For McLeod, the study of Commonwealth Literature, as it emerges in the 1950s and before it becomes transformed into Postcolonial Studies, is marked by several distinctive characteristics (pp. 10–16). The critique addressed here is that Postcolonial Studies remains far too tied to these characteristics. The following are of relevance in this regard: (A) While the study of literatures in English encompassed writers from the settler countries (the Dominions) as well as writers from countries then in the process of independence, the process of inclusion was selective. Thus, for example, neither US nor Irish writers formed part of this configuration. (B) While acknowledging differences among writers from the different nations, a sense of unity, of common inheritance, was presupposed as well, greatly favoring thereby the primacy of Great Britain within this body of literatures. (C) While promoting the importance and study of such literatures from outside Great Britain, in itself a significant political act at the time, the underlying critical disposition was that of liberal humanism. Thus, without bypassing the cultural differences among the different writers from the different locations, great emphasis was placed on what was of permanent and universal relevance in such writers, thereby maintaining the interpretative criteria at work in the traditional study of English literature.

the local concerns and contexts of non-Western literature. For such critics, postcolonialism is but the product of migrant non-Western intellectuals in the West who create thereby a new, academic variation of neocolonialism: raw textual materials from outside the West are imported into the West for postcolonial processing to be exported and consumed outside the West. This critique McLeod dismisses out of hand: behind it stands a romantic vision of and search for a history free from the effects of colonialism. Second, postcolonialism has been charged with creating for itself an undesirable and unworkable ghetto within the academy: a marginal space with the impossible task of dealing with a literature across a vast expanse of time and space. For these critics, the result is, again, a form of neocolonialism: a highly convenient addition to the curriculum without a proper sense of rationale or proper attention to impact. This critique McLeod also dismisses out of hand: the problem lies not with postcolonialism but with the academy. Third, given its dependence on poststructuralist thought, postcolonialism has been accused of taking up the path of anti-foundationalism: reality as a textual product, yielding a world of local knowledges, rather than as a product of economic and social conditions, allowing for a grand theory of knowledge and corresponding metanarratives. According to these critics, this is the work of Third World intellectuals enthralled with First World theory, who end up constructing reality in the light of their own fragmented image. This critique McLeod refutes: the relationship between postcolonialism and anti-foundationalism is a conflicted one. Fourth, postcolonialism has been charged with deploying a highly problematic division of time: a binary division of world history; a referential privileging of colonialism in such history; a bypassing of neocolonialism. For these critics, the result amounts to a neocolonial vision of global history. This critique McLeod refutes: properly defined, postcolonialism can obviate such objections. Lastly, postcolonialism has been portrayed as ignoring the larger framework of capitalism and modernity, with no concern for global economic conditions and the issue of class. Consequently, for such critics, postcolonialism finds itself in the service of capitalism, a complicity that its own proponents seek to hide—in effect, a neocolonial structure. This critique McLeod dismisses out of hand as well: postcolonialism is sharply aware of its relationship to capitalism and may serve as a form of resistance against it.

In conclusion, the proposed definition of postcolonialism, with its focus on literature and reading practices, on the British Empire, and on the diversity of imperial and colonial contexts within the empire, has been designed with all of these critiques in mind. Properly understood and deployed, it can indeed serve, McLeod would certainly argue, as an enabling term in the ongoing postcolonial discussion.

Critical Summary One finds in McLeod a sharp difference, both in terms of meaning and scope, between the overall conceptualization and the actual pursuit of the postcolonial. A high degree of variance exists, first of all, between the actual focus on literary texts and reading practices and the theoretical conception of the postcolonial field as a whole. For McLeod, the range of activities and the range of practices envisioned is quite broad, going far beyond the realm of literature and reading. These, however, are mentioned only in passing. On this score, McLeod follows, in principle, both Loomba and Gandhi as well as Ashcroft, Griffiths, and Tiffin and Deane. A high degree of variance exists as well between the actual focus on Great Britain and the theoretical reach of the postcolonial field as a whole. For McLeod, the range of imperial and colonial contexts envisioned is quite broad, going far beyond the confines of the British Empire, though not beyond the West as such. Once again, however, these are mentioned in passing only. On this score, McLeod stands, in principle, with Gandhi as well as Gugelberger, the *Dictionary*, Deane, and Sagar. Such contrast between practice and theory—admittedly rather surprising and ultimately problematic in a volume explicitly designed as a beginning in postcolonialism—is due, I believe, to McLeod's aversion to generalization and his concern for specifics. While comparative analysis is indeed lauded as a goal, homogenization is feared as a constant danger throughout, hence his own careful circumscription of practice in the volume.[53]

53. The following comments are in order: (A) The wide theoretical definition of Postcolonial Studies proposed is commendable, allowing in principle for a consideration of both cultural production and material matrix. The volume itself, however, does not move beyond the particular realm of literature within cultural production. (B) The wide theoretical extent of Postcolonial Studies posited is commendable, allowing in principle for a consideration of imperial–colonial formations other than that of Great Britain, though only within the West. Again, however, the volume itself does not move beyond the confines of the British Empire, and it certainly does not contemplate, at all, the possibility of transhistorical or transcultural application. (C) Quite attractive as well are the careful definitions of colonialism, imperialism, capitalism, and postcolonialism worked out in light of one another. In the end, however, I find that of postcolonialism offered, with its emphasis on the aesthetic, highly problematic, given the previous definitions of colonialism and imperialism adopted, which include a variety of other dimensions of control, including the political and the economic. I would also argue for a broader sense of both imperialism and colonialism. (D) Similarly quite attractive is the importance placed on diversity in postcolonialism, on the different contexts of imperialism and colonialism, and hence the need to pay particular attention throughout to specifics. Although left completely undeveloped, I find the ideal of a comparative analysis that is well grounded on the local and the concrete a most worthy aim.

Mapping the Optic

The preceding review of the literature on Postcolonial Studies has been carried out with two primary questions in mind: what is the operative definition of postcolonial analysis at work—its object? What is the proposed range contemplated for such analysis—its parameters? In all cases I have tried to supply the answers to such questions within the general intellectual context and overall line of argumentation of the work and critic(s) in question. At one level, the results bear witness to my beginning characterization of the field as highly diverse and conflicted. Not only are the answers to both questions quite varied and clashing, but also the frameworks and approaches behind their formulation prove quite disparate and discordant as well. At another level, the results reveal a number of recurring concerns within each question as well as certain standard positions within each concern. Anyone wishing to engage in postcolonial analysis—of one sort or another, to one degree or another—must take an explicit and critical position on both questions and do so in the light of the theoretical discussion.

Biblical critics interested in bringing together Biblical Studies and Postcolonial Studies are no exception in this regard. The same kind of critical and explicit stance should be expected of them as of anybody else. My own procedure in this matter will be to make my way through the enormously complex and divisive ground covered by these two questions with the aid of those recurring concerns and standard positions mentioned earlier. In so doing, I shall refer to stances alluded to as well as taken by the literature reviewed. Thus, I shall also be building, in more systematic fashion, on the critical comments offered with regard to each work surveyed. This I shall do first with regard to the import of postcolonial analysis and then with regard to its compass. I shall close with a brief comment regarding the role of religion in Postcolonial Studies.

Question of Meaning

Regarding the definition of the field as such, I see five issues as coming to the fore in recurring fashion. Listed in order of logical expansion, these are as follows: the force of the term; the nomenclature deployed; the terrain surveyed; the referential quandary; the nature of the encounter.

Force of the Term The term 'postcolonial', employed both as an adjective and as a substantive ('the postcolonial'), is used in different ways in the literature. Such variations may be profitably approached from an analysis of the term itself: linguistically, it is compound in nature—the prefix 'post' and the root 'colonial'; etymologically, both components are derived from Latin—the root comes from *colonia*, meaning a 'farm' or a 'settlement', with reference to a population that is sent from one place to another; the prefix represents the temporal preposition *post*, indicating what comes after. At a most basic level, therefore, the 'postcolonial' is what comes after the 'colonial'. The different usages of the term come about as a result of the specific force assigned to the prefix, the precise meaning of 'what comes after'.

Three major variations should be noted. The first takes the 'post' to mean what comes after the end of colonialism, that is, the aftermath of decolonization (*Dictionary*). Its signification is thus of a political and historical nature. The second takes the 'post' to refer to what comes after the onset of colonialism, thus including not only the aftermath of decolonization but also the entire project of colonization as well as the process of decolonization (Gugelberger; Sagar). Here the signification is also political and historical in nature, but far wider in range. The third regards the 'post' as marking what comes after a conscious awareness and problematization of the relationship of domination and subordination involved in colonization, regardless of the historical and political conditions in existence. In this view the 'postcolonial' moment can take place at any time within the project of colonization or in the course of its aftermath. Its signification is thus of a psychological and social nature.

All three variations are understandable and defensible. My own preference is for the third option: the postcolonial as conscientization, a realization of the problematic of domination and subordination in the geopolitical realm. Such conscientization can emerge within a political and historical colonial context or fail to emerge within a political and historical postcolonial context. Postcolonial Studies would thus involve a study of the problematic as such, regardless of situation. The other two usages I find problematic. The first option proves much too restrictive: the 'postcolonial' would only apply to the period following upon decolonization. This usage would bypass the question of neocolonialism and the discussion whether there was ever a 'postcolonial' moment as such in the historical and political sense. The second option becomes much too inclusive: the 'postcolonial' would encompass the entire phenomenon of colonization, from beginning to end, rendering the term 'colonial' entirely dispensable. To be sure, the understanding of 'postcolonial' as conscientization is not without its own difficulties: the term would constitute a synecdoche, reflecting both critical awareness and a historical–political period. Actually, my decided preference would be for a replacement of this term by a different category altogether, a more comprehensive expression, with 'imperial–colonial' as most attractive. One would speak, therefore, of Imperial–Colonial Studies or imperial–colonial discourse. The main obstacle in this regard would be the institutionalization of 'postcolonial' as signifier.

Nomenclature Deployed Howsoever conceived, the term 'postcolonial' inevitably involves mention of two other concepts as well, 'colonialism' and 'imperialism'. The relationship between these concepts, however, is far from clear. Indeed, at times no distinction whatever seems presupposed, and the two terms are used interchangeably. More often than not, however, a distinction is presumed, either implicitly or explicitly, with four major variations in evidence.

The first, which goes back to the Latin roots of the terms, receives its classic statement in the work of Edward Said, as mentioned in several of the works consulted (e.g., Ashcroft, Griffiths, and Tiffin 1998). While imperialism refers to the practice, theory, and attitudes of a dominating center over distant territory, colonialism denotes the implantation of settlements in distant territory by the dominating center. The operative distinction here involves physical presence, geographical and material, of the center in distant territory. The second and third variations belong together insofar as both introduce the element of temporal progress. The second, emerging out of the Marxist tradition, approaches the relationship from the point of view of economics and defines it in sequential terms: whereas colonialism implies mercantilism, intervention of the center in the peripheral economies by way of extraction, imperialism signifies capitalism, intervention by way of redrawing. Physical presence thus yields to economic domination, distinguished in terms of mode. The third, focusing on civilizational development, also posits a sequential relationship but now defined in organizational terms: whereas colonialism proceeds in loose and local fashion, imperialism attains structural and global coherence throughout (Deane). Hence, physical presence is replaced by civilizational control, distinguished in terms of degree. The fourth variation, exemplified by the work of Ania Loomba, employs the terms as indicative of source and impact: while imperialism refers to whatever has to do with the originating and dominating center, colonialism points to whatever has to do with the receiving and subordinate periphery. Thus, spatial considerations replace both physical presence and temporal progress, whether economic or civilizational, as the distinction at work.

I find the fourth variation to be the most attractive. Unlike the first, it is not tied to the question of settlement: one can speak of colonialism without necessary reference to physical presence of the center, as in the case of neocolonialism. Unlike the second, it is not tied to the question of economic framework: one can speak of imperialism without necessary reference to the development of capitalism, a unique historical phenomenon. Unlike the third, it is not tied to the question of civilizational sophistication: one can speak of imperialism without necessary reference to advanced organizational coherence. The distinction is linked, rather, to the question of power, of domination and subordination, and its spatial configuration. As a result, one speaks of imperialism and colonialism as constitutive components of one and the same phenomenon, with the former marking what transpires in the controlling center and the latter what transpires in the controlled periphery. From this perspective, there is no imperialism without colonialism and no colonialism without imperialism. Needless to say, the use of this variation would go hand in hand with my own stated preference for the category of 'imperial–colonial' as signifier for the field in question.

Terrain Surveyed Regardless of semantic force or nomenclature deployed, a most controversial and rather bitter dispute in Postcolonial Studies revolves around the question of the terrain to be covered and analyzed within such studies. The battle lines are clear, with three options clearly in view. Within this issue, a further question regarding the semantic force of the term 'postcolonial' comes to the fore, centering on the insertion of a hyphen within the term itself, 'post-colonial'.

The first option is characterized by emphasis on cultural production. This approach is very much associated with the work of cultural discourse theory, as represented by the triumvirate of Said, Spivak, and Bhabha. Under the influence of poststructuralism, this option foregrounds issues of representability and representation in imperial–colonial frameworks; its mode of discourse is theoretical in orientation and universalist in application (Gugelberger; Sagar). A distinction may be further introduced in terms of focus: a concern with works of literature in particular (Sagar) or with textual production in general (Gugelberger). The second option is marked by emphasis on historical context. This approach is very much distinctive of the critique leveled at cultural discourse theory, more often than not Marxist in orientation. Under the influence of social theory, this option highlights issues of social conditions, drawing on such fields as economics, politics, and sociology; its mode is materialist in orientation and localized in application. Such controversy generated at one point the use of the hyphen as a signifying factor in the discussion: inclusion would refer to cultural production; exclusion, to historical context—a distinction similarly conveyed by the use of 'postcolonialism' and 'postcoloniality' in other quarters. The third option, common in recent criticism, brings these two approaches together: engagement with issues of cultural representability and representation as well as issues of social conditions; attention to the theoretical and the material; incorporation of the universal and the local (Deane). For this option, the presence or absence of the hyphen becomes insignificant, a mere variation in linguistic usage with no semantic import.

I would argue for the third option as the most appropriate and fruitful. Analysis of imperial–colonial phenomena should address both cultural production and historical context: the representation of the imperial–

colonial is as important as its material foundations. Cultural production emerges out of such social conditions; social conditions are represented in and through cultural production. The main difficulty for this option, however, lies in the immensity of such a combined task: the breadth and complexity of the theoretical spectrum required as well as the scope and detail of the historical context(s) in question.

Referential Quandary No matter how the terrain of Postcolonial Studies is surveyed, whether in terms of cultural production or social context or both, a quandary regarding the application of such a relational type of analysis proves unavoidable—a dilemma that goes beyond the semantic force of the prefix, the use of the hyphen, or the nature of the relationship between imperialism and colonialism. This quandary has to do with the power and ramifications of reference present in any study of the relationship between center and periphery. Three positions come readily to mind in this regard.

The first position draws upon the categories of the postcolonial to capture and theorize the relationship between a center and a periphery. In so doing, emphasis is placed on the experience and reality of the periphery, its history and its life, not in its own terms but rather in terms of its relation to the life and history of the center, its reality and experience. Such categories bring out the hold and intrusion of the dominant (e.g., the history of the West) on the subjugated (e.g., the history of the non-Western world). From this vantage point, it is the relationship to the center, a relationship of subordination, that proves most significant for the periphery, and that becomes the focus of Postcolonial Studies. The second position counters that such invocation of the postcolonial forces the life and history of the colonized into the life and history of the colonizing, so that the reality and experience of the periphery is read in the light of the center and, as a result, all that pertains to it is treated as an appendix or hyphen to the center. Within the relationship, therefore, the center is granted a pivotal and privileged role. Such skewing of the reality and experience of the periphery through the filter of the center is regarded as calling into question the project of Postcolonial Studies. From this perspective, such analysis ends up reproducing, quite ironically, the outlook of the center. The third position clears a middle ground. It takes the impact of the center on the periphery as not only undeniable but also fundamental, so that recourse to the postcolonial becomes a pointed and fruitful way of acknowledging and theorizing this impact. At the same time, it does not regard such a framework as ruling out analysis of the periphery in its own terms, away from the center, whenever appropriate or imperative. From this vantage point, Postcolonial Studies emerges as one approach, and a most necessary one, to the periphery, but not the sole one, insofar as it posits more to the periphery than its relation to the center.

This third position I find most persuasive, and easily transferable into my own preferred interpretation of the imperial–colonial category as a spatial signifier. On the one hand, within any imperial–colonial phenomenon, the impact of the center, the imperial, on the periphery, the colonial, is massive and cannot be ignored. To make such a claim is not to rob the colonial of life and history, to reduce it to a mere appendix or hyphen of the imperial; it is to recognize, rather, the formidable web of domination and subordination at work. On the other hand, within any imperial–colonial phenomenon, the periphery can and should also be approached in its own terms—its own reality and experience, cultural production and social context, structures and contradictions. To make such a claim is not to ignore the centrality of empire, to succumb to repression or romanticism; it is to recognize, rather, the fact of separateness and localization in the colonial.

Within this third position, moreover, a series of corresponding temporal distinctions, building upon the base nomenclature of imperialism and colonialism, might prove helpful. Thus, in terms of the center, imperialism would be subdivided as follows: pre-imperialism; imperialism proper; post-imperialism and/or neo-imperialism. Similarly, in terms of the periphery, colonialism would be subdivided as follows: pre-colonialism; colonialism proper; post-colonialism and/or neo-colonialism. In each case, the middle category (imperialism or colonialism) would signify that stage of direct and formal political control over the territory in question. The first stage (pre-imperialism or pre-colonialism) would stand for whatever preceded the imperial–colonial framework in question, while the third stage (post-imperialism or post-colonialism) would indicate whatever follows upon the cessation of formal and direct political control, a situation that may very well involve continued control beyond the political (neo-imperialism or neo-colonialism). In addition, on each side of the imperial–colonial phenomenon, the forces of opposition have to be recognized and theorized as well (at the center, anti-imperialism; in the periphery, anti-colonialism). Within this overall classification, then, invocation of the postcolonial would seem de rigueur in the middle and last (if neo-imperialism and neo-colonialism are the result) stages, while analysis of the periphery in its own terms would seem essential in the initial and last (if post-imperialism and post-colonialism are the result) stages. At any point, however, whenever deemed in order, analysis of the periphery may be conducted in terms of its own life and history, without reference to the center, even within the middle stage.

Nature of Encounter Invocation of the postcolonial, howsoever defined or deployed, leads to a further controversy having to do with the mode of the encounter between center and periphery present in any imperial–colonial framework. Three tendencies can be readily outlined in this regard: the homogenizing; the localizing; and the multifarious.

On the homogenizing side, two variations, not mutually exclusive, are worth mentioning; both stress commonality. In one case, the encounter is portrayed as a clash between the oppressive forces of the imperial and the resisting forces of the colonial. In this scenario, unremitting oppression meets steadfast resistance, active or passive. In the second case, the encounter between center and periphery is depicted in such a way as to flatten the character of both center and periphery, rendering all empires as well as all colonies, whether controlled by the same empire or not, as functionally the same. On the localizing side, the emphasis is on distinctiveness. The more theoretical the approach to imperial–colonial frameworks, the less in touch it is with actual imperial–colonial frameworks. The answer lies in close, detailed analysis of such encounters. On the multifarious side, the stress is on balance between commonality and distinctiveness. Thus, while there may be recurring elements in imperial–colonial encounters, the variations need to be acknowledged and theorized as well. On the one hand, such encounters involve considerable ambiguity in both center and periphery, ranging from oppression–resistance to attraction–seduction. On the other hand, such encounters involve considerable variation in the constitution and practice of both empires and colonies, even when under the power of one and the same empire.

The third tendency is the most appealing by far. It avoids the temptation of reductionism—the channeling of imperial–colonial encounters into a totalizing model of interaction, operative throughout. It avoids the temptation of pointilism—the shunning of comparison among imperial–colonial encounters. It opts, rather, for a balance of general principles or common elements and unique details or distinctive components. Commonalities are neither favored nor eschewed. In effect, both commonalities and differences need to be acknowledged and theorized. The main drawback is clear: the immensity of the task required by such balance.

Question of Scope

Regarding the range of the field as a whole, I see two issues as recurrent: the sense of origins and the principle of uniqueness, both of which have a decisive impact on transhistorical and transcultural applicability. Both issues are, in turn, responsible for a number of outstanding lacunae in the field.

Sense of Origins A reading of the literature on postcolonialism reveals, in my experience, a very definite, and circumscribed, sense of origins. The preceding overview of such literature, representative and focused as it is, readily confirms this general impression. Two basic features should be noted in this regard.

First, the discussion centers prominently on the imperial–colonial formations of the West from the eighteenth through the twentieth centuries. Sometimes, the discussion does so in exclusive fashion, without any reference whatsoever to other imperial–colonial formations, whether in other historical periods or other cultural contexts. In some cases, a limited element of comparison is introduced by way of contrast to the earlier imperial–colonial formations of the West in the sixteenth and seventeenth centuries. At other times, the discussion pursues the comparative element more extensively, historically as well as culturally, by speaking of imperial–colonial formations as long-standing and wide-spread phenomena. Here the range of the discussion varies widely. Thus, one may find mention of formations contemporary with those of the West, such as the Ottoman Empire or the Japanese Empire; prior to those of the West but within the Western tradition, like the Roman Empire or its Greek precedents; or across the board, from antiquity broadly conceived to the present broadly conceived. However, even when imperial–colonial formations are described as recurring historical phenomena, in evidence across the spectrum of cultures, the discussion that follows swiftly moves on to focus on the more recent imperial–colonial formations of the West. By and large, therefore, comparative analysis has played a rather minor role in Postcolonial Studies. The result is clear: questions of transhistorical or transcultural applicability remain basically unaddressed.

Second, within this given focus on Western imperial–colonial formations in the course of the eighteenth through the twentieth centuries, the discussion centers prominently as well on one such particular formation, the British Empire. In effect, much of the literature comes out of this tradition, whether written by those from the imperial center or those from the colonial periphery, and foregrounds this tradition. Thus, the names and references mentioned, the cultural production and social context examined, the literature and scholarship consulted, all derive, by and large, from the life and history of the United Kingdom and its territorial possessions during the period in question. Therefore, even within its overriding concern for the Western formations, comparative analysis has played, by and large, a rather minor role in Postcolonial Studies. The result is, again, clear: questions of transhistorical or transcultural applicability remain essentially unaddressed.

Principle of Uniqueness Such emphasis on recent imperial formations of the West in general and on that of the British Empire in particular is, in my opinion, not at all the result of mere chance. Behind it—sometimes explicitly advanced; sometimes implicitly so—lies a principle: uniqueness. To wit: a claim that there is something radically distinctive about the recent imperial–colonial formations of the West that set them apart, as a group, from all other such formations, historically as well as culturally. This claim bears a further nuance: such distinctiveness is to be found most tellingly in the British Empire. This principle does not ultimately remove the recent Western formations as a variation of the imperial–colonial phenomenon, but it does place them on a different level altogether.

The key to this distinctiveness is always identified as the conjunction taking place during the time in question between the imperial–colonial formations of the West and the emerging forces of modernity and capitalism in the West. This collusion of geopolitical relations, on the one hand, and social/economic developments, on the other, separates these Western formations, as a collective, not only from the immediately preceding formations within the West itself but also from all other variations across historical periods and cultural contexts. The emphasis on the United Kingdom can be readily explained thereby. Since modernity and capitalism have their beginnings in the British Isles, only to move later on across the European subcontinent from North to South, the British formation emerges as the prime and leading example of this new, transmogrified, and unique phenomenon: the modern and capitalist imperial–colonial formation. Consequently, not only can this formation in general (the West) be approached and analyzed by itself, but also in particular (Great Britain); in both regards, therefore, comparative analysis plays but a rather minor role. The result, once again, is obvious: questions of transhistorical and transcultural applicability remain fundamentally untouched.

Resultant Lacunae The combination of a limited sense of provenance and the underlying principle of difference leads to a number of egregious lacunae in Postcolonial Studies. By lacunae, to be sure, I do not mean to say that there is no discussion whatsoever, only that such discussions are, comparatively speaking, rather minor in character. From my own context and interests, the following strike me as particularly significant:

Realm of Antiquity. Whenever the imperial–colonial formation is understood in broad terms, the world of the Roman Empire is unfailingly
invoked as a prime, even ideal, example of this phenomenon. Such
understanding often goes on to mention the Greek precedents of the
Roman Empire, as part of the often-posited 'Greco-Roman' tradition.
At times, the influence of this particular formation is underlined as well,
indeed as a prototype for future formations, especially in the West. This

historical trajectory is quickly made and quickly left behind. No analysis to speak of is undertaken either of the Roman Empire as such or of the relationship between this foundational formation and its later, deliberate imitations. What is true of the Roman Empire is true of all antiquity, whether with respect to the world of the Near East or the Mediterranean Basin or those of Africa, Asia, and the Pacific, or the Americas and the Caribbean. Such absence, however, is most conspicuous in the case of Greco-Roman antiquity, given the connections generally taken for granted between such formations and the later Western ones within a continuing 'Western' tradition. In Postcolonial Studies such histories and voices remain, for the most part, silent.

Latin America and the Caribbean. Although the beginnings of the Western imperial–colonial formations is dutifully traced to the sixteenth and seventeenth centuries—that is, to the early, expansionist and mercantile, formations of the Spanish and Portuguese Empires, extending to America and beyond (the African coasts and outlying islands and archipelagos; islands and archipelagos in the Pacific)—one finds hardly any analysis of these formations. Such examples are quickly noted and quickly abandoned. This absence is all the more remarkable, given the fact that these colonies undergo the process of upheaval, independence, and neo-dependence anywhere from one hundred and fifty to fifty years earlier than those of the other Western formations, with the exception of the United States and Haiti. In Postcolonial Studies, such histories and voices remain largely submerged.

Russia and the Union of Soviet Socialist Republics. Rarely does one find mention of the Russian Empire either among or alongside the imperial–colonial formations of the West from the eighteenth through the twentieth centuries. One is more likely to find, it seems to me, references to the Ottoman Empire or the Japanese Empire than to Russia and its ever-expanding move eastward. Just as rarely does one find mention of the Soviet Empire, the heir and continuation of the Russian Empire, among the imperial–colonial formations of the twentieth century. This omission is particularly hard to fathom, given the fact that the Soviet Union expanded and sought to expand ever westward, indeed globally, that it functioned as the undisputed leader of the 'East' in global opposition to the 'West', and that it endured much longer as an imperial–colonial formation than its counterparts in the West. Such allusions, when made, are quickly offered and quickly forgotten. In Postcolonial Studies such histories and voices further remain almost completely and strangely subdued.

The United States of America. More common, though by no means frequent, are references to the American Empire among the Western imperial–colonial formations of the nineteenth and twentieth centuries. Such recognition is generally accompanied by a further observation to the effect that the case of the United States proves rather unique within the history of the phenomenon, insofar as it constitutes, in sequential fashion, an example of both a Western colony (or group of colonies), as part of the British Empire, and a Western empire, after becoming a nation-state in its own right. Such mention is quickly advanced and quickly bypassed. This absence proves difficult to understand on several counts, since the United States: first, moves ever westward and southward through the duration of the nineteenth century, even contemplating expansion into the Pacific Ocean as well as into territories in the Caribbean, Central America, and Mexico; second, comes to embody, at the turn of the twentieth century, the epitome of modernity and capitalism; third, builds steadily, throughout the course of the twentieth century, a spectacular military complex and network; fourth, becomes the undisputed leader of the 'West' in global opposition to the 'East'. In Postcolonial Studies such histories and voices remain, for the most part, eerily dormant as well.

As mentioned earlier, these lacunae are significant to me on account of my own interests and context: first, as a student of early Christianity, whose origins and development take place within the imperial–colonial framework of Rome throughout the Circum-Mediterranean; second, as a product of Latin America and the Caribbean, born and raised within one of the last two territorial possessions of the Spanish Empire in the Western Hemisphere, Cuba, with separation coming only at the very end of the nineteenth century; third, as a subject of the Soviet imperial–colonial formation by way of a global outpost, Cuba; finally, as a part of the American imperial–colonial formation in two respects: to begin with, by way of territorial possession and neocolonial sphere of influence, given my origins in Cuba, the Caribbean, and Latin America; subsequently, by way of residence and citizenship, as denizen of a superpower that has now become a hyperpower, with a grand imperial strategy in the making. In all four respects, Postcolonial Studies becomes most attractive for me; however, the absence of such specific discourses proves at once frustrating and challenging.

Lacuna of Religious Discourse

This exposition of various lacunae in Postcolonial Studies leads me to a final observation regarding yet another noteworthy absence in the literature, quite evident in the works surveyed above. It is rare to find any mention of religion whether by way of cultural production or social matrix. It is almost as if religious texts and expressions did not form part of the cultural production and as if religious institutions and practices did not belong to the social matrix of imperial–colonial frameworks. I would argue, as a student of religion in general and of the Christian religion in particular, that religion is to be acknowledged and theorized as a constitutive component of such frameworks, and a most important one—as important as, say, literature or economics.

Concluding Observation

I undertook the writing of this essay, as explained in the Introduction, in order to secure adequate grounding and direction for the proposed confluence of Biblical Studies and Postcolonial Studies. This I sought to do by tracing the two fundamental questions of meaning and scope in Postcolonial Studies through a close reading of its introductory literature. This effort yielded a variety of issues in dispute and a spectrum of positions within such issues with respect to both questions. I should now like to conclude by summarizing my own stance regarding the proposed confluence.

Question of Scope

I subscribe to the view that imperial–colonial formations represent long-standing and wide-ranging phenomena, present across historical periods and cultural contexts. I see no reason why postcolonial analysis should be limited to the modern and capitalist formations of the West; I see comparative analysis as justified and in order. Such analysis can thus be gainfully extended to the world of antiquity in general and to the Roman formation in particular. Moreover, I see no reason why postcolonial analysis should not include the religious dimension; I see the analysis of religion as justified and in order. Thus, I hold that the study of early Christianity can be readily and fruitfully approached from such a perspective: a set of primarily religious responses developed from within and having to do with the imperial–colonial framework of Rome. Such study further comprehends, as stated at the beginning, the approach to such responses and their context on the part of Western critics through today as well as of non-Western critics since the 1970s.

Question of Meaning

Needless to say, such study should be undertaken in the light of and in full dialogue with Postcolonial Studies. Such study, I would argue, should: foreground throughout the unequal relationship of domination and subordination at work; address the imperial as well as the colonial spaces, the center and the periphery; examine both cultural production and material matrix; make room for pursuing the colonial in its own terms; and opt for diversity in recording the encounter between the imperial and the colonial. Finally, given its own emphasis on a relationship of inequality, such study should affect and be affected by other studies with a similar focus on unequal relations—Feminist, Liberation, Minority, Gay and Lesbian Studies. A tall order, indeed, but of the essence.

Bibliography

Adam, Ian, and Helen Tiffin
    1991   *Past the Last Post: Theorizing Post-Colonialism and Post-Modernism* (Hemel Hempstead, UK: Harvester Wheatsheaf).
Ashcroft, Bill, Gareth Griffiths, and Helen Tiffin
    1998   *Key Concepts in Post-Colonial Studies* (London and New York: Routledge).
Ashcroft, Bill, Gareth Griffiths, and Helen Tiffin (eds.)
    1989   *The Empire Writes Back: Theory and Practice in Post-Colonial Literatures* (London: Routledge).
    1995   *The Post-Colonial Studies Reader* (London and New York: Routledge).
Baldick, Chris
    1990   *The Concise Oxford Dictionary of Literary Terms* (Oxford and New York: Oxford University Press).
Barker, F., P. Hulme, and M. Iversen
    1994   'Introduction', in F. Barker, P. Hulme, and M. Iversen (eds.), *Colonial Discourse/Postcolonial Theory* (Manchester and New York: Manchester University Press): 1–23.
Boehmer, Elleke
    1995   *Colonial and Postcolonial Literature: Migrant Metaphors* (Oxford and New York: Oxford University Press).
Childers, Joseph, and Gary Hentzi (eds.)
    1995   *Columbia Dictionary of Modern Literary and Cultural Criticism* (New York: Columbia University Press).
Childs, P., and P. Williams
    1997   *An Introduction to Post-Colonial Theory* (London: Harvester-Wheatsheaf).
Deane, Seamus
    1995   'Imperialism/Nationalism', in Frank Lentricchia and Thomas McLaughlin (eds.), *Critical Terms for Literary Study* (2nd edn; Chicago and London: University of Chicago Press): 354–68.
During, Simon
    1985   'Postmodernism or Postcolonialism?', *Landfall* 39: 366–80.
    1987   'Postmodernism or Postcolonialism Today', *Textual Practice* 1: 32–47.
Gandhi, Leela
    1998   *Postcolonial Theory: A Critical Introduction* (New York: Columbia University Press).
Gray, Martin
    1985   *A Dictionary of Literary Terms* (York Handbooks; Beirut: York Press; Harlow: Longman Group Ltd.).

Green, Michael
1996   'Cultural Studies', in Michael Payne (ed.), *A Dictionary of Cultural and Critical Theory* (Oxford: Blackwell Publishers): 124–28.

Gugelberger, Georg M.
1995   'Postcolonial Cultural Studies', in Michael Groden and Martin Kreiswirth (eds.), *The Johns Hopkins Guide to Literature & Criticism* (Baltimore and London: The Johns Hopkins University Press): 581–84.

Judd, Dennis
1996   *Empire: The British Imperial Experience from 1765 to the Present* (London: HarperCollins).

Klor de Alva, J.J.
1995   'The Postcolonization of the (Latin) American Experience, a Reconsideration of "Colonialism", "Postcolonialism" and "Mestijaze"', in G. Prakash (ed.), *After Colonialism, Imperial Histories and Postcolonial Displacements* (Princeton: Princeton University Press): 241–75.

Loomba, Ania
1998   *Colonialism/Postcolonialism* (The New Critical Idiom; London–New York: Routledge).

McLeod, J.
2000   *Beginning Postcolonialism* (Beginnings Series; Manchester: Manchester University Press).

Moore-Gilbert, B.
1997   *Postcolonial Theory: Contexts, Practices, Politics* (London and New York: Verso).

Moore-Gilbert, B., G. Stanton, and W. Maley
1997   'Introduction', in B. Moore-Gilbert, G. Stanton, and W. Maley (eds.), *Postcolonial Criticism* (Longman Critical Readers; London and New York: Longman, 1997): 1–72.

Peck, John, and Martin Coyle
1985   *Literary Terms and Criticism* (How to Study Literature; London: Macmillan Education Ltd.).

Prakash, G.
1995   'After Colonialism', in G. Prakash (ed.), *After Colonialism: Imperial Histories and Postcolonial Displacements* (Princeton: Princeton University Press): 3–17.

Quayson, A.
2000   *Postcolonialism: Theory, Practice, or Process?* (Cambridge: Polity Press).

Sagar, Aparajita
1996   'Postcolonial Studies', in Michael Payne (ed.), *A Dictionary of Cultural and Critical Theory* (Oxford: Blackwell Publishers): 423–28.

Said, Edward
1978   *Orientalism* (New York: Vintage).
1993   *Culture and Imperialism* (London: Chatto & Windus).

Sarup, Madan
1989   *An Introductory Guide to Post-Structuralism and Postmodernism* (Athens: University of Georgia Press).

Segovia, Fernando F.
2000   *Decolonizing Biblical Studies: A View from the Margins* (Maryknoll: Orbis Books).

Selden, Raman
1989   *A Reader's Guide to Contemporary Literary Theory* (2nd edn; Lexington: University Press of Kentucky).

Slemon, Stephen
1994   'The Scramble for Post-Colonialism', in C. Tiffin and A. Lawson (eds.), *De-Scribing Empire: Postcolonialism and Textuality* (London: Routledge): 15–32.

Spivak, Gayatri Chakravorty
1985   'Can the Subaltern Speak? Speculations on Widow Sacrifice', *Wedge* 7/8: 120–30.
1990   *The Post-Colonial Critic: Interviews, Strategies, Dialogues* (ed. S. Harasym; London: Routledge).

Sprinker, M.
1995   'Introduction', in R. de la Campa, E.A. Kaplan, and M. Sprinker (eds.), *Late Imperial Culture* (London–New York: Verso): 1–10.

Spurr, D.
1993   *The Rhetoric of Empire: Colonial Discourse in Journalism, Travel Writing, and Imperial Administration* (Durham, NC, and London: Duke University Press).

Stevens, Bonnie Klomp, and Larry L. Stewart
1992   *A Guide to Literary Criticism and Research* (2nd edn; Fort Worth: Harcourt Brace Jovanovich College Publishers).

Storey, John
1993   *An Introductory Guide to Cultural Theory and Popular Culture* (Athens: University of Georgia Press).

Williams, P., and L. Chrisman
1994   'Colonial Discourse and Post-Colonial Theory: An Introduction', in P. Williams and L. Chrisman (eds.), *Colonial Discourse and Post-Colonial Theory: A Reader* (New York: Columbia University Press): 1–20.

Young, Robert C.
1995   *Colonial Desire: Hybridity in Theory, Culture and Race* (London: Routledge).
        Postcolonialism: An Historical Introduction (Oxford: Blackwell).

QUESTIONS OF BIBLICAL AMBIVALENCE AND AUTHORITY UNDER A TREE OUTSIDE DELHI; OR, THE POSTCOLONIAL AND THE POSTMODERN

Stephen D. Moore

> Driven by the subaltern history of the margins of modernity—rather than by the failures of logocentrism—I have tried, in some small measure, to revise the known, to rename the postmodern from the position of the postcolonial. (Bhabha 1994d: 175)

Prefatory 'Post-'script

Postcolonialism and postmodernism: one would be hard pressed by now to intone two more overdetermined, and overinflated, critical terms.[1] Is the 'post' in postcolonialism the same as the 'post' in postmodernism (cf. Appiah 1991),[2] so that the two terms are merely alternative names for the same phenomenon? At first glance, perhaps, it might appear that a case could be made for this position, particularly if 'postmodernism', or, better for our purposes, 'postmodernity', is understood as that which has replaced or displaced 'modernity' (to resort for the moment to a rather crude chrono-logic), the latter being understood in turn as the combined and cumulative product of the European Reformation, Scientific Revolution, and Enlightenment—together with the corollary colonization of the

---

1. The term 'postcolonialism', for instance, 'designates too many things, all at once', as Aijaz Ahmad complains. 'It is said to refer, first, to conditions that are said to prevail in the former colonies, such as India. But the same term is also made to refer to a *global* condition of the relations between the West and the Rest ... —so that "postcoloniality" becomes a "post" not only of colonialism but also of an indeterminate larger thing. At the same time, the term "postcolonial" also comes to us as the name of a *discourse* about the condition of "postcoloniality"', and a discourse that presumes a 'prior consent to theoretical postmodernity', what is more. 'Between postcoloniality as it exists in a former colony like India, and postcoloniality as the condition of discourse practised by such critics as Homi Bhabha', he concludes sardonically, 'there would appear to be a very considerable gap' (1996: 283, his emphasis). Postcolonialism's other discontents include Robert Young, who, although poles apart from Ahmad in other ways, proposes jettisoning the term 'postcolonialism' altogether and replacing it with 'tricontinentalism' (2001: 57).
2. Appiah's voice is but one in a cacophonous chorus that has addressed this perplexing relationship—and arrived at a range of incommensurate conclusions. See, in addition: Adam and Tiffin 1989; Ashcroft, Griffiths, and Tiffin 1995: Part IV ('Postmodernism and Postcolonialism'); Bhabha 1994d, 1996; Moore-Gilbert 1997: 121–30; Tiffin 1988; Quayson 2000.

non-European world. Colonial exploitation, not least the slave trade, has often been said to have enabled the economies of early (and not so early) modern Europe in the material realm, while in the psychic realm the non-European world, conceived as quintessentially 'superstitious' and 'primitive', served conveniently as the constitutive Other for Europe's dominant image of itself as quintessentially 'rational' and 'civilized' (cf. Moore-Gilbert 1997: 123). But if modernity is to be regarded as in no small part an effect of European colonialism, might not postmodernity and postcolonialism be regarded in consequence not only as natural allies but even as virtual synonyms?

To argue thus, however, would be to indulge in an overbenign reduction of the concept of postmodernity, or, to revert to the more common term, postmodernism.[3] As the latter term is now frequently used, it names much more than an anti-hegemonic reaction to or repudiation of the world-annexing impulses of European modernity. In its more bloated forms, indeed, postmodernism is a code word for the cultural logic of late capitalism (cf. Jameson 1991), whose signal features include mass culture, mass media, multinational corporations, and information technology—although, seen from the 'underside', as it were, this same set of features appear as the dissolution of traditional societies, asymmetrical systems of economic exchange, crippling national debt, limited access to technology, and so on. Postmodernism, thus distended, however, is, if anything, a synonym not for *post*colonialism so much as for *neo*colonialism. The latter term, which is less evocative, perhaps, of a state 'beyond' colonialism than of the West's continued domination of the Rest (cf. Nkrumah 1965; Young 2001: 44–56), better names the socio-economic and socio-political constraints within which the majority of the world's population conducts its daily affairs. I am reminded of a now misplaced magazine article that tells of a certain African village's recent attempts to honor the parousia of the CEO of Microsoft Corporation, a visitation preceded by a gift to the village of a state-of-the-art PC. Bill Gates arrived with his entourage to discover that the computer had been hooked up to the sole electrical outlet in the village, thereby becoming a shrine to the *deus absconditus* of neocolonialism, and a poignant symbol of the village's simultaneous inclusion in and exclusion from the benefits of global capitalism—or of 'postmodernism', in the distended sense. Far from being a synonym for 'postcolonialism', indeed, 'postmodernism', as neocolonialism, might instead be the primary phenomenon presently in need of postcolonial critique.

---

3. Not that these two terms are invariably synonymous either (see Moore 1989: 544–51), but it will not be necessary to tease them apart (again) here.

And yet there can be no clean subject–object separation of postcolonialism and postmodernism either, if for no other reason than that a third term regularly mediates between them in such a way as to muddy any clear distinction between them. That term is 'poststructuralism'.[4] In the minds of most who ponder such matters, poststructuralism (epitomized by, although by no means confined to, Derridean deconstruction) is quintessential academic postmodernism—postmodernism as academic discourse. And postcolonial theory—the most visible manifestation of contemporary postcolonial studies, itself epitomized by the names of Edward Said (1978a; 1993), Gayatri Chakravorty Spivak (1987; 1990; 1999), and Homi Bhabha (1994b)—is, for the most part, poststructuralist through and through.[5] Said's *Orientalism* (1978a), for instance, generally regarded as the charter document of postcolonial theory, makes strategic use of the analytic categories of Michel Foucault (but also those of Antonio Gramsci) to excavate the West's multi-discursive construction of the 'Orient'—although Said's dealings with Foucault, never entirely uncritical, have since been marked with increasing caution. Spivak's embrace of poststructuralist thought, primarily that of Jacques Derrida, has been less equivocal (the epithet 'feminist Marxist deconstructivist' memorably bestowed upon her by Colin McCabe in the foreword to *In Other Worlds* [Spivak 1987] seems apt, despite her own caginess about

4. A term that readily evokes a congeries of interrelated topoi: the systematic dismantling of 'metaphysical' concepts (origin, essence, identity, transcendence, etc.) and hierarchical oppositions (presence/absence, primary/secondary, central/marginal, white/non-white, masculine/feminine, heterosexual/homosexual, etc.); the meticulous analysis of the ways in which literary, critical, and philosophical arguments are invariably destabilized by the figures and tropes that they necessarily employ; the exposure of the exclusions, omissions, and systemic blind-spots that enable texts, and societies, to function; the unearthing of the constructedness of the most solid-seeming features of our cultural landscapes ('man', the body, insanity, gender, sexuality, race/ethnicity, etc.); the investigation of the ineluctable place of power in the fabric(ation) of truth and knowledge; the exploration of the radical internal heteronomy allegedly fissuring every human subject; the examination of the ways in which every text, independently of the conscious intentionality of any author, traverses countless other texts, ceaselessly recycling and rewriting them; and so on. See further, Moore 1994.

5. Excellent (if exacting) introductions to Said, Spivak, and Bhabha can be found both in Young 1990 and Moore-Gilbert 1997. More basic introductions to all three can be found in Hawley 2001. Moore-Gilbert has subsequently had a second shot at Spivak and Bhabha (Moore-Gilbert 2000), while Young has returned to Said (2001: 383–94). Full-length books on Said or Spivak include: Hussein 2002; Ashcroft and Ahluwalia 2001; and Morton 2002. Said has been an important interlocutor for a handful of biblical scholars, notably Sugirtharajah (1998) and Friesen (2001). For attempts at biblical exegesis in a Bhabhan mode, see Runions 2002; Thurman 2003; and Moore forthcoming. Bhabha plays a more effaced, although by no means insignificant, role in Brett 2000; Liew 1999; and Samuel 2002. Other than Donaldson's essay in the present volume, I know of no sustained biblical-critical engagement with Spivak's work.

being labeled), and the same is true of Bhabha, who is likewise heavily indebted to Derrida, as we shall see, but also to Jacques Lacan, and, to a lesser degree, to Foucault, Roland Barthes, Julia Kristeva, and even Louis Althusser (to add a 'structuralist' name to the familiar 'poststructuralist' litany).

Postcolonial theory (or colonial discourse analysis, to restore its original name to it) has comfortably assumed its appointed place (all *too* comfortably, some would argue; more on this below) within the Anglo-American academy alongside New Historicism, third-wave feminism, queer theory, cultural studies, and other theory-savvy critical movements that all, to a greater or lesser degree, bring critical sensibilities forged in the crucible of an often generic poststructuralism to bear upon assorted 'material' domains (history, not least the colonial variety; gender; sex and sexuality; popular culture), frequently in explicit reaction to the first, neo-formalist, putatively apolitical phase of French poststructuralism's appropriation in the anglophone academy. Said's *Orientalism*, in particular, can be regarded as a crucial catalyst in the politicization not just of Anglo-American poststructuralism but of the Anglo-American literary academy more generally,[6] a transformation that began in earnest in the early 1980s and has been unrelenting ever since.

Not surprisingly, perhaps, the spectacle of poststructuralism's systematic politicization, especially within the US academy, has itself elicited political critique, none more scathing, perhaps, than that of Aijaz Ahmad (1992), whose primary target happens to be postcolonial theory, the bull's-eye on the target being Edward Said. According to Ahmad (and the summary of his extended arguments that follows is a partial and rather freely paraphrastic one), postcolonial theory replicates troublingly within the Western academy the international division of labor characteristic of global capitalism, whereby raw materials generated in the Third World (in this case, the archival products of colonialism: administrative records, missionary tracts, traces of indigenous voices, and so on) are exported to the First World, where they are turned into refined or luxury products by a privileged intelligentsia (themselves thoroughly insulated from the harsh material realities of Third World existence) for consumption by a metropolitan elite of fellow-scholars and graduate students, which in fact constitutes their primary audience, all direct engagement with the extra-academic world, least of all the working class or underclass, even within the USA itself, being foreclosed almost as a matter of course.

---

6. Also worth noting in this regard is Said's once influential essay, 'The Problem of Textuality: Two Exemplary Positions' (1978b), which pitted a rhetorically politicized Foucault against a depoliticized Derrida.

Symptomatic of the complicity of postcolonial theory with late capitalist ideology, presumably (to echo Ahmad further, but also to extrapolate from him), would be the fact that some of the wealthiest Western universities, ornate pillars of the social and political establishment, reserve some of their most coveted and most lucrative positions for 'politicized' theorist-critics, not least leading postcolonial theorist-critics: Spivak holds a prestigious chair at Columbia, as did Said until his death in 2003, while Bhabha holds a no less prestigious one at Harvard (having ascended there in stages by way of the University of Sussex and the University of Chicago, his stock, like that of Spivak, formerly of the University of Pittsburgh, inexorably rising with that of postcolonial studies). Such allegations, while crude, can have a deep impact nonetheless. A few semesters ago, to recite a personal example, an Argentinian student in one of my courses read aloud, and in shocked tones, an excerpt from Ahmad's blistering broadside at the outset of a class discussion of postcolonial theory, after which many members of the class seemed to find it all but impossible to take the topic seriously.

Rajeswari Sunder Rajan, writing in *Critical Inquiry*, has attempted to respond on behalf of the accused (although the accusations he is countering are not those of Ahmad per se so much as the related ones of Arif Dirlik [1994]). 'The operation of global capitalism as cause', notes Rajan, 'is so pervasive that it is only too easy to establish that intellectuals in particular (and of every persuasion) are co-opted within its system' (1997: 597). He goes on to suggest that what would be of significantly more interest would be 'the identification of criticism or critics who could be considered exempt from the embrace of capitalism's reward system' (*ibid.*). Rajan does not altogether succeed, however, in deflecting Dirlik's (or Ahmad's) accusations, for there are rewards and rewards, and the rewards attaching to an endowed chair at Harvard or Columbia are one thing, while those attaching to, say, a position at an inner-city community college are another altogether (to remain for now within the USA, although the remuneration for such a position, even at entry level, would far exceed, even in real terms, that for a senior position at, say, the University of Havana, to cull but one example from a great many possible ones). But the argument now threatens to undercut itself, for faculty at community colleges and other institutions at the base of the US pyramid of higher learning typically lack the leisure to engage in research and publication, so that the only First World postcolonial intellectuals whose theoretical positions would, in accordance with the implicit canons advanced by Ahmad and Dirlik, be fully 'authenticated' by their institutional locations would be those whose voices would be altogether absent from published academic debate—unlike those of Ahmad and Dirlik themselves.

What *is* highly instructive, nonetheless (and both Ahmad and Dirlik serve to remind us forcibly of it), is how the USA can brazenly lavish its most exalted academic honors upon the very intellectual class that tends to be most critical both of its domestic arrangements and international operations, seemingly in the sure and certain knowledge that the pronouncements of such intellectuals, once they exit the academic sphere, will plummet silently into a bottomless well of public indifference (unlike those of the Dixie Chicks, say, whose moderate interrogation of Operation Iraqi Freedom raised a storm of public reaction). 'I always counsel people against the decision to go into the academy because they hope to be effective beyond it', literary theorist Stanley Fish announced at a much publicized moratorium on 'theory' recently staged at the University of Chicago (Eakin 2003: D9). For Ahmad, as we noted earlier, Said epitomizes theory's scandalous shortcomings. Yet it is precisely the late Edward Said who may be said to have constituted the outstanding contemporary exception to Fish's cynical rule: Said was a leading US academic intellectual whose outspoken (and theory-honed) views on Israeli-Palestinian relations in particular, expressed in numerous news-paper and magazine articles and radio and television interviews, and anchored in years of active service on the Palestinian National Council, made him a familiar and formidable name to an indeterminate but surely sizeable international public, many or most of whom had never heard of postcolonial studies.

And what of Homi Bhabha—interestingly enough, the only one of the more than two dozen academic luminaries assembled around the table at the Chicago colloquium on theory's alleged bankruptcy to venture a defense of theory's political efficacy (Eakin 2003: D9)? What I myself have encountered repeatedly in recent years, as have several of my immediate colleagues in neighboring theological disciplines, is that a striking number of students coming into our classes, international students in particular, with intense commitments to social justice, vernacular hermeneutics, liberative praxis, and activist politics, feel themselves personally addressed by Homi Bhabha and discover in critical categories such as colonial ambivalence, mimicry, and hybridity analytic tools that enable them to reconceptualize their own relationships to their frequently complex socio-cultural locations in ways that they experience as transforming and even empowering—as do I myself.

In the cultural crucible in which I spent my own formative years (that of postcolonial, hyper-Catholic, southern Ireland of the 1950s and 1960s), the Bible was an English book—*the* English book, indeed (cf. Bhabha 1994e: 102)—so much so that when in due course I went in search of a college degree program in Biblical Studies, the only real avenues open to me in the Irish Republic were the degrees offered at the University of Dublin, Trinity College, that enduring monument to British colonial rule in Ireland, founded by Elizabeth I in 1592 to educate the sons of the Protestant Anglo-Irish aristocracy and effectively closed to Catholics until the 1960s.

My training in Biblical Studies at Trinity was simultaneously an induction in Postcolonial Studies, although I was insufficiently aware of it at the time. In any case (although I would not want to make too much of it), it is my own (necessarily eroded) identity as a member of that most unlikely of postcolonial peoples—a nation of white West Europeans whose formative history includes some 800 years of colonial intervention (and not as agent, but as object)[7]—that equips me now with a keen appetite for pondering the complexities that characterize the often tortuous exchanges between colonizer and colonized during colonial occupation and after official decolonization (and not just in Ireland, of course), relations of domination and submission, coercion and co-option, attraction and revulsion (the very relations that most preoccupy Bhabha, as we shall see, and are the objects of his most incisive analyses)—and with tracing the Bible's ever-shifting place in this intricate web of exchanges.

Picking Up Bhabha's Thread

> And the holiest of books, the Bible, bearing both the standard of the cross and the standard of empire finds itself strangely dismembered. (Bhabha 1994c: 92)

To begin again, but differently: postcolonial studies, poststructuralism, biblical interpretation—at least one notable interfacing of these three reading practices has already occurred, and occurred not in a corner but in a text that, arguably, ranks alongside Said's *Orientalism* as, simultaneously, the most celebrated and most contested product of contemporary postcolonial studies. I speak of Bhabha's 1994 essay collection, *The Location of Culture*, and specifically of 'Signs Taken for Wonders' (originally published in 1985), the sixth of its eleven essays, and as such a centerpiece of sorts. Not unlike other essays of 1980s' vintage engaged in a fusion of poststructuralism and historiography—New Historicist essays in particular—this one too opens with an historical anecdote.[8]

---

7. In applying the adjective 'colonial' in blanket fashion to this entire 800-year span, I am aware that I am putting a simple spin on a complex issue. For an elaborately nuanced discussion of the ways in which the labels 'colonial' and 'postcolonial' may or may not be applied to Irish history, see Howe 2000: 7–20. Further primers on Ireland and postcoloniality include Lloyd 1993 and Kiberd 1995.

8. For the strategic role of the anecdote in New Historicism, see Graham and Moore 1997: 439–45. In brief, the classic New Historicist anecdote is assigned to blow a hole in the teleological (and frequently theological) metanarratives of traditional historiography, by infecting these over-plotted histories with elements of the contingent and the unassimilable. I would hesitate to ascribe an elaborate theory of the anecdote to 'Signs Taken for Wonders'

The date: May 1817. The place: a grove of trees 'just outside Delhi' (p. 102). An Indian catechist, Anund Messeh, has just arrived at the scene, having journeyed hurriedly and excitedly from his mission in Meerut, apparently in response to a report that a throng of some 500 souls, men, women, and children, are seated in the shade of the trees and engaged in scriptural reading and debate. The following exchange, attributed to Anund and an elderly member of the assembly by the *Missionary Register* of January 1818, whence Bhabha exhumed it, ensues:

> 'Pray who are all these people? and whence come they?' 'We are poor and lowly, and we read and love this book'.—'What is that book?'— 'The book of God!'—'Let me look at it, if you please'. Anund, on opening the book, perceived it to be the Gospel of our Lord, translated into the Hindoostanee Tongue, many copies of which seemed to be in the possession of the party: some were PRINTED, others WRITTEN by themselves from the printed ones. Anund pointed to the name of Jesus, and asked, 'Who is that?'—'That is God! He gave us this book'.— 'Where did you obtain it?'—'An Angel from heaven gave it us, at Hurdwar fair'.—'An Angel?'—'Yes, to us he was God's Angel: but he was a man, a learned Pundit'. (Doubtless these translated Gospels must have been the books distributed, five or six years ago, at Hurdwar by the missionary.) ... 'These books', said Anund, 'teach the religion of the European Sahibs. It is THEIR book; and they printed it in our language, for our use'. (Bhabha 1994e: 102–103)

In the space of some half a dozen sentences, the supplier of this divine book undergoes a rapid series of renamings that cascade in a dizzying descent. First, God himself is said to have provided the book out of his bounty, then his Angel, then a mere mortal, albeit a 'learned Pundit' and missionary, and finally the 'European Sahibs'. The transcendent Word has again become flesh—first brown flesh and then white flesh. Shimmering undecidably at the juncture of two incommensurate cultures, it belongs to both and neither at once.

The anecdote has barely begun to unfold, however; I shall return to it a little later. Its intense attraction for Bhabha is hardly surprising. Bhabha's intellectual idiom is a generic poststructuralism, as we noted earlier, Derridean primarily, though Lacan also looms large on the Bhabhan mindscape, as does Foucault on occasion, and assorted other Parisian *penseurs*. Sizeable swathes of Bhabha's text approximate the near illegible density of early Derrida. Without the Derridean decoder ring, indeed, Bhabha simply cannot be deciphered. And many of the Derridean mana-

---

(even within New Historicism, such a theory only comes to 'mature' expression in Fineman 1989), but Bhabha does attempt to blow some sizeable holes in the metanarrative fabric of nineteenth-century colonial discourse by means of his own anecdote, as we shall see.

words—not least *writing, inscription, doubling, repetition, the book, the text*—are also Bhabhan obsessions, not to say fetishes (fetishism itself being another Bhabhan obsession)—hence the allure of this anecdote for Bhabha, which he reads as an epiphanic scene insistently repeated, 'played out in the wild and wordless wastes of colonial India, Africa, the Caribbean', namely, 'the sudden, fortuitous discovery of the English book' (p. 102)—in this case the quintessential English book, the one that is at once the book of mission and the book of empire. What fascinates Bhabha is the way in which this found book, redolent with originary meaning and authority, universal and immutable, is inevitably and inexorably dislocated and evacuated, hallowed and hollowed at one and the same time, as it is subjected to linguistic and cultural reformulation and deformation—to reiteration, repetition, reinscription, doubling, dissemination, and dis-placement (to recite a deconstructive litany that is as familiar to the reader of Bhabha as to the reader of Derrida).

Bhabha is not without his own conceptual and terminological apparatus, however, drawn largely from Freud via Lacan—although, in hypereclectic fashion, also from a range of other theorist-critics as diverse as Fanon and Bakhtin—and given a highly distinctive inflection: *ambivalence, mimicry,* and *hybridity* are merely some of its better known categories (the Bhabhan mana-words, indeed).[9] Nor does he hesitate to declare his distance from Derrida on occasion, most notably seven pages into the essay under discussion, when he announces his 'departure from Derrida's objectives in "The double session"', the Derridean text he has been milking, and a strategic redirection of attention from 'the vicissitudes of interpretation' in the act of reading 'to the question of the effects of power' in the colonial arena (Bhabha 1994e: 108; cf. Derrida 1981). In the event, Bhabha does not stray very far from Derrida; we are immediately told that the announced 'departure' will actually constitute a 'return' to some underdeveloped themes in Derrida's essay. The question I wish to ponder here, however—hardly a novel question, I realize, although one that, so far as I am aware, has not yet been the subject of protracted reflection in the context of Biblical Studies—is whether or to what extent strategies of reading whittled in the laps of some of the master texts of the European philosophical tradition—for that is what Derrida's texts have by now become—or in the laps of some of the master texts of the European psychoanalytic tradition, in the case of Lacan, are adequate to the task of

---

9. In another essay that, in my own head at least, constitutes a companion piece to the present one, I have attempted to define each of these three analytic categories (definitions echoed in brief below) and 'apply' them to the Apocalypse of John (Moore forthcoming). In that essay, too, I summarize some of the principal criticisms that have been leveled against Bhabha's brand of postcolonial theory (criticisms also echoed in brief below).

analyzing European colonialism and its effects, including the mobilization and counter-mobilization of biblical texts in colonial arenas.

What Bhabha's deployment of poststructuralist, largely Derridean, thought does enable, arguably, is a more adequate appreciation of the *complexity* of the cultural space occupied by the Bible in British India. While Bhabha readily acknowledges that Said's *Orientalism* was seminal for his own project (1994b: ix), he just as readily takes Said to task for his (largely implicit) characterization of colonial discourse, epitomized by Orientalist discourse, as self-confident and self-consistent, monolithic and monologic, animated by a single unifying intention (the will to power), as well as for his corollary assumption that colonization itself is characterized by a one-sided possession of power on the part of the colonizer. Aided and abetted by Freud, as refracted through Lacan, but also through Fanon, Bhabha calls each of these assumptions acutely into question.[10] For Bhabha, colonial discourse is characterized above all by *ambivalence*. It is riddled with contradictions and incoherences, traversed by anxieties and insecurities, and hollowed out by originary lack and internal heterogeneity. For Bhabha, moreover, the locus of colonial power, far from being unambiguously on the side of the colonizer, inheres instead in a shifting, unstable, potentially subversive, 'in-between' or 'third' space between colonizer and colonized, which is characterized by *mimicry*, on the one hand, in which the colonized heeds the colonizer's peremptory injunction to imitation, but in a manner that constantly threatens to teeter over into mockery; and by *hybridity*, on the other hand, another insidious product of the colonial encounter that further threatens to fracture the colonizer's identity and authority.

What Bhabha does not address, directly at least, is what all of this might mean for the colonizer's book—which is, of course, to say the 'European' book par excellence, the Bible—but it requires but little reflection to see that it means the book's *deconstruction*. (Could Bhabha's essential Derrideanism lead us to expect anything else?) If Said's conception of colonial discourse and colonial power admits, in principle at least, of a Bible that can function more or less straightforwardly as an effective instrument of the colonizer's will to subjugate the colonized, Bhabha's conception of colonial discourse and colonial power conjures up a rather different Bible, a far more mercurial Bible, which, as it permeates the cultural space of the colonized, effortlessly adapts to its contours, is rewritten in the process of being reread, and thereby subverts the colonizer's claims on its behalf of univocity and universality.

---

10. Bhabha's relationship to Fanon is itself somewhat complex, because he also takes Fanon to task (specifically, the Fanon of *The Wretched of the Earth* [1961]) for his 'Manichaean' locating of power too asymmetrically on the side of the colonizer (Bhabha 1994a: 61–63).

In the face of the subtle hermeneutical spectacle with which Bhabha implicitly presents us, however, all sorts of uncomfortable questions arise, many of which have already been posed in one form or another by Bhabha's critics. Several touch on ostensibly universalizing moves in Bhabha's own text, most notably his exportation, lock, stock, and barrel, to the colonies of European psychoanalytic theory in the Freudian-Lacanian mode (see, e.g., Young 1990: 144; Moore-Gilbert 1997: 140–51). This colonial export business is merely one aspect of a problem that is much larger than Bhabha, however, that of the blanket application of 'First World' theory more generally to 'Third World' cultures. (In Biblical Studies, the analogue has been a kind of methodological imperialism in which only methods and theories manufactured in Europe or North America have been deemed adequate to the task of exegesis—and not only by the manufacturers themselves, resulting in an incessant stream of students from Africa, Latin America, and especially Asia to study in European and North American universities and seminaries.) And yet, in the case of Bhabha, what is most problematic, perhaps, is not his *use* of psychoanalytic theory per se but his failure to acknowledge its cultural specificity. In this regard, he has been compared unfavorably to Fanon, who also makes use of Freudian and even Lacanian categories, as we noted earlier, especially in *Black Skin, White Masks* (1967), but never uncritically or unselfconsciously.

Still more problematic in Bhabha's writings is the thorny issue of *agency*—although the limitations of his work in this regard are paradoxically bound up with its moments of greatest insight. Bhabha's basic approach to colonialism and its aftermath, it might be said, provides an exemplary, if incomplete, analytic model. To state it (all too) simply, critical approaches that concentrate exclusively on the 'outward' appurtenances of colonialism and its counter-effects, such as military interventions, administrative infrastructures, nationalist movements, civil disobedience, or armed insurrections—not to deny for a moment the importance of analyzing such fundamental phenomena—cannot account adequately for the immensely complex relations of collusion and resistance, desire and disavowal, dependence and independence that can characterize the exchanges between colonizer and colonized during colonial occupation *and* after official decolonization. Isolating and unraveling these often tortuous relations, tensions, and affiliations accounts for Bhabha's most impressive achievements, and his indispensable tools to this end have been those forged in the fires of poststructuralist thought.[11] As he himself has put it:

11.   *European* poststructuralist thought (to resurrect the earlier issue)? Yes, on the face of it, although Robert Young, for one, has made a spirited case against seeing poststructuralism as simply or straightforwardly European, Euro-American, or Western. 'In fact, the "high

> My growing conviction has been that the encounters and negotiations of differential meanings and values within 'colonial' textuality, its governmental discourses and cultural practices, have enacted, *avant la lettre*, many of the problematics of signification and judgment that have become current in contemporary theory—aporia, ambivalence, indeterminacy, the question of discursive closure, the threat to agency, the status of intentionality, the challenge to 'totalizing' concepts, to name but a few. (1992: 439)

Bhabha's psychoanalytic and poststructuralist version of postcolonial criticism is most in its element, one might say, when applied to 'normal' colonial relations, as opposed to overtly coercive colonial relations when the use of armed force is paramount. That is when Bhabhan concepts such as mimicry and hybridity come into their own. Both implicitly and explicitly, Bhabha ascribes considerable subversive potential to such phenomena. Yet where is this subversion, this sabotage, this resistance to colonial domination actually occurring? In the consciousness of the individual colonized subject? Or in his or her subconscious? Or unconscious? Or is its real locus instead in the tide of discourse that ebbs and flows between colonizer and colonized, causing the colonizer's identity and authority to be surreptitiously eroded in and through his discursive impositions on the colonized? Is the colonizer, then, the ultimate agent of his own discursive undoing? Characteristically, Bhabha never tackles such questions head on.[12]

'Signs Taken for Wonders', however, is one essay in which Bhabha is more than usually emphatic that the colonized are engaged in active subversion of the colonizer's discourse, in this case the colonizer's Scripture. Ostensibly, the encounter of the catechist Anund Messeh with the throng of five hundred outside Delhi in May 1817 is enacted amid *ruins*. As Bhabha reports, a letter from a representative of the Indian Church Missionary Society sent to London that same month expressed the desire that the Indian 'heathens', suitably catechized, themselves 'be made the instruments of pulling down their own religion, and of erecting in its ruins the standards of the Cross' (Bhabha 1994e: 106). Bhabha's

---

European theory" of structuralism and poststructuralism is of broadly non-European origin: structuralism was developed by the Prague school as an anti-western strategy, directed against the hierarchical cultural and racial assumptions of imperialist European thought. Many of those who developed the theoretical positions known collectively as poststructuralism came from Algeria and the Maghreb. Though structuralism and poststructuralism were taken up and developed in Europe, both were indeed alien, and fundamentally anti-western in strategy' (2001: 67–68; Young's chapter on Derrida, in particular [pp. 411–26: 'Subjectivity and History: Derrida in Algeria'], pushes this line of argument to the limit [and possibly over it]).

12. Even in the essay 'The Postcolonial and the Postmodern', whose subtitle is 'The Question of Agency' (1994d).

countervailing desire, understandably enough, is that of interpreting these ruins, or runes, differently, by reading *with* the natives assembled under the tree outside Delhi, and *against* the narrator of the *Missionary Register* anecdote, for whom these natives, seemingly, are a gormless, guileless, and generally ignorant lot.

To take up the anecdote where we earlier left off: '"These [Gospel] books", said Anund, "teach the religion of the European Sahibs. It is THEIR book; and they printed it in our language, for our use". "Ah! no", replied [his interlocutor], "that cannot be, for they eat flesh"' (Bhabha 1994e: 103). Bhabha remarks (and here I am both paraphrasing and amplifying his comment) that this 'canny' observation effectively challenges the assumption that the authority of the 'English book' is universal and self-evident by underscoring the cultural specificity and relativity of its provenance. Bhabha's exegesis of this canny rejoinder, and of the natives' subsequent declaration that they are willing to be baptized, but 'will never take the Sacrament [of the Eucharist] ... because the Europeans eat cow's flesh, and this will never do for us' (p. 104)— statements he characterizes as 'insurgent interrogations in the interstices' of colonial authority (p. 117)—occupies a further five pages of dense meditation. What is being accomplished under the tree outside Delhi, however, at least on Bhabha's account, is nothing less than the hybridization of the 'English book'. The colonizers' missionary strategy of distributing Hindi Bibles to the native populace, Bibles calculated to function as time bombs that will eventually decimate the natives' indigenous religious culture from within, has exploded in the colonizers' faces. 'After our experience of the native interrogation', claims Bhabha, 'it is difficult to agree entirely with Fanon that the psychic choice is to "turn white or disappear". There is the more ambivalent, third choice: camouflage, mimicry, black skins/white masks', he adds, reading Fanon against Fanon, and quoting Lacan: 'It is not a question of harmonizing with the background but, against a mottled background, of being mottled—exactly like the technique of camouflage practised in human warfare' (Bhabha 1994e: 120–21, quoting Lacan 1978: 99). And it is as a 'masque of mimicry' that Bhabha ultimately construes the anecdote of the encounter under the tree outside Delhi, a moment of 'civil disobedience' enacted openly under the eye of colonial power by means of the subtle strategy that he terms 'sly civility' (Bhabha 1994e: 121; cf. Bhabha 1994f).

And it is surely in 'civil' colonial encounters such as this one—and most of all in 'textual' encounters—that Bhabhan theory is at its most persuasive, if it is ever to be persuasive at all. For if it is to be objected—as indeed it has been (e.g., Moore-Gilbert 1997: 134–35)—that, in the larger scheme of things, any amount of colonial ambivalence, mimicry, or hybridity did not, in the end, effectively hamper British administration and exploitation of India, it is no less evident that the colonizers at least failed to impose their religious ideology uniformly upon the Indian populace.

In the end, however, Bhabha does not seem to know quite what to do with the Bible. 'And what is the significance of the Bible?', 'Signs Taken for Wonders' eventually inquires, only to answer lazily 'Who knows?' (p. 121), a shrug of the shoulders all the more surprising for the fact that the essay has already implicitly provided an answer. The significance of the Bible in the Indian colonial situation, it has suggested, was that it was an especially fraught site of simultaneous compliance and resistance (the Indian Bible thus turns out, not altogether unexpectedly, to be a Bhabhan Bible). That it could, and did, function as a colonialist instrument of coercion and co-option hardly needs belaboring. But the extent to which it could simultaneously function as an instrument of native resistance in that situation is further suggested by a final excerpt from the *Missionary Register* of May 1817, which Bhabha quotes, although without comment, thereby ending his essay. The author of this excerpt is yet another missionary to the Indians (this one British, unlike Anund Messeh), who can hardly contain his frustration:

> Still [every Indian] would gladly receive a Bible. And why? That he may store it up as a curiosity; sell it for a few pice; or use it for waste paper .... [A]n indiscriminate distribution of the scriptures, to everyone who may say he wants a Bible, can be little less than a waste of time, a waste of money and a waste of expectation. For while the public are hearing of so many Bibles distributed, they expect to hear soon of a corresponding number of conversions. (Bhabha 1994e: 122)

In the colonial context, the practice of bartering the European Book of books without first having read it, or especially of employing it as waste paper,[13] might well be construed as the epitome of a *materialist* reading of the colonial Bible, a singularly canny affirmation of the ineluctable materiality of this Sign of signs, and hence its cultural specificity and relativity. Simultaneously and consequently, however, these highly charged gestures might also be construed as the epitome of a *resistant* reading of the colonial Bible, ones that resist precisely by refusing to read—or, more precisely still, perhaps, resist by resolutely remaining at the level of the material signifier, the papery substance itself—wondrously thin, almost transparent, yet wholly tangible—refusing its translation, its sublation, into a transcendental, transcontextual, transcultural signified: arguably an

---

13. Or worse? South African liberation theologian Itumeleng Mosala, on a visit to Drew Theological School in February 2000, began his public lecture with an eyebrow-raising narrative of two opponents of apartheid contained in a single, bleak prison cell, one bereft of toilet tissue, among other things, but furnished with twin Bibles, of the difficult decision facing each prisoner in consequence, and of the symbolic stakes in each course of action.

apt model (although only one of many) for a biblical critical practice that would aspire to be 'postcolonial' and 'poststructuralist' at once—or to put it another way, perhaps, 'political' and 'postmodern' at once—and as such might boldly pick up the thread that Homi Bhabha so abruptly drops at the end of 'Signs Taken for Wonders', and patiently pick at it until some of the dense knots that bind the biblical texts to diverse colonial contexts—knots themselves constituted by elaborate acts of reading—begin to unravel.

Bibliography

Adam, Ian, and Helen Tiffin (eds.)
  1989   *Past the Last Post: Theorizing Post-Colonialism and Post-Modernism* (Hemel Hempstead, UK: Harvester Wheatsheaf).
Ahmad, Aijaz
  1992   *In Theory: Classes, Nations, Literatures* (London: Verso).
  1996   'The Politics of Literary Postcoloniality', in Padmini Mongia (ed.), *Postcolonial Theory: A Reader* (London: Arnold): 276–93.
Appiah, Kwame Anthony
  1991   'Is the Post- in Postmodernism the Post- in Postcolonial?', *Critical Inquiry* 17: 336–57.
Ashcroft, Bill, and Pal Ahluwalia
  2001   *Edward Said* (London and New York: Routledge).
Ashcroft, Bill, Gareth Griffiths, and Helen Tiffin (eds.)
  1995   *The Post-Colonial Studies Reader* (London and New York: Routledge).
Bhabha, Homi K.
  1992   'Postcolonial Criticism', in Stephen Greenblatt and Giles Gunn (eds.), *Redrawing the Boundaries: The Transformation of English and American Literary Studies* (New York: The Modern Language Association of America): 437–65.
  1994a   'Interrogating Identity: Frantz Fanon and the Postcolonial Prerogative', in Bhabha 1994b: 40–65.
  1994b   *The Location of Culture* (London and New York: Routledge).
  1994c   'Of Mimicry and Man: The Ambivalence of Colonial Discourse', in Bhabha 1994b: 85–92.
  1994d   'The Postcolonial and the Postmodern: The Question of Agency', in Bhabha 1994b: 171–97.
  1994e   'Signs Taken for Wonders: Questions of Ambivalence and Authority under a Tree outside Delhi, May 1817', in Bhabha 1994b: 102–22.
  1994f   'Sly Civility', in Bhabha 1994b: 93–101.
  1996   'Postmodernism/Postcolonialism', in Robert S. Nelson and Richard Shiff (eds.), *Critical Terms for Art History* (Chicago: University of Chicago Press): 307–22.

Brett, Mark
    2000   *Genesis: Procreation and the Politics of Identity* (London and New York: Routledge).
Derrida, Jacques
    1981   'The Double Session', in Jacques Derrida, *Dissemination* (trans. Barbara Johnson; Chicago: University of Chicago Press): 173–286.
Dirlik, Arif
    1994   'The Postcolonial Aura: Third World Criticism in an Age of Global Capitalism', *Critical Inquiry* 20: 328–56.
Eakin, Emily
    2003   'The Latest Theory Is That Theory Doesn't Matter', *The New York Times*, April 19, D9.
Fanon, Frantz
    1961   *The Wretched of the Earth* (trans. Constance Farrington; New York: Grove Press).
    1967   *Black Skin, White Masks* (trans. Charles Lam Markmann; New York: Grove Press).
Fineman, Joel
    1989   'The History of the Anecdote: Fiction and Fiction', in H. Aram Veeser (ed.), *The New Historicism* (London and New York: Routledge).
Friesen, Steven J.
    2001   *Imperial Cults and the Apocalypse of John: Reading Revelation in the Ruins* (Oxford: Oxford University Press).
Graham, Susan Lochrie, and Stephen D. Moore
    1997   'The Quest of the New Historicist Jesus', *Biblical Interpretation* 5: 438–64.
Hawley, John C.
    2001   *Encyclopedia of Postcolonial Studies* (Westport, CT: Greenwood Press).
Howe, Stephen
    2000   *Ireland and Empire: Colonial Legacies in Irish History and Culture* (Oxford: Oxford University Press).
Hussein, Abdirahman A.
    2002   *Edward Said* (London: Verso).
Jameson, Fredric
    1991   *Postmodernism, or, The Cultural Logic of Late Capitalism* (Durham, NC: Duke University Press).
Kiberd, Declan
    1995   *Inventing Ireland* (London: Jonathan Cape).
Lacan, Jacques
    1978   *The Four Fundamental Concepts of Psychoanalysis* (trans. Alan Sheridan; New York: Norton).
Liew, Tat-siong Benny
    1999   *Politics of Parousia: Reading Mark Inter(con)textually* (Biblical Interpretation, 42; Leiden: E.J. Brill).

Lloyd, David
    1993   *Anomalous States: Irish Writing and the Postcolonial Moment*
                (Durham, NC: Duke University Press).
Moore, Stephen D.
    1989   'The "Post-" Age Stamp: Does It Stick? Biblical Studies and the
                Postmodernism Debate', *Journal of the American Academy of
                Religion* 57: 543–59.
    1994   *Poststructuralism and the New Testament: Derrida and Foucault at
                the Foot of the Cross* (Minneapolis: Fortress Press).
    Forthcoming 'Revelation', in F.F. Segovia and R.S. Sugirtharajah (eds.), *The
                Postcolonial Commentary on the New Testament* (New York: T. & T.
                Clark).
Moore-Gilbert, Bart
    1997   *Postcolonial Theory: Contexts, Practices, Politics* (London: Verso).
    2000   'Spivak and Bhabha', in Henry Schwarz and Sangeeta Ray (eds.), *A
                Companion to Postcolonial Studies* (Blackwell Companions in
                Cultural Studies; Oxford: Blackwell): 451–66.
Morton, Stephen
    2002   *Gayatri Chakravorty Spivak* (Routledge Critical Thinkers; London
                and New York: Routledge).
Nkrumah, Kwame
    1965   *Neo-Colonialism: The Last Stage of Imperialism* (London: Heine-
                mann).
Quayson, Ato
    2000   'Postcolonialism and Postmodernism', in Henry Schwarz and
                Sangeeta Ray (eds.), *A Companion to Postcolonial Studies* (Black-
                well Companions in Cultural Studies; Oxford: Blackwell): 87–111.
Rajan, Rajeswari Sunder
    1997   'The Third World Academic in Other Places; or, the Postcolonial
                Intellectual Revisited', *Critical Inquiry* 23: 596–616.
Runions, Erin
    2002   *Changing Subjects: Gender, Nation and Future in Micah* (Playing the
                Texts, 7; Sheffield: Sheffield Academic Press).
Said, Edward W.
    1978a   *Orientalism: Western Conceptions of the Orient* (New York:
                Vintage).
    1978b   'The Problem of Textuality: Two Exemplary Positions', *Critical
                Inquiry* 4: 673–714. Revised version in Edward W. Said, *The World,
                the Text, and the Critic* (Cambridge, MA: Harvard University
                Press, 1983): 178–225.
    1993   *Culture and Imperialism* (New York: Vintage).
Samuel, Simon
    2002   'The Beginning of Mark: A Colonial/Postcolonial Conundrum',
                Biblical Interpretation 10: 405–19.
Spivak, Gayatri Chakravorty
    1987   *In Other Worlds: Essays in Cultural Politics* (London and New
                York: Methuen).

1990   *The Post-Colonial Critic: Interviews, Strategies, Dialogues* (ed. Sarah Harasym; London and New York: Routledge).

1999   *A Critique of Postcolonial Reason: Toward a History of the Vanishing Present* (Cambridge, MA: Harvard University Press).

Sugirtharajah, R.S.

1998   *Asian Biblical Hermeneutics and Postcolonialism: Contesting the Interpretations* (The Biblical Seminar; Sheffield: Sheffield Academic Press).

Thurman, Eric

2003   'Looking for a Few Good Men: Mark and Masculinity', in Stephen D. Moore and Janice Capel Anderson (eds.), *New Testament Masculinities* (Semeia Studies, 45; Williston, VT: Society of Biblical Literature Publications): 137–63.

Tiffin, Helen

1988   'Post-Colonialism, Post-Modernism and the Rehabilitation of Post-Colonial History', *Journal of Commonwealth Literature* 23: 169–81.

Young, Robert J.C.

1990   *White Mythologies: Writing History and the West* (London and New York: Routledge).

2001   *Postcolonialism: An Historical Introduction* (Oxford: Blackwell).

GOSPEL HAUNTINGS: THE POSTCOLONIAL DEMONS OF NEW TESTAMENT CRITICISM

Laura E. Donaldson

> I should have liked to establish a transferential relationship with the Rani of Sirmur. I pray instead to be haunted by her slight ghost, bypassing the arrogance of the cure. (Spivak 1999: 207)

If postcolonialism operates with the resources of a history shaped by colonization against the legacy of colonialism (Spivak 1995b: xxxi),[1] then a significant weakness of its contemporary critical practice is the reluctance—or even refusal—of critics to assume the importance of gender and sexuality to any understanding of these conflicted and contradictory 'resources'. Although these issues are often acknowledged in footnotes and even occasionally in a separate chapter, they are still given no substantive role within the formations of colonialism. Postcolonial cultural studies has also discouraged the deployment of gender as a theoretical rubric by linking it to a narrowly defined Euro-American, middle-class feminism. However, this view ignores not only the diversity of Western feminisms but also the recent proliferation of women's advocacy movements in the 'Two-Thirds' and 'Fourth' Worlds.[2] In her 2000 Wellek Library Lectures, Gayatri Chakravorty Spivak contends that the old postcolonial model—'very much "India" plus the Sartrian "Fanon"'—is no longer adequate as the 'master model for transnational to global cultural studies on the way to planetarity' (2002: 85); on this I will say more at the end of this essay. A major reason for the inadequacy of the 'old' postcolonial paradigm is its obstinate refusal to acknowledge women except by subsuming them under the more general category of 'the colonized'.

Of course, the specific issue in this essay is the issue of gender within the context of postcolonial Biblical Studies. I will weave one possible tapestry for their interrelationship that takes its warp and weft from the biblical

---

1. Spivak has also described postcolonialism as a 'persistent dredging operation' whose critical machinery keeps the 'apparently crystalline disciplinary mainstream' from becoming 'muddy' (Spivak 1999: 1). In *Postcolonialism: An Historical Introduction*, Robert Young (2001) echoes Spivak in his description of postcolonialism as a set of conceptual resources rather than a 'theory', or the deduction from a number of axioms of a historical model applicable to an indefinite number of empirical descriptions (cf. Spivak 1999: 64).

2. The successful grassroots movement by First Nations women in Canada to overturn the discriminatory portions of the Indian Act, the Chipko anti-logging movement, the protests against oppressive dowry practices in India, and Wangari Maathai's Green Belt movement in Kenya are several examples of such political mobilizations.

figure of Mark's 'Syro-Phoenician' and Matthew's 'Canaanite' woman—a character who has elicited an unusual amount of critical attention from feminist and postcolonial biblical critics. The woman's 'demon-possessed' daughter has generated much less commentary, however, and it is precisely her 'ethical singularity' that I wish to address. For Spivak, who first used this term in her translators' introduction to a collection of stories by Mahasweta Devi (Spivak 1995b), ethical singularity emerges from a vision of 'impossible justice' through specific encounters with a single figure: the ethical functions as a problem of relationship rather than knowledge (1995a: 70). She advocates such deep engagement with a singular figure to guard against facile appropriations of the oppressed by well-intentioned radicals: 'The object of ethical action is not an object of benevolence, for here responses flow from both sides' (1995b: xxv). Or, to use a more uncanny metaphor, establishing a relationship of ethical singularity to the figure of the demon-possessed daughter means allowing oneself to become haunted by this extraordinary subject. Moreover, since I will argue that one of her social and symbolic ancestors is the Ghostwife, or Medium, of Endor, it also means discerning *all* the ghosts, wherever they might lead.

Through the work of such intellectuals as Jacques Derrida, Gayatri Chakravorty Spivak, Avery Gordon, and Sharon Patricia Holland, spectrality has become a powerful trope for acknowledging the presence of the invisible in the ordinary world of the visible. As Spivak so trenchantly summarizes:

> You crave to let history haunt you as a ghost or ghosts, with the ungraspable incorporation of a ghostly body, and the uncontrollable, sporadic, and unanticipatable periodicity of haunting ... It is not, then, a past that was necessarily once present that is sought. The main effort is to compute with the software of other pasts rather than reference one's own hallucinatory heritage. (1995a: 70)

Although mixing references to parapsychology and information technology in the same sentence might seem bizarre, it is vintage Spivak asking her audience to consider how haunting interrupts the hegemonic through 'hallucinatory' confrontations with other histories. This transformative effect is precisely what postcolonial and feminist criticism has hoped to achieve, although spectrality and haunting require one to engage with these altered realities on deeper levels than mere intellect. To understand this more clearly, however, I want to explore the ethically singular haunting of the demon-possessed daughter in the Gospels of Matthew and Mark.

Marked

> By asserting that disability is a reading of bodily particularities in the
> context of social power relations, I intend to counter the accepted
> notions of physical disability as an absolute, inferior state and a
> personal misfortune. Instead I show that disability is a representation, a
> cultural interpretation of physical transformation or configuration, and
> a comparison of bodies that structures social relations and institutions.
> Disability, then, is the attribution of corporeal deviance—not so much a
> property of bodies as a product of cultural rules about what bodies
> should be or do. (Thompson 1997: 6)

In Mark 7.24-30, readers meet the 'woman of Syro-Phoenician origin'
(*gyne hellenis syrophoninissa*), a mother who ventures alone into the region
of Tyre so that she might ask Jesus to exorcise the demons from her little
daughter. Jesus refuses, and his scornful retort to the woman 'bowed down
at his feet' seems to display an ethnic prejudice against those who are non-
Jewish: 'Let the children be fed first, for it is not fair to take the children's
food and throw it to the dogs' (7.27).[3] One gauge of this comparison's
offensiveness is the refusal of Matthew to repeat it. The woman remains
undaunted by this stinging rebuff, however, and reminds Jesus that even
puppies under the table eat the children's crumbs. This response ultimately
convinces him to change his mind: 'Then he said to her, "For saying that,
you may go—the demon has left your daughter". So she went home, found
the child lying on the bed, and the demon gone' (7.29-30).

In *The Gospels in Context*, Gerd Theissen clarifies Jesus' comments by
noting that his rejection of the woman expresses the social and political
bitterness festering between Jews and non-Jews in the largely agricultural
border regions between Tyre and Galilee. The Roman Empire required
enormous imports of grain and other foodstuffs to support its expansionist
regimes—a demand that placed a heavy burden on growers to export their
crops rather than make them available to the local, and largely poor,
populace. As Theissen notes, in the struggle over food, the rural Jewish
population of Hellenistic cities such as Tyre usually suffered greatly (1991:
74).[4] Conversely, the woman's ability to speak Greek probably signifies a
high level of education and her daughter's access to a mattress ('she ...
found the child lying on the bed') membership in a relatively wealthy,
urban class (pp. 61–80). The geopolitical terrain of Jesus' journey into 'the
region of Tyre' consequently emulates many aspects of the disparities
common to the contemporary postcolonial world.

---

3. All biblical citations are taken from the New Revised Standard Version.

4. Theissen recommends that we hear Jesus' statement to the woman as 'Let the poor
people in Jewish rural areas be satisfied first' rather than one akin to ethnocentrism.

Orthodox Christian interpretations of Jesus and the Syro-Phoenician woman have perceived it as justifying a global mission to the 'Gentiles'[5] and elevating the mother herself to a 'model of that lively and courageous faith that constitutes a proper response to Jesus' (Donahue 2000: 910). For example, the Pseudo-Clementines began their interpretation of this story where the Gospel of Mark stops: the woman's 'pagan' husband abandons her, but she steadfastly remains a Christian and even betroths her daughter in marriage to a poor Christian. For the Pseudo-Clementines, the Syro-Phoenician woman vividly illustrates that one must be prepared to sacrifice class standing and even cultural status for the sake of the faith.[6] Viewing the woman as either an enabler of Christian salvation history or an icon of pietistic individualism has serious limitations, however, and some biblical critics have used postcolonial perspectives to tell a very different story. R.S. Sugirtharajah approvingly cites the 'postcolonial reclamation' of the narrative by Japanese feminist scholar Hisako Kinukawa, who views the Syro-Phoenician woman as rattling the exclusive ethnic zones erected around communities at the time (Sugirtharaja 2001: 238). Richard Horsley remarks upon the woman's appearance without male protectors and speculates that she is 'a poor, widowed or divorced woman alone in the world with a possessed daughter'. As such, she functions as a representative of all who are threatened with similar circumstances (2001: 213). Such disparate views of the Syro-Phoenician woman have led Kwok Pui-lan to observe that she 'stands at the boundaries of the privileged and the marginalized' (1995: 75), and to advocate a biblical criticism able to acknowledge such contradictions.

Although each of these views offers crucial perspectives on the character of the mother, none of them includes her daughter as a crucial element. I wonder how these postcolonial analyses of Mark's Syro-Phoenician woman might change if they placed the demon-possessed daughter at the center. Ato Quayson has recently proposed 'relocating' postcolonialism through the discourses of disability (2002: 228), and I would argue that this extraordinary daughter displaces and reconfigures both anti-colonial and postcolonial readings of the story through her own struggle with 'demon-possession'. In the final part of the essay, I intend to dispute this description of the daughter as 'demon-possessed' and therefore, 'dis-abled'—but because I recognize the importance of this condition to any interpretation of the daughter, I first want to investigate how her disability

---

5.   Richard Horsley persuasively argues that the NRSV translation of *hellenis* as 'Gentile' misleadingly imposes on the text a later dichotomy between Jew and Gentile as essentialist markers of religious-ethnic identity (2001: 212).

6.   As cited in Theissen (1991: 71).

creates an enabling violation not only of normative Christian but also of anti-colonial discourse.

In her response to Elly Elshout's presentation on 'Women with Disabilities', Hebrew Bible scholar Carole Fontaine observes that the dignity of the disabled and their status as valued members of diverse communities is denigrated by the Bible's continuous depiction of them as objects of divine action: 'They serve as marvelous plot-devices that show off the power of God or the Anointed One. In effect, they form part of the group of God's "special interests" in the New Testament: like Romans, tax-collectors, and women, they show how remarkable is Jesus's broad-based concern and willingness to interact with society's "throwaways"' (Elshout 1999: 439). For Fontaine, this 'relentless [biblical] characterization of the disabled as objectified beneficiaries of divine healing' actually *de*humanizes them and tragically robs these figures, as well as their real life counterparts, of their potential to grow and mature in the Christian faith (p. 439). Documentary film-maker and scholar Sharon L. Snyder articulates a similar view. According to Snyder, both of the biblical testaments perform a kind of erasure through their insistence on healing: 'The old banishes cripples from religious visibility through segregation, while the new manages to erase disability through the promise of a miraculous cure' (2002: 183). These two responses are directly germane to any reading of the demon-possessed daughter.

As one whom the text does not allow to speak, the daughter can neither testify on her own behalf nor control whether or not Jesus heals her. Her silent witness insistently calls the abled to investigate rigorously their own complicity in oppressively naturalized ideologies of health. Gospel readers must likewise examine why these narratives (and the institutions based on them) manifest such anxiety about those who manifest disabilities. Mark's demon-possessed daughter offers one possible answer in the way that 'demon-possession' and the ventriloquism attending her status as a female child evokes a profound vulnerability to external forces. As Rosemarie Garland Thompson notes, the disabled body stands for a self gone out of control as well as individualism run rampant: it confirms the cultural other lying dormant within the self, 'threatening abrupt or gradual transformation from "man" to "invalid"' (1997: 43).[7] In *Extraordinary Bodies*,[8]

---

7. Garland uses 'man' as a signifier for the Enlightenment ideology of individualist rationalism where one is autonomous, self-contained, and master of bodily as well as all other boundaries.

8. Thompson's ground-breaking 1997 book launched the field now known as Disability Cultural Studies. Its title references Mary Douglas' discussion of the anomalous, or extraordinary, in *Purity and Danger: An Analysis of the Concepts of Pollution and Taboo* (1966). Thompson articulates disability as a pervasive ideological discourse structuring a wide range of thought, language, and perception in a predominantly abled culture.

Thompson articulates disability in terms of Mikhail Bakhtin's notion of the carnivalesque or disorderly body as a disturber of the social order. Bakhtin's framework allows one to envisage the disorderly body—and, I would add, the disorderly mind-spirit—as agents capable of transforming cultural discourses rather than as always only passive victims (Thompson 1997: 38). Thompson suggests an interpretation of disability 'not as discomforting abnormalities or intolerable ambiguities', but rather as 'the entitled bearers of a fresh view of reality' (p. 38). The demon-possessed daughter becomes the entitled bearer of a fresh view of reality through the disturbing question that she elicits: when and why does the exorcism of this character's disability enact its own form of repression? This is a particularly urgent query for postcolonial biblical criticism, since some scholars have perceived a strong connection between colonial oppression and forms of mental illness that one might easily interpret as demonic possession.

Neo-anti-colonialism

> The neocolonial anticolonialist still longs for the object of a conscientious ethnography, sometimes gender marked for feminism. (Spivak 1999: 191)

The spectacular figure of the Gerasene man (Mk 5.1-20; Mt. 18.18, 23-27; Lk. 8.22-25), chained alone and howling among the tombs of the dead, has always occupied a compelling place in the Christian imaginary; his story, and that of Jesus' casting his demons into a nearby swineherd, has also functioned as an exceptionally effective 'plot-device' to highlight Jesus' messianic power. In recent scholarship, however, some biblical critics have begun to interpret the story within the social and historical context of Roman imperialism. For example, John Dominic Crossan observes that the tale of the Gerasene man explicitly codes demon-possession in the literal terms of Roman imperial occupation (their name is Legion, the military unit of Roman colonization), and Jesus' exorcism of them, therefore, constitutes nothing less than an 'individuated symbolic revolution' against the Roman Empire (1995: 91). In *Jesus and Empire* (2002), Richard Horsley appeals to both linguistic and historical evidence for his anti-colonial interpretation of the Gerasene. Horsley notes that the initial exorcism in Mark (1.21-28) does not reveal Jesus 'casting out' (*ekballein*) the demons, but rather 'vanquishing' (*epitiman*) them. Here, language is crucial, since previous biblical texts deployed 'vanquish' to represent Yahweh coming in judgment against imperial powers that had oppressed or subjugated Israel (p. 100). Further, according to Horsley, the story of the Gerasene yields important insights into the daily lives of people in Galilee and the surrounding regions, who had experienced the burning of villages by Roman legions as well as the slaughter or enslavement of their parents and grandparents (p. 100). While they use slightly different methodologies, both Horsley and Crossan reach a similar conclusion—that 'the ultimate significance of Jesus' exorcisms was the defeat of Roman rule' (p. 102)—and both place these acts securely within an anti-colonial framework.

It is tempting to draw parallels between the Gerasene man and the demon-possessed daughter. After all, like many villages on the outskirts of Tyre, the one hosting the meeting of Jesus and the Syro-Phoenician mother probably suffered greatly from Rome's particular form of extractive colonialism. Both imperial and Tyrian taxation rates were onerous and included notorious 'in-kind' taxes often amounting to half a farmer's harvested yield. Given this context, Jesus' healing of the demon-possessed daughter seems similar to that of the Gerasene man in connoting an anti-colonial act. As illuminating as this hermeneutic might be, however, it also imposes a unitary meaning on the demoniac episodes that actually occludes the much more uneven and unsettling processes at work. In his essay 'Jesus and the Demoniacs', Christian Strecker worries that the 'functional rationalism in this [anti-colonial] approach reduces the complexity of the phenomenon in an alarming way, pushing indigenous reports to the sideline as well as the beliefs and the direct experiences of the people concerned' (2002: 122). I share this concern. More particularly, I affirm that the 'direct experiences' of the Gospels' 'demon-possessed' characters include gender as well as indigeneity: perspectives that destabilize the tightly contained polarities of the anti-colonial and reconstellate along the much more shifting, diffuse, and often contradictory boundaries of the postcolonial.

Crossan's interpretation of the Gerasene demoniac and his exorcism as anti-colonial fails to acknowledge how strongly (pun intended) gender inflects the story. While the Gerasene wails 'at the top of his voice', the demon-possessed daughter is mute; while he is frenziedly active, she lies unmoving on her mattress; while he inhabits the narrative as vividly as he inhabits the tombs, she is absent from the narrative proper. Such stereotypical male and female attributes refute any attempt to yoke men and women indiscriminately together under the master term of 'the colonized'. Indeed, at least one critic has interpreted the Gerasene as displaying 'a demoniac excess of male strength', and described his cure as healing 'an excess of maleness': 'The man is now ordered and civil, formerly naked he is now dressed, formerly dangerous in his strength he is now fit for society' (Kermode 1979: 135). The Gerasene's exorcism thus converts his hypermasculinized, disorderly—according to Thompson, disabled—body to a docile, abled one 'fit for society'.

The biblical demand that the Gerasene become 'fit for society' bears a close resemblance to the colonialist demand that indigenous peoples become 'civilized'. Each demand has motivated an oppressive ideology of coercive curing: the Gerasene from wild masculinity; and indigenous peoples from a perpetual state of wild 'barbarism' to which would-be healers often ascribed exaggeratedly sexual characteristics. Rather than threatening an abrupt or gradual transformation from 'man' to 'invalid', then, the story of the Gerasene demoniac instead narrates an abrupt transformation from 'invalid' to 'man'. In this case, Jesus' exorcism actually domesticates and neutralizes the disorderly extraordinary, and the ultimate result is the confinement of this potentially subversive state to the ordinary (one might even say 'hegemonic') world.

The provocative connection that the story of the Gerasene makes between colonization and hypermasculinity needs further exploration by biblical scholars. At the very least, it intimates an inseparable connection between gender and the construction of an anti-colonial hermeneutics. The imbrication of gender with the *post*colonial becomes clear when one reads the narratives of the demon-possessed woman juxtaposed to that of the demon-possessed man. The text of Matthew yields one important clue for the gendered difference of the demon-possessed daughter from the Gerasene man in its identification of the Syro-Phoenician mother and daughter as 'Canaanites'. A loosely grouped congeries of peoples, the 'Canaanites' were the original inhabitants of the land now occupied by the Israelites and, as such, were placed under a *charam*, or a 'devotion to destruction' by Yahweh. In *Postcolonial Feminist Interpretation of the Bible*, Musa Dube asserts: 'To intertextually characterize a foreign woman as a "Canaanite" is to mark her as one who must be invaded, conquered, annihilated' (2000: 147). Because of Matthew's characterization, Dube interprets the mother's exchange with Jesus as a 'land possession type scene' disseminating both imperialist values and gender images that reinforce women's oppression.

More specifically, I argue that the 'demon-possession' of the Canaanite daughter's depiction associates her with one of the Bible's most hidden histories: that of its indigenous women. An important hallmark of many indigenous spiritual traditions is their use of ecstatic states or altered forms of consciousness as especially powerful sites of knowledge: 'In a state of ecstasy or altered consciousness an individual may find that he/she may lose the ability to think or speak in an ordinary way. Other means of perception and communication take over then' (Beck and Walters 1977: 98). Silence may not always mean an inability to speak, and in her muteness the daughter enunciates a witness more haunting than mere words could offer. Rather than evoking the illness pejoratively identified in the Christian text as 'demon-possession', the daughter might instead signify a trace of the indigenous; and rather than manifesting a deviance subject to the regimes of coercive (Christian) curing, she might also be experiencing the initial stages of a vocation known to indigenous peoples for millennia as shamanism.

'Shamanism' is a term coined by Euro-American anthropological discourse to cover a wide variety of spiritual roles and practices in indigenous cultures.[9] As such, it is sometimes applied problematically, but nevertheless remains a useful and consistent conceptual shorthand. In *The Sacred*, their excellent volume on the cultures and spiritual traditions of indigenous peoples, Peggy Beck and Anna Lee Walters (Pawnee/Otoe) describe shamanism as the process through which individuals seek the sources of the sacred and practice special ways of knowledge in order, for example, to cure illness, maintain the ceremonial calendar, ensure hunting successes, or seek lost objects. They also note that the most powerful spiritual leaders are often those forced by illness or a compelling dream or vision to become a shaman, whether they desired this role or not:

> A typical description of how this happens is that the shaman-to-be suddenly gets very sick, falls unconscious or begins to 'act crazy'. Perhaps the man or woman 'hears things', complains of voices speaking at night, or perhaps he/she runs away and won't speak to anyone for a period of time. Sometimes these things keep happening to an individual on and off for a number of years. At first the individual does not understand what is happening. Later, when the individual is older and has a greater understanding of sacred ways and practices, he/she may see that these afflictions and pains, the voices and the strange dreams, are trying to tell him/her something. (Beck and Walters 1977: 97)

Although they are not directly represented, the Canaanite daughter's afflictions and pains also tell readers that biblical narrators and redactors have clearly underestimated the capacity of the Bible's indigenous characters to talk back, albeit silently and indirectly, to their subjugators.[10] Of course, my interpretation that the daughter's state might connote something other than demonic possession is just that—an informed speculation. It is meant as a subversion of the ideologically motivated and much more troubling conclusion that is naturalized and universalized as 'God's Word' in Mark and Matthew. The notion of the Canaanite daughter as an emergent shaman possesses deep roots, however, and gains

9. The etymology of *shaman* comes from *saman*, a word in the language of the Siberian Tungus people, whom anthropologists have viewed as providing the prototype of a 'shamanistic' vocation.

10. The question of whether the subaltern can speak looms very large in this discussion, and I will say more about this in the conclusion of the essay. A fuller analysis of the complexities of and revisions to Spivak's initial question can be found in my essay 'The Breasts of Columbus', in Donaldson and Kwok (2001).

some plausibility when we read her story with that of her ancestress, the *'ishshah ba'alah 'owb*, 'a woman possessing a ghost or spirit', who is more familiarly known to biblical readers as the Ghostwife or Medium of Endor.

A Postcolonial Ghost Story

> Then Saul said to his servants, 'Seek out for me a woman who is a medium, so that I may go to her and inquire of her'. His servants said to him, 'There is a medium at Endor'. (1 Sam. 28.7)

> Ghost stories attempt to bring the dead back to life [and] ... are offered as an alternative—or challenge—to 'official' dominant history. (Brogan 1998: 17)

The story in 1 Sam. 28.3-25 is one of the most remarkable in the Hebrew Testament, and its vivid portrayal of the interaction among the Medium of Endor, King Saul, and the prophet Samuel has inspired many great artistic moments, including the opening scenes of Shakespeare's *Macbeth*. Unlike those of Macbeth, however, Saul's difficulties emerge from his earlier failure to complete the *charam* that Yahweh has ordered against the Canaanite people known as the Amalekites.[11] Because of this lapse (at least according to the Deuteronomistic narrator), Yahweh repudiates Saul and refuses to communicate with him when the Philistine army threatens to overrun the Israelites. In desperation, Saul asks his servants to locate 'a woman who is a medium' so that he might consult her about the outcome of the looming battle. They immediately reply that there is just such a woman living in the village of Endor. Saul seeks advice from this medium and asks her to raise the spirit (*elohim*) of the deceased prophet Samuel so that he might discern how best to engage militarily with the Philistines. She successfully channels the irascible Samuel, whose first words to Saul are, 'Why have you disturbed me by bringing me up?' (28.15). Through the medium's aegis, Samuel delivers a terrible message: Saul and his sons will not only lose the conflict with the Philistines but also their lives. Stricken by this news and falling 'full length on the ground' (28.20), Saul's corpse-like state mimics his soon-to-be real life fate. The medium, who has been largely overshadowed by the dramatic dialogue between Saul and Samuel, convinces the troubled king to eat and places a feast before him and his servants: 'Then they rose and went away that night' (28.25).

---

11. In 1 Sam. 15, we discover that Saul fulfills Yahweh's directive by killing all the people, but sparing the best of the sheep and cattle. He also took their leader, King Agag, prisoner instead of executing him on the spot.

Both linguistic and comparative studies point to the fact that this apparently well-known female spiritual practitioner was not an isolated phenomenon in early Israelite religious life. For example, Phyllis Bird notes that the highly unusual pairing of feminine–masculine order of the Hebrew term, *'ishshah ba'alah 'owb*, testifies to the predominance of women in the guild of those who communicate with the dead (1997: 112). Other feminist biblical critics have suggested that, while the books of Samuel describe few official roles for women, the Medium of Endor hints that they still retained networks of considerable power outside the centralized governmental and religious establishment.[12] This research has revised biblical criticism's knowledge of women and gender in ancient Israel and constitutes a promising source of new, potentially transformative insights. However, neither Bird nor other feminist scholars mention the ethnic status of the medium and her ambiguous position in relation to Saul and the Israelites—a gender-only analysis facilitating the erasure of Canaanite women from the sacred text. A reading of the medium that does interrelate gender analysis with her indigenous heritage reveals a very different message: the persistence, rather than the disappearance, of the indigenous, or Canaanite, woman. To explore this fully, however, it is necessary to examine the medium's encounter with Saul much more closely.

The chapter in 1 Samuel recounting the medium's story begins with the statement of two 'facts': the death of Samuel and the edict by Saul banning all mediums and wizards from the land. The phrase 'mediums and wizards' most certainly stands in for those indigenous spiritual leaders—or, one could argue, shamans—who inhabited the land of Canaan before the arrival of the Israelites. Their banishment attests to the power they held amongst their own people as well as their ability to attract supporters from the new group of Israelite settlers. When a disguised Saul shows up at her door, the surprised medium of Endor quickly reminds him of his repressive acts: 'Surely you know what Saul has done, how he has cut off the mediums and the wizards from the land. Why then are you laying a snare for my life to bring about my death' (1 Sam. 28.9)? The medium assents publicly to the ban, but also signals that some have managed to escape Saul's brutal state apparatus. For example, the speed and confidence with which Saul's servants direct him to the medium indicates that some established circuits of Canaanite religious knowledge have evaded the Israelite conquest and official proscription of their spiritual leaders. Likewise, her very success in conjuring the ghost of Samuel suggests that, while her public role might have been officially censored, the medium lost none of her power or spiritual gifts. In a manner akin to a photographic

---

12. See e.g., Jo Ann Hackett (1992: 85–95).

negative, then, the story of Saul and the Medium of Endor ironically and inversely attests to the endurance of Canaan's indigenous spirituality.

Questions about the medium's identity abound, but it seems likely that she was a person of mixed Philistine and Canaanite heritage. The location of the ancient village of Endor on the border between Philistia and Israel has prompted Hebrew Bible scholar David Jobling to argue that she might be Philistine, or at least of mixed Philistine–Israelite blood (1998: 186). The 'Philistines', who gave the land of Palestine their name, were a bold seafaring people from the north known for their iron chariots and agile military tactics. While the Israelites never completely defeated them— although David did thwart many of their expansionist ambitions—the Philistines emulated the Canaanites in becoming the repository of all that was Other to the Yahwists. More importantly, the Medium of Endor's successful practice of necromancy (conjuring the dead) makes it just as likely that she possessed a significant heritage from the region's indigenous peoples, and the biblical narrative does yield important clues about her geopolitical location. Joshua 17.12, for example, reveals that the town of Endor stubbornly resisted Israelite attempts to conquer it: 'Yet the Manassites could not take possession of those towns; but the Canaanites continued to live in that land.' When the conquerors subsequently prevailed, putting the inhabitants of Endor to corvée, or forced labor, the text states that even then they 'did not utterly drive them out' (17.13). These postcolonial contexts for the Medium of Endor exist as one of the Hebrew Testament's 'hidden transcripts', or record of suppressed voices concealed in plain sight.

Political anthropologist James C. Scott first articulated this notion in his illuminating study *Domination and the Arts of Resistance* (1990), which documents the 'infrapolitics of the powerless'. Scott observed that the process of domination generates a hegemonic public conduct as well as a backstage discourse consisting of what cannot be spoken in the face of power (p. xii). He included in this subterfuge such behaviors as rumors, gossip, songs, gestures, pilfering, poaching, clandestine tax evasion, foot-dragging, and intentionally sloppy work for landlords—and I would surely add haunting the very authorities that banned one's spiritual traditions. As Scott notes, these hidden transcripts share certain qualities: each expresses ideological insubordination openly, albeit in disguised form; each is specific to a given social site and particular set of actions; and each hides behind anonymity or innocuous understandings of their conduct (pp. xii– xiii). The most likely social sites for recovering hidden transcripts will tend to be those actual or symbolic locations that are subjected to the least amount of surveillance. The house of a non-Israelite woman in a small borderlands village would hardly represent a noticeable threat to the kingly establishment of Saul. After all, the Bible's historical books raise up much more important, male rivals for his kingdom: the prophets, of whom

Samuel is one of the most powerful representatives; the priestly house of Eli; the young shepherd boy David; and his most bitter military enemy, the Philistines. In the face of these threats, the survival of women's indigenous knowledge remains of little consequence, and this is probably why 1 Samuel's narrator presents her story with a minimum of interference: 'When he writes of her religious function, he does so objectively, indicating she was competent, that she could do what she claimed to do; and at the end of the chapter he limpidly tells of her goodness' (Jobling 1998: 189).

This judicious attitude belies such misogynist and ethnocentric commentaries as Eugene Peterson's recent book *First and Second Samuel* (1999), in which he derisively compares the medium's spiritual and technical expertise to contemporary New Age 'channeling' and declares that she offers a spiritual experience without the 'inconveniences' of relationship and commitment (1999: 126). In this scenario, Saul is reduced to 'sneaking around the back alleys of Israel looking for a witch to replace God' and his encounter cannot offer any 'saving truths'. Peterson's disparaging of the female medium's shamanistic power as 'new age channeling' and her vocation as a 'witch' reiterates in more contemporary form the Christian Testament's discursive colonization of the Canaanite daughter as 'demon-possessed'. The concept of spirit-possession as sacred knowledge production is censored by both of these interpretations. Unlike the silenced daughter, however, the Medium of Endor refuses both subjugation and 'healing'. Hidden in plain sight, she constructs her own version of poetic justice and witnesses to the 'survivance' of indigenous women as well as all others expelled from the official texts of the Hebrew and Christian Bibles.[13]

Biblical Hauntologies

> *What is* a ghost? What is the *effectivity* or the *presence* of a specter, that is, of what seems to remain 25 ineffective, virtual, insubstantial as a simulacrum? ... Let us call it a *hauntology*. (Derrida 1994: 10)

> Following the ghosts is about making a contact that changes you and refashions the social relations in which you are located. It is about putting life back in where only a vague memory or a bare trace was visible to those who bothered to look. It is sometimes about writing ghost stories, stories that not only repair representational mistakes, but also strive to understand the conditions under which a memory was produced in the first place, toward a countermemory, for the future. (Gordon 1997: 22)

---

13. 'Survivance' is a neologism coined by Gerald Vizenor (Ojibwe) combining both survival and endurance.

Historical and discursive colonization depend on the creation of ghosts. Indeed, the layering of one society upon another only occurs through physical and symbolic violence requiring either the deaths of conquered peoples or their social suppression and assimilation. Colonization trans- forms them, in other words, into ghosts: 'That special instance of the merging of the visible and invisible, the dead and the living, the past and the present' (Gordon 1997: 24). In this context, a poetic (and uncanny) description of postcolonial feminist criticism might be allowing ourselves to be haunted by those ghosts whose suffering undergirds the routine banalities of daily life. If, as Avery Gordon notes, haunting is a way of life, a method of analysis, and a type of political consciousness that must be passed on or through (p. 183), it offers postcolonial feminist criticism a means not only to repair the 'representational mistakes' that have led to the transparency of the colonized and women but also to begin creating a more opaque 'countermemory' for the future. To be haunted by (rather than interpret) the spirit-possessed daughter and the Medium of Endor moves one beyond mastery into a deeply moving relationship: 'Being haunted draws us affectively, sometimes against our will and always a bit magically, into the structure of feeling of a reality we come to experience, not as cold knowledge, but as a transformative recognition' (p. 8). These biblical ghosts mark the possibility of turning around—or converting—all those in an ethically singular relation with them.

The countermemory of this reverse conversion propels us out of colonial and misogynist discourse into something more akin to 'planetarity', Spivak's admittedly Utopian displacement of postcolonial critique. She proposes 'the planet' to overwrite the globe—and one might just as easily substitute a globalized colonialism and neocolonialism that seeks to impose the same system of exchange everywhere (2002: 72).

> The globe is on our computers. No one lives there. It allows us to think that we can aim to control it. The planet is in the species of alterity, belonging to another system; and yet we inhabit it, on loan. It is not really amenable to a neat contrast with the globe. I cannot say 'the planet, on the other hand'. When I invoke the planet, I think of the effort required to figure the (im)possibility of this underived intuition. (p. 72).

For Spivak, the planet thus becomes a sign of the uncanny, because it robs one of the ability to feel 'at home'. Just as the Christian Testament's spirit-possessed daughter haunts normative readings of her alleged 'demon-possession', the apparition of the planet haunts readings of the globe that perpetuate historical amnesia about all those who are missing in its dominant social texts. Similarly, just as the Medium of Endor persists in spite of every attempt to purge the public transcripts of her presence, the planet haunts the globe as the specter of that which resists assimilation into globalizing regimes of either religious faith or capitalist neocolonialism. Both of these women likewise haunt my vision of postcolonial feminism. The spirit-possessed daughter and the Medium of Endor signify the textual remnants of an ancient indigeneity and invite readers to construct a radically altered future from this glimpse of a possible biblical past. They gesture toward a planetary future in which the disappeared will be found, the missing welcomed home, and there will finally be no need for ghosts.

Bibliography

Beck, Peggy V., and Anna Lee Walters
    1977   *The Sacred: Ways of Knowledge, Sources of Life* (redesigned edition; Tsaile, AZ: Navajo Community College Press).

Bird, Phyllis A.
    1997   *Missing Persons and Mistaken Identities: Women and Gender in Ancient Israel* (Overtures to Biblical Theology; Minneapolis: Fortress Press).

Brogan, Kathleen
    1998   *Cultural Haunting: Ghosts and Ethnicity in Recent American Literature* (Charlottesville and London: University of Virginia Press).

Crossan, John Dominic
    1995   *Jesus: A Revolutionary Biography* (San Francisco and New York: HarperSanFrancisco).

Derrida, Jacques
    1994   *Specters of Marx: The State of the Debt, the Work of Mourning, and the New International* (trans. P. Kamuf; New York and London: Routledge).

Donahue, John R.
    2000   'Mark', in J.L. Mays (ed.), *The HarperCollins Bible Commentary* (San Francisco and New York: HarperSanFrancisco): 901–24.

Donaldson, Laura, and Kwok Pui-lan (eds.)
    2001   *Postcolonialism, Feminism, and Religious Discourse* (New York: Routledge).

Douglas, Mary
    1966   *Purity and Danger: An Analysis of the Concepts of Pollution and Taboo* (New York and Washington, DC: Frederick A. Praeger).

Dube, Musa
    2000   *Postcolonial Feminist Interpretation of the Bible* (St. Louis: Chalice Press).

Elshout, Elly (facilitator)
    1999   Roundtable Discussion: 'Women with Disabilities—A Challenge to Feminist Theology', in Alice Bach (ed.), *Women in the Hebrew Bible: A Reader* (New York and London: Routledge): 429–58.

Gordon, Avery
  1997   *Ghostly Matters: Haunting and the Sociological Imagination* (Minneapolis and London: University of Minnesota Press).
Hackett, Jo Ann
  1992   '1 and 2 Samuel', in Carole A. Newsom and Sharon H. Ringe (eds.), *The Women's Bible Commentary* (Louisville: Westminster/John Knox; London: SPCK): 85–95.
Holland, Sharon Patricia
  2000   *Raising the Dead: Readings of Death and (Black) Subjectivity* (Durham, NC, and London: Duke University Press).
Horsley, Richard
  2001   *Hearing the Whole Story: The Politics of Plot in Mark's Gospel* (Louisville, London, and Leiden: Westminster John Knox).
  2002   *Jesus and Empire: The Kingdom of God and the New World Disorder* (Minneapolis: Fortress Press).
Jobling, David
  1998   *1 Samuel* (Berit Olam: Studies in Hebrew Narrative & Poetry; Collegeville, Minnesota: The Liturgical Press).
Kermode, Frank
  1979   *The Genesis of Secrecy: On the Interpretation of Narrative* (Cambridge, MA, and London: Harvard University Press).
Kwok, Pui-lan
  1995   *Discovering the Bible in the Non-Biblical World* (The Bible & Liberation; Maryknoll, NY: Orbis Books).
Peterson, Eugene H.
  1999   *First and Second Samuel* (Westminster Bible Companion; Louisville: Westminster/John Knox Press).
Quayson, Ato
  2002   'Looking Awry: Tropes of Disability in Postcolonial Writing', in D.T. Goldberg and A. Quayson (eds.), *Relocating Postcolonialism* (Oxford: Blackwell): 217–30.
Scott, James C.
  1990   *Domination and the Arts of Resistance: Hidden Transcripts* (New Haven and London: Yale University Press).
Snyder, Sharon
  2002   'Infinities of Forms: Disability Figures in Artistic Traditions', in S. Snyder, B.J. Brueggemann, and R. Garland Thompson (eds.), *Disability Studies: Enabling the Humanities* (New York: Modern Language Association of America): 173–96.
Spivak, Gayatri Chakravorty
  1995a   'Ghostwriting', *Diacritics* 25 (2): 65–84.
  1995b   *Imaginary Maps: Three Stories by Mahasweta Devi* (New York and London: Routledge).
  1999   *A Critique of Postcolonial Reason: Toward a History of the Vanishing Present* (Cambridge, MA, and London: Harvard University Press).

2002   *Death of a Discipline* (Wellek Library Lectures; New York: Columbia University Press).

Strecker, Christian
2002   'Jesus and the Demoniacs', in W. Stegemann, B.J. Malina, and G. Theissen (eds.), *The Social Setting of Jesus and the Gospels* (Minneapolis: Fortress Press): 117–33.

Sugirtharajah, R.S.
2001   *The Bible and the Third World: Precolonial, Colonial and Postcolonial Encounters* (Cambridge: Cambridge University Press).

Theissen, Gerd
1991   *The Gospels in Context: Social and Political History in the Synoptic Tradition* (trans. L.M. Maloney; Minneapolis: Fortress Press).

Thompson, Rosemarie Garland
1997   *Extraordinary Bodies: Figuring Physical Disability in American Culture and Literature* (New York: Columbia University Press).

Young, Robert
2001   *Postcolonialism: An Historical Introduction* (Oxford and Malden, MA: Blackwell Publishers).

MARGINS AND (CUTTING-)EDGES: ON THE (IL)LEGITIMACY AND INTERSECTIONS OF RACE, ETHNICITY, AND (POST)COLONIALISM

Tat-siong Benny Liew

W.E.B. Du Bois once identified the twentieth century as that of the 'color line' (1996: xx). Others will no doubt point to other 'Cs' to characterize those hundred years, like the collapse of the communist experiment or the 'conclusion' of colonialism (in the doubled sense of colonialism's cessation in the form of territorial occupation and its culmination in the form of global capitalism). Both of these phenomena have contributed to the proliferation of nationalism, postcolonialism, and/or the emphasis on race/ ethnicity. In addition, both communism and colonialism were inseparable from the color conflict referenced by Du Bois. After all, the Black Civil Rights movement that erupted in the United States in the 1960s was deeply entangled with the anti-Vietnam War movement, the Third World Liberation Front, and the subsequent institutionalization of various 'ethnic studies' programs within many college and university curricula.

Race, ethnicity, and (post)colonialism have not only remained important at the dawn of the twenty-first century, their continuing academic influence has also been felt within Biblical Studies. In 2002, for example, we saw the publication of Shawn Kelley's *Racializing Jesus*, Gay L. Byron's *Symbolic Blackness and Ethnic Difference in Early Christian Literature*, and R.S. Sugirtharajah's *Postcolonial Criticism and Biblical Interpretation*. Before I talk about these and other texts to address the intersections of race, ethnicity, and postcolonialism in New Testament studies, I would like to spend some time suggesting that these three terms have parallel as well as intertwined lives within the larger world of academic studies.

Common Crisis of Legitimacy, Criss-Crossing Lives

Race

Scholars debate when the (general) concept of race—what we can tentatively define as the categorization of human beings in terms of phenotypical peculiarity like skin color, skull size, hair type, and/or nose shape—first came into being. They agree, however, that race as an ideology was first crystallized, if not created, in modernity (roughly since the fifteenth or sixteenth century). For instance, as Robert Miles articulates the continuities between the modern conception of race and the phenotypical recognitions that already existed in the Greco-Roman world, he nonetheless accentuates the discontinuities between them (1989: 11–40; see also Goldberg 1993: x; Childs and Williams 1997: 189–90). Among other things, pre-modern representations of phenotypical differences were attributed to climate, neutralized by geographical distance, and not necessarily tied to a hierarchical ranking of humanity. Moreover, Greco-Roman and modern representations of others were separated by the medieval obsession with religious difference, particularly because of the mighty Islamic Ottoman Empire. For Miles, not only does the modern ideology of race belong to a different register qualitatively (like its emphasis on biological inheritance, scientific validation, and hierarchical differentiation), it also distinguishes itself quantitatively in terms of its mass dissemination made possible by the printing press.

For many, the appearance of the word 'race' in the English language in the modern period testifies to the (re)construction of the ideology.[1] According to Goldberg, race is not just an aspect but is itself emblematic of modernity (2002: 97–100; see also Goldberg 1993). Its concomitant racial hierarchy, for example, illustrates and implements the modern will to power and order (Foucault 1970; Foucault 1997: 213–35; Appadurai 1993; Stoler 1995; Stoler 2002: 140–61).[2] The periodization of this (re)construction, along with numerous scientific/ideological shifts since modernity's onset (like genetics, the arbitrary choice of different phenotypical markers that lead to contradictory groupings, and the close relations between race and racism), have led many to question if the very concept of race is even legitimate.[3] Michael Banton, for example, argues that race is constructed by and out of white anxiety (1959) and refers to it as a 'folk concept' (1979). Miles, to give one more example, argues from the rise of both racial logic and capitalism in modernity that race is actually an alibi for class and economy. Race, for Miles, as a system of categorization, is a means for another purpose, namely, 'the process of allocating resources and services' (1989: 3). It is customary, therefore, among many academics to express

1. According to Ashcroft, Griffiths, and Tiffin, 'race' was first used in the English language in a poem by William Dunbar in 1508, but first used as biological or phenotypical categorizations by Immanuel Kant in 1764 (1998: 199–200).

2. As we New Testament scholars learn from Goldberg how modernity and racism have a shared basis in philosophical liberalism, we should also remember that, along with the colonized people of Africa, Asia, Australia, and the Americas, Jews were one of the main targets of modern racism (Bauman 1989; see also Stoler 1995: 196–97).

3. Mohanram, extending what Judith Butler says about the designation of only certain body parts as 'sexual' parts (Butler 1990: 114), sees defining race by skin color as just another example of arbitrary power (1999: 144).

their conceptual hesitation or reservation by putting the word 'race' in either italics or quotation marks (Goldberg 1993: ix).

As the construct of race is being questioned and deconstructed, many so-called 'racial minorities' are adamant about its continual use and thus its very real effects and affects on daily lives (Childs and Williams 1997: 191–92). The most memorable illustration in this regard is arguably how recurrent refusal of cab service faced by Blacks in New York City will not change with their eloquent speech on the 'immateriality' of race (Gates 1992: 147). The point here is not to dispute the connection between race and class but rather that neither can be subsumed by or reduced to the other. In other words, 'race [still] matters' (West 1993). The constructed categories of race (like black or Asian) should and can become the rallying point to resist and contest the contents and power relations implied by those very categories. Others, without denying at all the importance of racial(ized) resistance, proceed to manipulate and meddle with even the constructed categories. Vijay Prashad, for instance, points to historical instances of what he calls 'Afro-Asian connections' to attack the idea(l) of cultural purity (2001). In contrast, he argues for a new coalition and (con)fusion of subordinated racial groups. Prashad's ultimate aim is thus not a color-blind society but a creation of 'new skins' (2001: ix-xi, 65) to challenge dominant raciology and struggle for justice and democracy.

This crisis of legitimacy surrounding the concept of race is, however, far from over. One of its latest and fiercest interrogators is Paul Gilroy (2000), a black *trans*-Atlantic intellectual whose work is well known in both the United Kingdom and the USA. Unlike others who aim to deconstruct race mainly in the context of modernity, Gilroy moves from modernity to focus on the present postmodern and global context to advocate for the discarding of race. According to Gilroy, there is a negative and positive reason for his present and contextual stance 'against race'. Negatively, the effectiveness of race resistance is now much diminished because global capitalism is able to co-opt the black body as yet another marketing tool, as well as another product that can be sold and bought. Globalization's apparent opposite emphasis on (local) particularities (like gender, generation, or sexuality)—which are also partly enhanced by marketing research for sales niche—has also made racial(ized) solidarity increasingly difficult without freezing or essentializing race. The seductive power of this conservative and authoritarian step is evidenced for Gilroy by the widespread appearance of race-related, if not race-based, ultranationalism. Positively, removing raciology (whether from majority or minority perspectives) may open a door to a greater community or a planetary humanism.

Gilroy further opines that computer and digital communications, coupled with cellular/molecular/genomic developments (despite their reconstructing of raciology and biological determinism), are also contributing to the possibility of a new and postracial humanism. Gilroy is referring here to two specific phenomena. First, the new techno-ability to break through what Kaja Silverman calls 'the threshold of the visible world' (1996) by literally getting under your skin to scrutinize images and scan codes. Second, the new techno-ability to live out what Donna J. Haraway calls 'the cyborg manifesto' (1991: 149–81) by engineering and engrafting humanity with and as machinery. If I may play on yet another book title, Gilroy thinks that it is now time again to move 'past the last post' (Adam and Tiffin 1990). Beyond postmodernism and postcolonialism is what Gilroy calls a postracial and planetary humanism. Probably because Frantz Fanon is among the first to emphasize that race is a psychological if not an objective reality for Blacks (1961; 1967), Gilroy makes a special point to suggest that this postracial and planetary humanism is already part of Fanon's vision (2000: 46, 70–71).

It becomes clear as soon as one gets past the first chapter of Gilroy's book (2000: 11–53) that his postracial polemic is mainly a response to ultranationalist emphasis on racial purity and its almost fascist form of solidarity as soldiery (2000: 54–176).[4] While I share Gilroy's concerns, I also need to make a clarification. I have already referred to Gilroy's own admission that genetics might be a new form of biological determinism; let me add here that recent studies have shown that computer and digital communications are also far from color-blind (Kolko, Nakamura, and Rodman 2000; Nakamura 2002; Wong and Lee 2003). What Gilroy illustrates by shifting focus onto the present postmodern and global context is actually Fanon's argument that raciology is not static but mutates constantly (1970: 41–54). If so, Gilroy's stance on ultranationalism notwithstanding, I would suggest that instead of going beyond or 'against' race, one needs to stay alert to race and its shifting and shifty logic. The question is not whether race will or should continue to play a role but what kind of role race will or should play in the future.[5]

Ethnicity

In Gilroy's view, the aforementioned movement of biopolitics from 'dermal' to 'nano' was interfaced by what has been known as the 'New

---

4.   In one sense, Gilroy here is merely following up on a concern that motivates his writing of *The Black Atlantic* (1993), where he argues for a black diasporic identity that is cross-national and cross-ethnic. What is new is that this anti-national stance has now turned into an even more polemical 'anti-race' rhetoric.

5.   Laura Chrisman's critique of Gilroy's previous book, *The Black Atlantic*, is actually still applicable here. According to Chrisman, Gilroy's problem has partly to do with his own essentializing of nationalism (2003: 76–78). That is to say, for Gilroy, nationalism is by definition purist, exclusivist, and incapable of otherwise. Similarly, Gilroy's 'against-race' polemic is premised on race as by definition pure and thus exclusive.

Racism' (2000: 32–33). Very briefly, 'New Racism' was coined by Martin Barker (1981) to refer to the conservative attempt in the UK to change the form of its dominant raciology in the 1970s. This is done by removing the biological base and bravado of race talks. Instead of racializing in terms of inborn or inherent inferiority, 'New Racism' justifies itself by the 'pragmatic' reasoning that a nation or nationalism cannot function with a conglomeration of conflicting cultures. To put it another way, healthy national(ist) ecology requires cultural homogeneity as well as territorial specificity. Each race should have its own place. What we have here is therefore a sliding of race as a phenotypical classification to race as a cultural(ist) phenomenon. Race is now eliding with ethnicity.[6]

The year 1969 marked the appearance of two influential studies on ethnicity: Fredrik Barth's introductory essay to his edited volume *Ethnic Groups and Boundaries* and Yulian Bromley's Leningrad lecture on 'Ethnos and Endogamy' (Banks 1996: 17).[7] Bromley's Soviet-based anthropological theory became available in English in a subsequent paper (1974), where he presents the idea of an 'ethnosocial organism'. According to Bromley, ethnicity results from a dynamic interaction between an ethnic core (some cultural and psychological traits that are shared and recognized, but of unknown origin) and its surrounding environment (mainly economic, but also political). Ethnicity then is, for Bromley, persistent and yet pervious.[8] Barth, on the other hand, understands ethnicity as a construct for group differentiation and focuses correspondingly on the construction and maintenance of boundaries (1969). Such boundary work is, in Barth's opinion, primary. It will influence and determine ethnic contents, which are for Barth only secondary.

Since 1969, scholars have used ethnicity increasingly to talk about populations within nations of the geopolitical West as a correction and/or a cover for race.[9] This development was undoubtedly related to both the Civil Rights movement in the USA and the mounting tension caused by Asian and Caribbean population growth in the UK (multiplying offspring

---

6. Stoler, on the basis of her anthropological and historical work, argues that this so-called 'New Racism' is in fact not new but has been operating in European colonies long before the 1970s (2002: 97). If so, what we have here is another instance of influence that goes not from the metropole to the colony but the other way around. For more on the analysis of this 'New Racism', see Balibar and Wallerstein (1991: 17–28).

7. Banks points to a reference in the *Oxford English Dictionary* to a use of 'ethnicity' in 1772 but ends up suggesting W. Lloyd Warner and Paul S. Lunt as the first ones who used the term in its contemporary sense in 1942 (1996: 4–5).

8. Note that Bromley makes a point to state that race is not ethnicity and is insufficient for making ethnic distinctions (1974: 63).

9. I am using 'correction' to refer to a recognition that race is more cultural than biological and 'cover' to refer to a shifting attention from racism to what is supposedly a more 'neutral understanding' of social and cultural characteristics.

of immigrants who were first allowed in to supplement Britain's labor shortage after the Second World War). Because Barth and Bromley are both anthropologists, their use of ethnicity may first be seen as a non-colonialist way to refer to so-called 'tribal groups' of the non-West. Ironically, ethnicity has since become (at least partially) a 'buzz word' to signify problems of 'tribalism' both inside and outside of the West (Jenkins 1986). Not only does ethnicity obstruct the nation-building of the USA and the UK, it also leads to (recalling Gilroy above) ultranationalism in places like Bosnia and Rwanda. In other words, ethnicity is now a problem for and of nationalism.

This use of ethnicity betrays that it is often a label for groups who are not in power. As Brackette F. Williams points out, ruling groups do not acknowledge their own ethnicity (1989: 426; see also Ashcroft, Griffiths, and Tiffin 1998: 81–82). This parallels, of course, Ishmael Reed's experience of how his white students in California tend to become somewhat lost when they are asked to write about their ethnic background (Reed, Wong, Callahan, and Hope 1989) as well as Richard Dyer's insight that whiteness operates through invisibility (1988: 44–45). If whiteness is not a race or an ethnicity, then race and ethnicity share the common fate as labels for those who are lost in the history of unequal power relations. There is yet another characteristic that is shared by race and ethnicity. Both terms are popular and prevalent, but their meaning, usefulness, and validity are also often in question.

Working in the lingering shadows of both Barth and Bromley, scholars have been studying and understanding ethnicity in two opposing, though not necessarily mutually exclusive, ways. Some emphasize that ethnicity is a result of external domination; others emphasize that ethnicity is a result of internal group processes. In short, the contrast is between an external (political) force and an internal (cultural) glue. Approximately (but by no means absolutely) corresponding to these contrasting emphases is another set of contrasting emphases: ethnicity as instrumental or primordial. Admittedly, the significance of these differences is diminished when they are viewed as varying degrees of emphases rather than binary opposites. The stakes do get higher with the need or desire to distinguish an ethnic group from a non-ethnic group. Without enough specificity from the two 'axes' identified above (external/internal; instrumental/primordial), debates rage as to whether, to name just two examples, sexual dissidents like gays and lesbians (Epstein 1987) or a black religious group like the Rastafarians qualify as ethnic. For some, ethnic identities thus become fuzzy enough to be called 'hollow categories' (Ardener 1989: 69) or 'puffed up balloons' (Chapman 1992: 235). There is also the question of whether ethnicity is larger, smaller, or just plain other than race. While scholars agree generally that the terminology and ideology of race precede those of ethnicity, they simply cannot agree on the relationship between the two.

Because of these questions and confusions, some advocate to restrict if not abandon the use of the term (Blu 1980: 226–27; Just 1989: 76), while others foretell of its decline and disappearance (Ardener 1989: 211). For Banks (1996: 6, 182, 186), it is an academic construct at best and a parasitic concurrency or counterfeit at worst (dependent on race and nationalism). There is also Stephen Steinberg, who, in a way similar to what Gilroy does with race, opposes ethnicity on democratic grounds (1981).

What can we make of these points of contention, particularly the relationship between race and ethnicity? If Rastafarians qualify as an ethnic group, it would imply ethnicity as a subcategory of race, and Blacks as a race may be divided into several ethnic qua religious groups. This is also the understanding of many Asian North Americans, thus resulting in the call for a 'panethnicity' among them (Espiritu 1992). This understanding has the effect of preventing race from masking or covering over differences. Chinese, Koreans, and Vietnamese may all be Asians, but they are not all alike. Others, in contrast, subsume race within ethnicity (Glazer and Moynihan 1975; Banton 1998). They see race as nothing more than a transitional concept and thus, for reasons different from Gilroy's, nevertheless contribute to the momentum of trying to go 'beyond race'.

Michael Omi and Howard Winant are resolute that race must not be incorporated by or collapsed with ethnicity (1994; see also Takaki 1994; Rogin 1996). Speaking out of the multicultural context or contest of the USA, they point out that time and generation will not remove visible phenotypical differences; thus, racial minorities like Blacks and Asians in the USA will not be able to assimilate in ways that other white ethnic minority groups (like Italians or Irish) have. Targeting particularly Robert Park and his Chicago School of Sociology, Omi and Winant argue that a failure to recognize the difference between race and ethnicity will blind one from achieving a helpful socio-political analysis of structural power. I will further argue that race, because of its unfortunate but undeniable entanglement with racism, highlights the issue of power that ethnicity at times (particularly when ethnicity as an internal process is overemphasized) fails to communicate. Stuart Hall has proposed that the term 'ethnicity' is deployed to disavow the realities of racism (1988). This is particularly so since 'ethnic' may function as 'an all-purpose adjective to mean "exotically different"' (Banks 1996: 162), as in advertisements for 'ethnic food', 'ethnic jewelry', or the ever-elusive 'ethnic flavor'.

One should not, however, deduce from Omi and Winant that race is fixed and ethnicity is fluid. As Viet Thanh Nguyen reminds us with precisely the example of the Irish, phenotypical differences are 'something that we learn to see' (2002: 169). Noel Ignatiev has shown in his book and suggested by the book's very title, *How the Irish Became White* (1995), that the Irish were black before they turned white in the eyes of the dominant beholders (see also Curtis 1971). The same is true of the Jews, who used to

be a black race but are now being perceived and conceived as another
(white) ethnic group (Moose 1978). Stoler has recently argued that white
Europeans in colonial Indonesia were defined not by skin color alone but
also by 'other tenuously balanced assessments of who was judged to act
with reason, affective appropriateness, and a sense of morality' (2002: 6).
Given Prashad's vision for racial (con)fusion, we can add South Asians as
yet another example. As Mohanram's experience illustrates, South Asians
have been racialized as black, brown, or just right, depending on the place
and/or time (1999: xi-xiii; see also Gunew 1993: 455; and Brett 1996b: 10).
As St. Clair Drake and Horace R. Cayton argued as early as 1945, people
see with their emotions as well as their eyes; therefore, when people refer to
skin color, '[s]ometimes they do not mean color at all' (1945: 503n). My
point here is to neither dismiss Omi and Winant's concern nor invalidate
their argument but to acknowledge the complexity involved in race and in
its relationship with ethnicity. From this point on, I will often resort to the
popular designation 'race/ethnicity' to acknowledge rather than answer
these conceptual challenges.

Postcolonialism

The successive emergence of race and ethnicity in modernity points readily
to their entanglements with (post)colonialism. Statistics showing colonialism's programmatic development in the modern period need not be
rehearsed or recycled here (Said 1978: 39–41; Said 1993: 6; Childs and
Williams 1997: 10),[10] but I want to establish a conceptual connection
between (post)colonialism and race/ethnicity that goes beyond a con-
temporality in modernity that may merely be coincidental.[11] Fanon is
known for suggesting that race is central to colonialism (1970: 41–54).
According to Fanon, it is racism that helps turn people into objects to be
used by the colonizers. In other words, a(n) (illegitimate) construction of
race justifies 'an[other] otherwise illegitimate access to property and power'
(Stoler 2002: 24; see also Lloyd 1991). The influence and legacy of this
Fanonist (dual-)trail is evident in Albert Memmi and, more recently,
Goldberg (not to mention in Said's work on orientalism). Both Memmi

10.   This temporal overlap is why Homi Bhabha states in an interview that 'what was some
people's modernity was somebody else's colonialism' (Olson and Worsham 1999b: 17). See
also Dussel 1996.

11.   Note that in arguing for the conceptual connections between race and empire, I am
(again) not denying the connections between race and class or those between colonialism and
capitalism. Reducing relations that are multidimensional and multidirectional to any one-to-
one formulation is detrimental to understanding. The complex web of relations among
colonization, racism, and capitalism can be seen in the operation of the plantation; see, for
example, Curtin 1990 and Blackburn 1997. For an analysis of this same web of relations in a
more recent time, see Harvey 1989.

and Goldberg have basically made these two areas their foci of research and writing (Memmi 1965, 2000; Goldberg 1993; Goldberg and Quayson 2002).[12] A recent reader on race and racism has chosen to make colonialism one of its six major sections (Back and Solomos 2000: 257–372), while two recent but separate accounts on decolonization have given consistent attention to the abolition of slavery and the end of racial segregation (Betts 1998; Chamberlain 1999).

This connection between racializing and colonizing is perhaps even better seen in the profession(alizing) of anthropology (see also Childs and Williams 1997: 187–88). In the last decade, individual anthropologists have publicly acknowledged their discipline's role in fashioning race (Khare 1992; de Waal 1994: 28) and founding empire (Comaroff and Comaroff 1991: 1.xii-xiv; see also Said 1989). To make my point, I will just illustrate the former with the work of one dead and the latter with the work of one living anthropologist. Both cases will show that race and empire are imbricated with each other as they are also embedded within the discipline of anthropology.

Eugene Fischer, a close friend of Martin Heidegger and a card-carrying member of the Nazi Party, was the director of the Kaiser Wilhelm Institute for Anthropology, Genetics, and Eugenics. His brand and blending of (physical) anthropology and (racial) science were partly developed in his fieldwork in the German colony of South West Africa in 1908 (Gilroy 2000: 142; Weinreich 1999: 27, 31–33, 216–18). Almost half a century after Fischer, Peter Pels writes about a subdiscipline within anthropology called the 'anthropology of colonialism', wherein the genitive functions both subjectively and objectively (1997; see also Stoler 2002: 22–23; Stocking 1991; van Bremen and Shimizu 1999). According to Pels, anthropology has been a form of and a performance for colonial intelligence. Colonial rule has been developed on the basis of anthropological knowledge, and anthropology has been done with the colonial technique of observation, objectification, and ordering power. In other words, anthropology's

---

12. While it is true that with seeing race (often) comes the conceiving of a colony, the relation between race and colonialism is not always so straightforward. Though it is undeniable that race has been a basis and a means for colonial expansion, race has also been a reason for rejecting such expansionist ideology (Mehta 1997). This is so when nations are understood to be closed units integrated by racial and cultural 'purity'. This argument for and against colonial expansion on the basis of race is one of those 'tensions of empire' (Cooper and Stoler 1997). I should point out here that racism also has its tensions. For example, Goldberg has identified the tension between a 'naturalist/static' and a 'historicist/ evolutionary' conception of race (2002). This tension, according to Goldberg, leads to another tension of empire. The tension is whether colonial or state rule should operate on the basis of coercion-based amalgamation or capital-based assimilation.

embroilment with colonialism involves not only its purpose but its very method.

It is important for my purpose here to note that the last major section of Pels's essay concerns 'ethnicization and its fragments' (1997: 174–77), for I want to be more specific about the connection between ethnicity and (post)colonialism. In addition to Barth and Bromley, one of the first major schools that theorized ethnicity is the Manchester School (Banks 1996: 24–39). If Barth and Bromley are distinguished by their respective focus on boundary and an organic, 'ethnosocial' interaction, the Manchester School is known for its concern to study ethnic changes that are brought about by colonialism and urbanization. Earlier I mentioned the connection between 'tribal' and ethnic groups via Jenkins (1986). In Banks' estimation, the Manchester School is also most responsible for substituting within the discipline of anthropology the colonialist terminology (if not, as I pointed out, the ideology) of 'tribal' with ethnic groups. This long tradition of the Manchester School is still visible today by the consistent commitment on the part of the Manchester University Press to publish volumes that approach (post)colonialism from various angles (for example: Barker, Hulme, and Iversen 1994; McLeod 2000; Chrisman 2003).

In addition to anthropology, another avenue to argue for the association between race/ethnicity and colonialism is that of nationalism. First of all, nations and colonialism have a mingled relationship. Nations, both colonial and postcolonial, are formed and reformed as colonialism waxes and wanes. Second, as I have mentioned, Gilroy sees a link between ultranationalism and racial purity, while others focus on the amplifying buzz around ethnicity with the end of formal European colonization. Race/ethnicity becomes therefore a source of contention as former colonies turn into new, postcolonial nation-states and as formerly colonized peoples move into the nation-states of their previous colonial masters. We should in this regard place our earlier discussion of 'New (that is, culturally based) Racism' in the UK against people of Caribbean and South Asian descent as an aftermath of post-1945 immigration in the context of (post)colonialism. Once we remember that the end of the Second World War also effectively marks the end of the British Empire, we will recognize that sights of race/ethnicity are seldom removed from (post)colonial sites.

According to Jenny Sharpe, when people refer to the USA as 'postcolonial', most are referring to the presence of racial/ethnic minorities within its borders rather than its past as a British settler colony or its status as a neocolonial superpower (1995). Sharpe goes on to suggest that while this understanding of the 'postcolonial' helps explain the phenomenon of 'internal colonization' in the USA, it does not shed light on the neocolonial hegemony that the USA exercises around the world. In other words, race/ethnicity must not be read in (post)colonial terms only within the confines of one nation but also within the context of transnational power relations (see also Dobrin 1999: 116–19). It is thus well worth our pondering what 'new reality' Nathan Glazer and Daniel P. Moynihan might have had in mind when they stated in 1975 that 'a new word [ethnicity] reflects a new reality' (1975: 5).[13]

The beginning of postcolonial studies, and thus the popularization of the term postcolonial, is often associated with the publication of Said's *Orientalism* in 1978.[14] Since the adjective generally or at least partially refers to people or places that have gone through the trauma of colonial conquest, it is easy to see how the word, like race and ethnicity, is not likely to be embraced as a self-description by those who have been colonizers.[15] More importantly, many have also questioned the legitimacy of the 'postcolonial', both as a term and as a concept.[16] Childs and Williams have done an excellent job summarizing various aspects of this debate (1997: 1–25). Simply put, the time, place, person, and meaning of the 'postcolonial' have all been subjects of suspicion, interrogation, and contestation.

What is most pertinent for my purpose here is how this legitimacy crisis of postcolonialism points to its multidimensional and multidirectional (de)construction and operation. Postcolonialism is many things: a socio-political movement; a discursive, ideological, and cultural formation; and, perchance, a yet-to-be-realized form of government. Correspondingly, or perhaps even consequently, it is often difficult, if not impossible, to have any clear divisions between the colonizer and the colonized. This is not to deny the power differentials between colonizer and colonized but only to disclose that colonization and domination can and do go in more than one single direction and that they involve more than one area of human activity. This is also not to initiate a debate over who or what is most colonized or victimized but to instill sensitivity against colonization and

---

13. Sharpe's argument that national identity is inseparable from international politics is, in a way, already if arguably inadequately presented in Said's thesis on orientalism, and how the West forms an identity by differentiating itself from the Oriental Other (1978; see Pollock 1993). For more recent works on the construction of the colonizer's identity through its construction of the colonized, see Baucom 1999. Amidst this identity talk, one should always remember Said's Foucauldian or political emphasis. That is to say, identity construction or racialization (of both colonizers and colonized) is always related to matters of national and international governance or governmentality. Judging from the emphases of two recent anthologies on postcolonialism and the USA (King 2000; Singh and Schmidt 2000), Sharpe's salient suggestion has certainly caused a stir if not exactly found an echo.

14. Supposedly, the first use of the term 'postcolonialism' occurred in a British paper in 1959 referring to India's independence in 1947 (Sugirtharajah 2002: 2).

15. This is part of the puzzle or the furor around the debate which Sharpe addresses, namely, if and how the USA should be considered 'postcolonial'.

16. Admittedly, by using the adjective 'postcolonial' here I am already simplifying the debate over the legitimacy of and the differences between the nouns 'postcoloniality' and 'postcolonialism'.

domination in all forms and disguises. Postcolonialism is 'the critical counter-point of [any] incomplete forms of decolonization' (Hesse 2002: 163).

I have argued that race/ethnicity and postcolonialism are conceptually connected with, or maybe even embedded in, each other. Now I would like to propose that there are also productive differences between the two. As shown by Sharpe (1995), I would suggest that postcolonialism provides, first of all, a theoretical framework to read race/ethnicity in a wider, international nexus of sociocultural and colonial politics. Acknowledging the USA as an imperial center, for example, certainly complicates the position(ing) of racial(ized) minorities in the USA. Yet, as the crossed circuits of race and ethnicity may function to complement and challenge each other (ethnicity exposes intraracial differences as race encounters ethnic difference with the latter's occasional oblivion to power and the political), race/ethnicity and postcolonialism must not be collapsed into one and the same thing. Colonization and domination are not restricted to matters of race or even ethnicity (particularly given the uncertainties over the qualifications of ethnic parameters). One should at least think of issues involving gender, generation, class, sexuality, and religion—to name just the most obvious. The point here is that postcolonialism, in its multidimensional and multidirectional complication, cannot and should not be reduced to any form of (over)simplicity or singularity.[17] Correspondingly, neither race nor ethnicity is a unitary idea. Their contacts and overlaps with other identity factors have not only caused minority writers to address their concerns through, say, gender and

---

17.   I should spell out at least one of the implications of this statement. I have in mind here that postcolonial endeavors are not restricted to people of a certain race, ethnicity, gender, genealogy, class, sexuality, religion, and so on. What I am targeting is a form of determinism, essentialism, and reductionism that sees, for instance, all white people as colonizers. I will in fact go so far as to suggest that even beneficiaries of colonialism are capable of postcolonial vision and mission. In a sense, then, I do agree with Sugirtharajah that postcolonialism frees people from racial/ethnic ghettos (2001: 272), but I will extend this to include also people who have been recipients of colonial privilege. As Dawn Duncan points out, limiting the postcolonial discussion to those who pass the place (people from outside Europe) or race (people of color) test is just another form of essentialism (1994; 2002). Duncan's focus is mainly on the Irish (who have, as we mentioned, changed from being a black race to a white ethnic group), thus her argument intersects in many ways the intricacies between race and ethnicity. One should remember, however, that colonial domination takes place in many forms and directions and is not limited to matters of only race and ethnicity. I therefore do not see why an English [-speaking?] person, for instance, cannot be one with postcolonial sensibilities and commitments. I personally do not think that this broadening of postcolonial consideration will necessarily bring about the relativizing and thus the sanitizing of European colonialism.

sexuality, they will also ensure that race and ethnicity will in one way or another always be with us (Nguyen 2002: 6, 166).

This warning against unitariness or singularity should, of course, also apply to the relations between race/ethnicity and postcolonialism in terms of the direction of productive challenge. If postcolonialism helps frame the analysis of race/ethnicity, points to forms of domination beyond race/ethnicity, and exposes the myriad ways in which race/ethnicity intersects with other identity factors, is there something in the emphasis or theorization of race/ethnicity that contributes to our understanding of postcolonialism?

Given the connection between race/ethnicity and (post)colonialism, the changing but continuing problem of racism and ethnocentrism reminds us that the 'post' in postcolonialism must not be read romantically and naïvely to mean that colonialism is a thing of the past. Like racism and ethnocentrism, colonialism also mutates into different forms. An intentional focus on race/ethnicity may further emphasize the need not to confine colonialist endeavors to European nations. In addition to the clear but past example of Japan, one can, for instance, look at the present relations between China and Tibet or Taiwan.

I want to mention one more contribution that race and ethnicity theories may contribute to postcolonial (de)construction and operation. There is a tendency, or at least a temptation, to see postcolonialism as the correction of past colonialism in the sense of elimination. Whether one understands the prefix 'post' in terms of 'beyond', 'anti', 'since', or any combination of the three, the temptation is always there to equate postcolonialism with a return to nativism (Chow 1993: 27–54). We must not confuse 'unthinking Eurocentrism' (Shohat and Stam 1994) with 'undoing Europe' in the sense of unveiling 'untainted natives'. As Sugirtharajah suggests, postcolonialism means eclecticism (2001: 272). It is important to remember that orientalism is partly characterized by 'its promotion of the distant past as normative' and by 'a pattern of dichotomies' (Rocher 1993: 242–43). It is also important to remember Gilroy's argument that 'slaughter' (those who are for colonial expansion) and separation (those who are against colonial expansion) are but two sides of the same (racial) logic (2000: 106, 138). Essentializing group difference in a way that completely ignores history is indeed 'probably the most damaging part of the orientalist bequest to postcolonial politics' (Breckenridge and van der Veer 1993b: 12). The nostalgia for and/or to be a 'pure native' actually carries traces of a colonial past.

These traces of a colonial past refer not just to the ahistorical and essentialist ideology of nativism but also to the legacy of history. A postcolonial condition is the peculiar phenomenon that transnationalism is no longer conditioned on travel. If the East has come to the West, the West has also gone to the East. One may be able to change the course of history;

one cannot erase it. What I think is helpful in the theorization of race/ethnicity is that it points not to an essence but to the mobilization of meaning *in* history. What gets emphasized is the historicity and the specificity of their be(ginn)ing. This is particularly true of ethnicity, its primordial part(y) notwithstanding. In fact, I think the inside/outside tension in the making of ethnicity (between 'political force' and 'cultural glue') can be transformed into a temporal tension to speak to the two historical be(gin)ings of a postcolonial: the one before *and* the other after the onset of colonialism. Ethnicity's 'interactional' approach, involving 'both self-ascription and ascription by others' (Edelman 1996: 25 n2), points in a way to the inseparable convergence of these two histories in the postcolonial.

Addressing the Cross, and Cross-(Ad)dressing

Despite continual debates on the meaning and legitimacy of race/ethnicity and postcolonialism, academic studies of the New Testament that employ these concepts as interpretive foci and categories have, by the end of the twentieth century, gained a degree of legitimacy and validity. This is so even if these issues and practices have not exactly moved from the margins to the center of the discipline. Their legitimate if marginal status is evidenced by the fact that within the two-volume *Dictionary of Biblical Interpretation* (Hayes 1999), one can find entries on 'Afrocentric Biblical Interpretation' (Felder 1999), 'Armenian Biblical Interpretation' (Cowe 1999), 'Asian Biblical Interpretation' (Kuan 1999), 'Cross-cultural Biblical Interpretation' (Sugirtharajah 1999a), 'Hispanic American Biblical Interpretation' (Segovia 1999), and 'Postcolonial Biblical Interpretation' (Dube 1999).[18] The inclusion of these entries should not, however, obscure the absence of entries such as 'European Biblical Interpretation' or 'Euro-American Biblical Interpretation'. Instead, what we find are numerous entries on particular European and Euro-American scholars of the Bible, such as Adolf Deissmann (Bullard 1999), Rudolf Bultmann (Morgan 1999), or Krister Stendahl (Brooten 1999). What this illustrates is, of course, the (colonial?) politics of recognition, and thus the racial/ethnic transparency or invisibility of white Bible scholars. The recent develop-

18.   One can actually add to this list, depending on how one defines ethnicity, other entries such as 'Evangelical Biblical Interpretation' (Osborne 1999), 'Gay/Lesbian Interpretation' (Stone 1999), and 'Orthodox Biblical Interpretation' (Stylianopoulos 1999). This is certainly an improvement compared to their complete absence in the *Dictionary of Biblical Interpretation* that appeared only eight years earlier (Coggins and Houlden 1990; cited in Sugirtharajah 1991: 2).

ment of whiteness studies in the larger academic circles has yet to have any impact in the world of biblical or New Testament studies.

Differences and Similarities, Between and Within

I hope my earlier, more theoretical discussion on race/ethnicity and postcolonialism will further sensitize New Testament scholarship to the ways in which these terms are embedded in and imbricated with each other. It is interesting that, unlike postcolonialism (for example, Donaldson 1996a: 3–6; Sugirtharajah 2001: 245–50, 265–71; Sugirtharajah 2002: 2, 11–42), the concepts and constructions of race and ethnicity have received very little theoretical attention within New Testament scholarship.[19] Most proceed as if those terms have certain given realities, or at least distinct definitions, that are readily accessible to all readers. Some are content with providing a simple working definition and/or referencing a couple of resources for readers to pursue on their own (Byron 2002: 2, 20, 22). Several exceptions that prove the rule may be Mark G. Brett's introduction to his edited volume on *Ethnicity and the Bible* (1996b), Philip F. Esler's paper on Galatians (1996), Sze-Kar Wan's essay on Paul's collection for the Jerusalem church (2000a), and Kelley's recent book on raciology and modern biblical scholarship (2002: 19–31). None of them, however, does anything with the complex relations between race and ethnicity.

Brett acknowledges the complexity of the matter in a brief footnote (1996b: 11 n. 26). Despite its brevity, I think Brett's footnote wittingly or unwittingly unveils at least part of the rationale behind this silence. Brett writes, 'Whether such diversity [Banton's theorization of racial classification in terms of lineage, type, subspecies, status, and class (1998)] has parallels in the ancient world is a matter for detailed historical investigation.' In other words, if race is a modern construct, contemporary New Testament scholars may well talk about using race as a place or location of reading, but can we talk about reading race in the ancient New Testament texts themselves? It is the question of anachronism, and thus, yet once more, the haunting of illegitimacy, which points back to the (colonial?) reality or politics of recognition within the profession. As a way to subvert the disciplinary gaze of the dominant, many appropriate or take advantage of the complex relations between race and ethnicity without articulating or acknowledging the issues involved in that complexity. For example, Byron consistently and deftly talks about color (rather than race)

---

19. This is not only true of biblical scholars. Scholars in other fields who use race/ethnicity as their interpretive lens have also been more willing to depend on more 'empirical' work within sociology and history rather than theory. See Cheng 2001: 25–26.

and ethnic differences in early Christian literature; how she sees the relationship between color and ethnicity is left unexpressed.[20]

Another interesting difference between New Testament scholars who use race/ethnicity as an interpretive category and those who use postcolonialism is that it has been more likely for the former to neglect the latter than the other way around. Part of the reason has to do with the simple fact that postcolonialism appears, as we have seen, later on the larger academic scene than race/ethnicity. While earlier texts on race/ethnicity involve only one or two references to colonial or imperial dynamics (Felder 1989: xii, xiv; Sugirtharajah 1991: 2), more recent texts on race/ethnicity tend to include in their indexes either the topic of 'postcolonialism' or authors who work on the topic (Kelley 2002; Byron 2002). This mutual but somewhat 'imbalanced' influence involves, however, not just chrono-logic but also has much to do with a 'post-o-phobic'. I will use (admittedly, out of context) another terse comment near the end of Brett's introductory essay—where the adjectives 'post-colonial', 'postmodern', and 'extreme' appear in a rather quick succession—as a tell-tale sign (1996b: 22). What is at work here is the lingering suspicions on the 'play(fulness)' of postmodernism, with which postcolonialism is often linked (see Moore: this volume). Many New Testament scholars committed to racial/ethnic justice in and around the globe are not sure if postmodernism's or postcolonialism's tendency to (over)emphasize textuality, hybridity, and multiplicity is not a fragmentation of, or even a flight from, politics.[21]

Having said that, many New Testament scholars (myself included) do see race/ethnicity and postcolonialism as interdependent and interrelated issues. Like Goldberg within the larger world of humanities and law, an increasing number are working to integrate these two issues within New Testament studies.[22] I have already dealt with their overlaps in a broader and more theoretical level; let me now briefly discuss how New Testament

20. Note in this regard the challenge issued by a classics scholar, Roger S. Bagnall, who emphasizes the need for greater conceptual clarity on what we mean by ethnicity in antiquity (1988). To answer that challenge, must one, or should one, work through contemporary theories on ethnicity, as well as contemporary discussions on the complex relations between ethnicity and race?

21. I should point out that this anxiety or hesitation is shared by certain postcolonial critics. See, for example, Said 2002: 11; Sugirtharajah 2001: 272–75; and Chrisman 2003: 1–5. Despite the two very understandable reasons given above, I will still emphasize the importance to converge (not collapse) the interpretive optics of race/ethnicity and postcolonialism. Sugirtharajah has given a couple of very instructive examples of how the tunnel vision on race/ethnicity ends up (dis)missing certain colonial dynamics in one's reading of the New Testament (2002: 92, 98).

22. Several pioneers in this effort are worth mentioning. They include Dube (1999; 2000); Segovia (1998; 1999; 2000a; 2000b), and Sugirtharajah (1991; 1998a; 1998b; 1999a; 1999b; 2001; 2002).

scholars who focus on these issues tend to share similar sentiments and strategies in their interpretive endeavors.

First, there is an attempt to read race/ethnicity and/or (post)colonialism in the biblical text. David Sim, for instance, begins his reading of ethnicity in Matthew by arguing for the importance of ethnicity in the New Testament (1996: 171–84). For Sim, more than the actual appearance of the word *ethnos* in the New Testament, there are a couple of related reasons to focus on New Testament ethnicities: (1) the Jewish claim of being a chosen people, and thus their commitment to be a distinct(ive) community; and (2) the church's attempt to reach or welcome Gentiles, despite its beginning as a Jewish sect. This attempt to mission and evangelize cultural others on the part of the early church, which also finds its way onto the pages of the New Testament, becomes for Donaldson a reason and obligation to read (post)colonialism in the New Testament (1996a: 6–8). In addition, Segovia talks about the need to take into serious consideration the thought that the Bible was first written, collected, and circulated in the context of (successive) empire(s) (1998: 56–58). One manifestation of these conceptual connections is a focused reading on specific characters in the New Testament to find or locate the (marginalized) other in a narrative, whether in racial/ethnic and/or (post)colonial terms. For example, both Clarice Martin (1989) and Abraham Smith (1995) read Acts 8.26-40 by identifying the black identity of the Ethiopian eunuch as their point of departure. In a similar manner, Dube marks the Canaanite woman of Matthew 15.21-28 as the colonized ethnic other in her 'postcolonial feminist' interpretation (2000).

Second, there is an agenda to expose the ideological bias of much dominant biblical scholarship, whether in racist, ethnocentric, and/or colonial terms. Kelley has most recently done so in terms of racist assumptions embedded in Hegelianism, Heideggerianism, and Romanticism, and their respective influence on the Tübingen School of Ferdinand Christian Bauer, the existentialist demythologization of Rudolf Bultmann, and the parable scholarship of Robert Funk and John Dominic Crossan (2002).[23] A little earlier, John Riches argued for the productivity but also the cultural prejudice of much European and North American biblical scholarship (1996; see also D. Martin 2001; and Alexander 2001). Starting with the Reformation, Riches focuses on the important question of religious pluralism via the History of Religions School. Out of his many examples, I will concentrate on his first two. For Riches, Luther's reading

---

23. Reading Kelley's book has caused in me a chain reaction. Now I cannot help but wonder about the racial and colonial implications of that chain of thought and scholarship that goes from Hegel to Karl Marx and Max Weber. This is particularly so since both Marx and Weber have been influential in New Testament studies. I have in mind here, just to name a few examples, Fernando Belo, Gerd Theissen, and Wayne Meeks.

of Romans simultaneously implies an internal liberty from 'works-righteousness', a freedom from the hegemony of the Church of Rome, as well as a hegemonic evangelism that defames and enslaves other (particularly Jewish) cultures and religions as 'false'. Like Kelley, Riches sees in Bauer a Hegelian influence. As Bauer sought to justify theology's place in the modern academy, Hegel's influence results in Bauer reading texts like 1 Corinthians 2.10-16 as Hegel's *Geist* and understanding the culture of Protestantism as the zenith of all cultural developments. If Luther sees Protestantism as the only true religion, Bauer conceives it as the most mature.

Riches frames his examples of 'cultural bias' by attributing them to the problem of 'annexation' (1996: 433, 446–47). He means by that the tendency to universalize one's inevitably cultural reading of a biblical text because of the power of (over)identification. In other words, analogy between one's culturally determined experience and the biblical text turns too easily into similarity, uniformity, unity, and finally seizure, custody, and univocity. In his discussion of E.P. Sanders, Riches mentions the need 'to preserve a certain neutrality' in scriptural interpretation (1996: 443). He further compares, with at least a degree of approval, Sanders' 'functionalist' approach to Paul and Palestinian Judaism to an anthropologist's commitment to an emic (of those participating inside) rather than an etic (of those observing from the outside) interpretation. For Riches, despite its bias and even 'colonising tendencies', historical criticism may still be of use to those from the so-called 'Third World', precisely because 'historical argument and scrutiny may … help to undermine the distortions to which the overpressing of cultural analogies can lead' (1996: 447).

I mention all of this not only because I have already discussed Pels's 'anthropology of colonialism', but also because Segovia has adamantly argued that the historical-critical method, because of its very idealization and claim of neutrality and objectivity, is a colonizing ideology (2000a).[24] My goal here is not to pit Riches and Segovia against each other, to instigate a fight, or to condemn one and commend the other. Instead, I want to underscore the differences that exist among New Testament scholars who are equally committed to issues of race/ethnicity and/or postcolonialism. Both Riches and Segovia view univocity and universality in interpretation as disagreeable, yet methodologically they do not agree

---

24. In addition to Segovia's critique of these methods' obsession with 'the original context', one might add to that critique their obsession with 'the original language(s)' or philology. See in this regard the thought-provoking essays on philology in the context of Indian literatures and politics by Vinay Dharwadker (1993) and David Lelyveld (1993).

on whether the root problem is too much identification or too much distantiation, a misuse or a misunderstanding of history.[25]

Finally, New Testament scholars who focus on race/ethnicity and postcolonialism share the aim of celebrating the agency of the racial/ethnic and/or postcolonial other. It is important to point out that this other can be the one represented or embedded in a New Testament text and/or the one (re)reading the New Testament text. The agency of the critic or interpreter is clear in all cases, but the same cannot be said of the biblical character or writer. That is to say, while race/ethnicity and/or postcolonialism provide/s a positive place or perspective for the interpreter to plot her or his reading, his or her reading of the racial/ethnic relations and other power dynamics within a biblical text may or may not be positive. There are at least two sets of differences that we must sift through here. There is a difference between reading the New Testament from a perspective of race/ethnicity/postcolonialism and reading race/ethnicity/ (post)colonialism in the New Testament. There are also differences in critiquing racism, ethnocentrism, and colonialism on the basis of the New Testament, in the interpretation of the New Testament, and in the New Testament. Since postcolonial New Testament criticism has only been developing within the last decade, I do not have the hindsight or the ability to trace any perceivable trend. If we look at the first couple of anthologies on postcolonial biblical criticism (Donaldson 1996b; Sugirtharajah 1998b), all of the different accents and angles mentioned above seem to be present concurrently. This contemporaneous blooming of a hundred flowers is, I would argue, an inheritance from the earlier development of a racial/ethnic optic within Biblical Studies. Conveniently, three anthologies edited by three different racial/ethnic minority scholars of the New Testament from

---

25. I wonder if adding a little adjective to both positions might not help clarify or even clear the difference between Riches and Segovia. If Riches is talking about too much *implicit* identification and Segovia is complaining about too much *explicit* distantiation, then they may actually be talking about the same thing. This does not, however, resolve their difference on the use or validity of historical criticism. I should also point out that Segovia, in another essay, does speak in support of a certain distantiation. I have in mind here his intercultural criticism or diaspora hermeneutics that 'read[s] the biblical text as an other ... [and] argues for *distantiation* from it as a working desideratum' (1995: 58, 69; emphasis mine). How this explicit 'distantiation' differs from other *implicit* identifications that Segovia decries is something that I am not able to ascertain. This is especially so since Segovia ends by (seemingly?) denying the actuality of that explicit 'distantiation' as but 'an unavoidable filtering of the one world or entity by and through the other, of the text by and through the reader' (1995: 70). Text-as-Other thus seems like a(nother) 'noble dream' (Novick 1988) that Segovia lures us into, and then immediately wakes us out of. What is at issue is the difference between the ludic and the programmatic, or the distance between what is imaginable and what is (im)practicable.

the USA can illustrate my argument that there is a definitive directional drift or division within this earlier interpretive movement.

The first anthology I have in mind is the volume edited by Cain Hope Felder (1991a), which is also the first anthology on African American biblical interpretation. In his pithy preface (1991b), Felder outlines the problem, the goal, and the method of African American biblical interpretation. Since dominant exegetical and hermeneutical methodology serves to maintain Eurocentrism by erasing black presence out of the Bible, (re)discovering black presence in the Bible will recapture the racial/ethnic pluralism that is part of the Bible's universalist vision. In terms of methodology, intertextual allusions within the Bible show an affinity with how Scripture has been and can be understood by African Americans. These three theses then become the framework by which the anthology is organized. Three essays in Part 1 address the question of 'goal' by discussing, clarifying, and largely affirming the vision and thus the authority of the Bible. Two essays in Part 2 focus on 'method' with their historical exploration on the sources and styles with which African Americans have interpreted the Bible in the past. Part 3, with three essays, seeks to correct the 'problem' by mapping out the geographical overlaps between ancient biblical lands and North Africa, pointing out the absence of color prejudice in the biblical world as well as simply 'outing' the pervasive presence and positive portrayals of Blacks in the Bible. Finally, three last essays make up Part 4, which not only provides additional examples of African American biblical interpretation but also peruses biblical passages that have been linked with the very issue of slavery.

Things had certainly changed or become complicated by the time another anthology, *African Americans and the Bible*, came on the scene a decade later (Wimbush 2001a). The massive difference in length notwithstanding, this anthology also reflects clear changes as to how African Americans function as an interpretive lens of the Bible. This is evident in even a cursory reading of Wimbush's introductory essay (2001b). For Wimbush, the Eurocentrism dominating biblical scholarship is no longer just the erasure of black presence in the Bible but the elimination or at least limitation of black present. Wimbush argues that Biblical Studies should begin with 'some fundamental self-inventorying' on the part of African Americans (2001b: 9). Wimbush's emphasis on time thus implies a commitment to and a curriculum of 'reading race reading scripture' instead of 'reading race in scripture'. In other words, Wimbush is more concerned with how African Americans read and make meaning with the Bible rather than what the Bible says or does not say about Blacks. Far from affirming the Bible's place and plea for racial/ethnic inclusion, Wimbush's goal is to study society and culture, or what he calls 'social textures', via their (inter)relations with 'sacred texts'. The Bible is therefore displaced in a sense. At the very least, its authority is not an obsessive or obsessing question. As Wimbush indicates, the making of meaning or 'worlding' that he and this anthology focus on may well involve 'going beyond and against' the Bible (2001b: 22).[26] In fact, this investigation of 'worlding' necessitates, according to Wimbush, a critical inquiry of the very concept(ion) of 'sacred texts' (2001b: 16).

Unlike Felder, Wimbush makes no claim about the affinity between how African Americans and biblical writers use Scripture. If anything, Wimbush goes out of his way to state that 'African Americans are not somehow the people of the most profound insight into the interpretation of any particular part of the Bible' (2001b: 28). In terms of methodology, Wimbush proposes a multidisciplinary approach in general and a linkage between Biblical Studies and African American studies in particular. For Wimbush, identifying black persons in the pages of the Bible should now give way to interpreting 'darkness' (the 'worlding' of humans despite or even through trauma, typified by the marronage and meaning-making of African Americans) as the very pivot of Biblical Studies.[27]

A year later, the very first anthology that uses Asian American as an interpretive lens to study the Bible was published as the last and final issue of the journal *Semeia* (Liew and Yee 2002). With contributors of Asian descent but of different ethnic origins (Chinese, Japanese, Korean, Filipino, and South Asian), the purposes and emphases of this anthology, as indicated by Liew's introductory essay (2002a), are amazingly akin to those articulated by Wimbush. There is a special appeal to connect Biblical Studies with Asian American studies, as well as a more general emphasis on a transdisciplinary participation and practice in biblical interpretation. Rather than 'finding' Asian Americans in the Bible, this anthology focuses on reading readers as much as on readers reading. It also seeks to demonstrate the differences within the Bible, disclose its oppressive and liberating potentials, and thus demand an interrogation of why people need and what people mean by 'Scripture'. Finally, as evidenced by the title of the anthology, *The Bible in Asian America*, it is more interested in the wider racial/ethnic and sociocultural picture associated with the Bible

---

26.   I am using the term 'worlding' here *without* the connotation of colonial dynamics that is being suggested by Spivak (1985). For Spivak, 'worlding' is closely akin to Said's orientalism. It refers to the colonial project of representing and ruling the other in the process. The change from Felder to Wimbush is also detectable in comparing Frank Snowden's studies (1970; 1983) and Byron's study (2002) of 'symbolic blackness' in the Greco-Roman world. Bryon presents a more varied picture and thus a more ambivalent attitude towards the New Testament and other early Christian literature.

27.   It is worth pointing out that while Felder's introduction only has one appearance of the word 'imperialistic' (1991c: 6), Wimbush's introduction is peppered with not only words like 'colonial', 'postcolonial', 'colonized', 'conquerors' (2001b: 1, 7, 10, 11, 13), but also references to postcolonial studies (2001b: 31n 14, 32n20).

than just the Bible as a literary text. It is more concerned with what Asian Americans have made of the Bible than what the Bible may or may not have to say about Asian Americans. The parallels between these two recent anthologies, published a year apart, suggest to me a definite diversification, if not a radical reorientation, in biblical scholarship that uses race/ethnicity as an interpretive category.[28] Fortunately for those who venture into a postcolonial criticism of the Bible, we have from day one benefited from these developments.

Evaluations and Suggestions
With the growing attention to both the ideology and the politics of New Testament studies, I am happy to see the parallel and intertwined developments that use race/ethnicity and/or postcolonialism as an operative optic. For me, these two viewpoints and emphases cannot be subsumed one into the other, neither can they be synthesized into one. I do think, however, that New Testament studies can gain much as scholars shift back and forth between these two perspectives and explore where and how they converge and/or diverge. As these two optics supplement and subtend each other, let me focus on several subjects that I see to be of particular interest and importance to the operation of both.

Vernacular It seems to me that the question of exotic essentialism (that is, nativism) is always in the background in discussions and developments of the vernacular. The vernacular emphasis, as shown by Sugirtharajah (1999c: 11–13), functions within postcolonialism as one way to avoid the collapsing of the metropole and the former colony.[29] Moreover, despite Sugirtharajah's repeated warnings and disclaimers (1999c: 14–16; 1999d; 2001: 7, 279; 2002: 77), his own statement that vernacular hermeneutics 'being nearer home and getting closer to the roots' (1999c: 13) seems to betray a contradictory impulse.[30] How does one showcase a 'native'

---

28. I am unable to say much about Latina/o biblical interpretation here partly because, to my knowledge, there is not yet a Latino/a anthology that focuses on the Bible. Segovia did suggest, however, that similar shifts and changes have taken place in Latina/o reading of the Bible (1999). I am afraid even less has been published on Native Americans and their use of the Bible. For a couple of recent attempts, see Weaver (1996) and Donaldson (1999).

29. That is, of course, at best just part of the picture. Postcolonialism's commitment to expose colonial dynamics at various levels also results in the entry of class and gender within studies of the former colonies. This is part of what motivated the worthwhile studies on the subaltern, as Sugirtharajah himself partially points out (2002: 22). Another reason given by Sugirtharajah for his work on the vernacular is to give, or rather acknowledge, the agency of the colonized (2001: 5–6).

30. What about his closing comments on Gustavo Gutiérrez and Elsa Tamez? Is his statement that they did not use 'any specific Latin American theological nuances, or indigenous cultural resources' (Sugirtharajah 2002: 112) meant to be a criticism? If so, why?

(whatever that means) without wittingly or unwittingly selling or promoting an implicit form of nativism? Sugirtharajah's own desire for and fear of the vernacular betray the simultaneously elusive, equivocal, and evident power that comes with the vernacular's implicit investments in purity, peculiarity, monopoly, and marketability.[31] Rather than issuing warnings or disclaimers, I would suggest that explorations of the vernacular be done in a way that makes visible the larger sociocultural, political, and colonial factors that contribute to the development of a particular vernacular way of being and reading. More importantly, I would suggest that such explorations seek to expose whenever and wherever possible how a vernacular points to or betrays within itself traces or hints of 'impurity'.

The dilemma presented by the vernacular and essentialism is equally difficult for those who use race/ethnicity as an interpretive category. Within racial/ethnic studies (to use just one example from the metropole), where 'Asian American' doubles effectually—despite academic argument to the contrary (Sumida and Wong 2001: 7 n. 5)—as both an identity description and a political designation, controversies over authenticity become practically inevitable. After all, how does one tell another Asian American (in racial/ethnic terms) that he or she is not an Asian American (in political terms) when there is a range of political ideologies (including reading ideologies) available? How and since when does a particular politics embody a special racial/ethnic 'essence'? Is it not a form of social regulation for a particular political position (borrowing Riches' terms mentioned above) to 'appropriate' and 'annex' a racial/ethnic description? Most of us have learned by now that language constitutes rather than just reflects reality, so nomenclature is never just benign. In addition to the need to be vigilant about the positive and negative power of the vernacular, the question of essentialism also confronts us with the need to rethink what one means by, say, 'Asian American' biblical interpretation.

Diaspora Precisely as one way to prevent essentializing, arresting, or absolutizing cultures and identities, many New Testament scholars who emphasize race/ethnicity and/or postcolonialism have come to embrace what is now known as the diasporic identity. Diasporic interpretation may be where racial/ethnic and postcolonial optics most readily converge.

---

31. Sugirtharajah has authored or edited four volumes that have, in varying degree, to do with the vernacular in biblical interpretation (1991; 1998a; 1999b; 2001). The fact that all of these volumes were published by three different publishers of the geopolitical West within a short time-span also renders problematic Sugirtharajah's own claim that biblical hermeneutics in the vernacular, unlike liberation hermeneutics of the Third World, is not popular in the West (1999c: 11–12).

There are a number of texts that I can refer to here (such as Segovia 2000b; Sugirtharajah 2002: 179–99), but I am going to get at this through Daniel Boyarin's *A Radical Jew: Paul and the Politics of Identity* (1994). I do so for three reasons. First, New Testament studies on race/ethnicity and/or postcolonialism should not, but nevertheless tend to, ignore or forget the importance of the Jewish question. Second, Boyarin's text has been very influential on New Testament scholarship that deals with ethnicity and postcolonialism. In Brett's edited volume on ethnicity, for example, Boyarin's text has occupied a major portion of three essays, including Brett's introduction (1996b: 11, 16–20), John M.G. Barclay's essay on Paul (1996: 206–13), and Riches' essay on the 'cultural bias' of European and North American biblical scholarship (1996: 441, 444–46). In Segovia's introductory essay to his edited volume on diasporic readings of the Bible, he also refers to Boyarin's text as one early model (2000c: 24–29). Third, it takes me back to yet another text that I have referred to earlier, Gilroy's *Against Race* (2000). Seemingly adopting opposing positions on the desirability of race/ethnicity, Gilroy and Boyarin agree on a similarly supportive stance regarding the diaspora.

I assume most readers are familiar with Boyarin's thesis about Paul, so I will be brief. Starting with Paul's pronouncement in Galatians 3.28 but eventually working with Romans, Boyarin argues that Paul, motivated by a Hellenistic idea(l) of univocity and universality as well as armed with a Neoplatonic dualism and an allegorical hermeneutics, seeks to reform Judaism's ethnic particularity by promoting through Christ a human unity and uniformity. This, Boyarin argues, Paul does by turning 'fleshly' differences (like ethnicity and gender) into matters of 'spiritual' indifference. What New Testament scholars tend to talk less about is Boyarin's final chapter, where he proposes the diaspora as a way to synthesize and balance Pauline sameness and rabbinic difference. A diasporic identity, according to Boyarin, esteems rather than erases ethnic difference, but it also prevents ethnic difference from possessing power and territory (as in Israel today) and thus from becoming oppressive.

I have already mentioned how Gilroy's postracial humanism is in large measure a response to his discomfort with ultranationalism's emphasis on citizenship as soldiery and (racial) purity. As it turns out, his reconfigured 'planetary humanism' is related to his use of diaspora to talk about 'the dynamics of identity and belonging constituted between the poles of geography and genealogy' (2000: 122). Like Boyarin, who sees the diaspora as a way to move beyond autochthony, Gilroy sees the diaspora as an 'outer-national' concept that problematizes 'the spatialization of identity' and 'the ontologization of place' (2000: 122–23). Disconnecting notions of culture from those of rootedness results for both Boyarin and Gilroy in a dynamic understanding of culture that is intercultural and transcultural but never acultural. Gilroy adds that the idea of diaspora also unsettles notions of citizenship by literally providing a third space or location within a nation-state that straddles between assimilation and deportation.

Brett and Wan are two Bible scholars who have taken Boyarin to task for his particular promotion of diaspora.[32] While Brett questions Boyarin's stance on land with the situation of the Australian Aborigines (1996b: 4–5),[33] Wan brings up the example of Asian Americans (2000b: 118–21). What both Brett and Wan point to is Boyarin's own indifference to difference. What Boyarin (dis)misses in his euphoric rhetoric on the diasporic is that there are not only different diasporas (Wan) but also different postcolonial locations (Brett). Aborigines in Australia certainly occupy a different postcolonial location from that of diasporic Jews, but their location is also different from that of the (postcolonial) white settlers

---

32. Wan, a New Testament scholar, also proceeds to challenge Boyarin's reading of Galatians (2000b: 122–27). According to Wan, Paul's statement in Gal. 3.28 is less about erasing ethnic differences but more about erasing power differentials between Jews and Gentiles in the church community (2000b: 126–27). As Wan reminds Boyarin of the larger context of Galatians (that of the Roman Empire and thus the minority status of both Jews and Jesus-followers), he himself seems to have lost sight of precisely that context as he reads Galatians affirmatively as another example of Pauline self-emptying of power (that is, vis-à-vis the gentile Galatians). Reading Galatians in *multiple* contextual and power differentials, another Jewish scholar, Màrk Nanos, has since argued that Paul's position is ironic because, as a circumcised Jew, he failed to recognize his own secured position and thus the liminal and threatening position being occupied by his Galatian 'converts' (2002). Without circumcision, these Galatian 'converts' were not proselyte Jews and were therefore liable to the sanction of the empire should they refrain from their previous pagan and emperor worship. Paul, in the eyes of Nanos, is like Wan. Both Paul and Wan contextualize the Galatian 'problem' in only the ethnic context of Jews and Gentiles. In contrast, the Galatian 'converts' might be, at least according to Nanos, contextualizing their dilemma in the colonial context of the Roman Empire. This scholarly debate over Galatians turns out then to be yet another illustration of or argument for the importance of intersecting race/ethnicity and (post)colonialism in one's interpretive endeavor. Contemporary Pauline scholarship, particularly with the rise of the much affirmed but by no means less problematic 'new perspective', provides *one* excellent entry way to explore race/ethnicity and (post)colonialism within New Testament studies; see, for example, Matlock 1998 for a potentially provocative point of departure. Saying that does not mean, however, that Paul is the only place for exploring race/ethnicity and/or postcolonialism in the New Testament. One of my disappointments with Brett's edited volume is that the essays on ethnicity in the New Testament are, for all practical purposes, completely dominated by the paradigm of Pauline and deutero-Pauline studies. The only essay that is not supposedly on Paul (Sim 1996) is nevertheless responding to the same question of Jewish-Christian relations that has been dominating Pauline scholarship since the pioneering work of Stendahl (1976) and Sanders (1977).

33. The issue of land and place is a controversial one within postcolonial debates. In contrast to Boyarin and Gilroy, there are scholars inside and outside the theological disciplines who emphasize the importance of land claims for postcolonials. For an example of the former, see Dube 2000; for an example of the latter, see Mohanram 1999.

of Australia.[34] Within the US context, Native Americans also occupy a very different postcolonial location from those of, say, Wan's Asian Americans.

What I am getting at is the need to scrutinize the relations of these different locations, which I think the resort to vernacular is also partially pointing to. We must not, however, (over)simplify these differences as only differences of race/ethnicity.[35] The tension between postcolonials in a 'First World' and those in the Third World context is, as Mohanram reminds us (1999: 177–79), 'legible' in the published interview of Spivak by three other female Indian professors of English (Spivak 1990: 67–74). The tension has mainly to do with the different postcolonial locations between these four women who otherwise have so much in common. Spivak is living and working in diaspora (USA), while her three counterparts live and work in Delhi, India. Spivak is surprised by the premise of the very first question, namely, the differences between a diasporic intellectual and 'native intellecutuals' (Spivak 1990: 67). Unprepared to give an answer, Spivak ends up insisting on the postcolonial status of all four of them (which the interviewers do not actually dispute) and denouncing nativism. While I find myself agreeing with Spivak on both counts, I still wonder if there is not a need to theorize or think through the implications of these two locations. In other words, are there or are there not other differences besides a naïve and negative nativism that distinguish an Indian American and an Indian after India's independence in 1947? Trinh T. Minh-ha has, of course, made the memorable and indisputable observation that there is a 'First World' in every 'Third World' and a 'Third World' in every 'First World' (1991: 148). Trinh does not say, however, that these 'first worlds' are the same or that these 'third worlds' are interchangeable. Sugirtharajah has enriched biblical scholarship tremendously with his many volumes on Third World and diasporic scholarship of the Bible (1998a; 1998b; 1999b; 2001; 2002). He has, however, always dealt with these topics in separation from each other and has yet to tease out the relations of these two postcolonial locations.[36]

34. For an example of postcolonial biblical criticism that deals with the Australian context, see Boer 2001. Since Boer deals mainly with the Hebrew Bible, one may also want to take a look at Huie-Jolly 2002, although the context shifts to that of the Maori in New Zealand.

35. For too long and too often, race/ethnicity has been used to cover up other types of differences, both within one's own racial/ethnic community and in other racial/ethnic communities. Sadly, this practice has been true for people on both sides of the colonial divide. See, for example, Spivak 1988 and Stoler 2002: 24–25, 38.

36. Using Sol Plaatje of South Africa and Du Bois of the USA as a case study, Chrisman has recently argued for the need to analyze the different and complex relations between these as well as among other postcolonial locations (2003: 89–106).

Another reason for not reducing differences in postcolonial locations to race/ethnicity is the fact that differences also exist within each diaspora. Given my beginning allusion to global capitalism and Wan's example, one must not (dis)miss the fact that the Asian American diaspora is itself a plurality in terms of class (Ong 1999; Wong 1995). There are Asian Americans who are, to name just a few examples, academics (like Wan), entrepreneurs, factory workers, 'guest'-workers, or unemployed refugees. The way Boyarin (dis)misses class difference within his euphoric rhetoric of the diasporic is, in my view, one of the most serious problems of his book. This problem is evident not only in Boyarin's (utter) silence on the slave-and-free pairing within Galatians 3.28, it is also explicit in how his concern with geography (his criticism of autochthony) leads to and/or results from a kind of genealogical amnesia and class blindness. Many people in the present, like Jews of the past, do not get to choose their diaspora(s), and their situations are far less idyllic or idealistic than what is imagined by Boyarin.

Sexuality These differences point to the need for an investigation of different postcolonial locations as well as for intersections within New Testament studies to go beyond that of postcolonialism and race/ethnicity. Since this volume will have essays dealing with postcolonialism's intersection with issues of class and gender, I will focus on identifying another identity factor that has so far seldom been on the radar screen of New Testament scholarship, whether the interpretive lens is that of race/ethnicity or postcolonialism. I have mentioned that diasporic studies in some ways have been the most sensible and successful meeting place for race/ethnicity and postcolonialism. Many should be familiar with how the word 'diaspora' is etymologically related to the sowing or scattering of seed. This sowing or scattering of seed is, within the context of the Greco-Roman world, both an agricultural as well as a sexual act (Fehribach 1998: 53–56). Stefan Helmreich has in that sense correctly wondered if the idea of the diaspora is unfortunately linked to sperm and masculinism (1993). In response, Gilroy suggests etymologically linking the word 'diaspora' with spore (the reproductive body in bacteria, fungi, and non-flowering plants) instead of sperm, which might result in a 'gender-free' or 'asexual' reproduction that is more liberating (2000: 126).

Despite Gilroy's suggestion, his conversation with Helmreich is clearly moving from issues of gender to those of sexuality. Many studies have pointed to the intersecting and intertwining relations among race/ethnicity, postcolonialism, and sexuality (Hyam 1990; Parker, Russo, Sommer, and Yaeger 1992). Since race/ethnicity has long been a premise and/or a process of the colonial divide, sexual relations between colonizers and colonized have also long been another one of those 'tensions of empire'

(Cooper and Stoler 1997). Such relations have been simultaneously encouraged as a show of power and prohibited as a threat to racial/ethnic purity. As a result, sexual relations between colonizers and colonized have always been unruly under colonial rule.

Sander Gilman has suggested that a major part of pathologizing racial difference is by way of sexuality (1985). Colonized and/or racial/ethnic others are often labeled as 'feminine' as well as sexually 'deviant'. Because of such stereotyping, some colonized and/or racial/ethnic others feel the need to (over)compensate by (over)emphasizing their 'masculinity', and thus also their aversion to homosexuality (Eng 2001; Gilroy 2000: 196–97; Kim 1998; Nguyen 2002: 66–70). Boyarin himself, for example, has argued in a later book that the (hetero)sexist bias in Freud's psychoanalysis is related to his attempt to displace his own experience as a colonized and feminized Jew as well as his own (homo)sexual desires for his friend Wilhelm Fliess (1997: 189–359).[37]

By emphasizing this convergence of racism/ethnocentrism, sexism, heterosexism, and colonialism, I am not saying that every one of them is interchangeable or that any one is reducible. I am, however, questioning the routine of addressing each in complete separation from or omission of the others.[38] As Bhabha suggests, intersections are different from additions; intersection is 'about adding to without adding up' (Olson and Worsham 1999b: 24–26). Not only does colonial domination work at the intersections, its power also compounds and multiplies by working at different sites. Stoler's two recent and closely related anthropological works on race and colonialism (1995; 2002) have argued—by employing and extending Foucault—that the 'education of desires', or the management of sex and sentiment, shapes the making of race (and class) in the colonies. If sexuality is foundational to race/ethnicity and colonialism, then its vilified form, homosexuality, may help us recognize race/ethnicity and (post)colonialism in surprising ways. As we discussed, the line between queer and race/ethnicity has already been blurred as a result of a controversial attempt of political ethnogenesis on the part of some queer activists (see Halley 2000). We have also seen recently a couple of volumes that begin to explore the interrelations between postcolonial and queer theories (Campbell 2000; Hawley 2001).

Returning to the discussion between Helmreich and Gilroy on diaspora and gender, I wonder if our conversation about sowing seed or scattering

---

37. For an earlier discussion of how Freud displaces the perceived threat of his own male and Jewish body onto the female body, see Gilman 1993.

38. Moose has called European racism a 'scavenger ideology' that is ready to annex anything within its reach to strengthen its own project (1978: 10). Given the way racism/ethnocentrism, sexism, heterosexism, and colonialism are embedded within and imbricated with each other, I wonder if the 'scavenger ideology' title should not be fitting for all of them.

sperm in the Greco-Roman context should not sometimes be more rather than less gender-specific (their shared concern over masculinism notwithstanding). After all, this act in the Greco-Roman context can be between two men (Hallett and Skinner 1997; C. Williams 1999; Nussbaum and Sihvola 2002). Thus it can be, in direct contrast to Gilroy's suggestion, sexual but non-reproductive. In other words, diaspora might be another queer thing. Queer readings of the New Testament are, of course, hard to find; even harder to find are queer readings of the New Testament that simultaneously deal with issues of race/ethnicity and/or postcolonialism.[39] Stephen D. Moore has recently attempted such an intercourse by interweaving the book of Revelation with 4 Maccabees and the discourse of Irish nationalism (2001: 173–99). Theodore W. Jennings, Jr., and Liew have also argued that the interaction between the Roman centurion and the colonized Jesus in Matthew 8.5-13 is understandable only by identifying the person who suffers from paralysis as the centurion's 'boy-love' (2002).

Before I move on, I want to comment briefly on the potential intersection among race/ethnicity, postcolonialism, and sexuality within Acts 8.26-40. Byron is certainly right that African American scholars have done much important work on the episode (2002: 6). Byron is also right that Wimbush's work on the Ethiopian Moses (1992) has been instructive (2002: 6), but I wonder if it is also not true that this particular work of Wimbush on asceticism and blackness has contributed in another sense to a blindness on the Ethiopian's 'other' identity as eunuch in Acts 8. Here I actually also disagree with Smith, his admirable attempt to go beyond identifying the eunuch as black notwithstanding, that too much attention has been paid to the body of the Ethiopian eunuch (1995: 228). I would argue that not enough attention has in fact been given. Should we not, for example, associate the eunuch's power (suggested by Smith) with his body, or more precisely, his sexuality? Eunuchs in the Greco-Roman world were not known for their asceticism or as asexual beings. Instead, their bodies were often a sign of sexual ambiguity (queerness?) and attraction (though this was admittedly mingled with fear and even contempt). They were generally perceived to be human sex toys or pets of royalty, and their power was generally understood to be derived from the sexual thrills and pleasures they provided for their kings and queens. In other words, I am

39. For whatever reasons, more work has been done on the Hebrew Bible and sexuality, although it has mainly been done with little attention to issues of race/ethnicity. See, for example, Boer 1999; Stone 2001. For a better example in this regard, see Goss and West 2000 (but note the numerical imbalance between essays written on the Hebrew Bible and those on the New Testament in this volume). For a critique of these studies from a racial/ethnic perspective, see Liew 2001. For a specific example that deals with sexuality and the New Testament but does not deal with race/ethnicity (despite the author's emphasis on autobiography and his own interracial marriage), see Staley 1999.

suggesting that scholars have promoted the Ethiopian's identity at the expense of his sexuality. What we have here is exactly an intersection where race/ethnicity (black Ethiopian), postcolonialism (a narrative written in the context of the Roman Empire—with whom the Ethiopians were constantly at war—about a meeting of divine and Ethiopian royal forces), and sexuality (eunuch) come together. How would this passage read differently if New Testament scholars would pay more careful and courageous attention to precisely this intersection?[40]

Psychoanalysis The fact that Boyarin's book on Jewish masculinity and (homo)sexuality devotes a major portion to Freud and psychoanalysis brings up another neglected aspect on New Testament studies that focus on race/ethnicity and/or postcolonialism, namely, psychoanalysis. This is true, for example, of the three race/ethnicity-centered anthologies I mentioned earlier. Felder (1991a) contains no mention of or reference to psychoanalysis. Liew and Yee (2002) contain one essay on 'an Asian American Rereading of a Classic Pastoral Care Text' (Clark 2002: subtitle). Out of Wimbush's encyclopedic volume, there is but one brief mention of Freud (Parks 2001: 662). Likewise, no mention is made of Freud, Lacan, or psychoanalysis in Brett (1996a), Byron (2002), or (despite his focus on race and modernity) Kelley (2002). Is this relative absence of psychoanalysis because of Freud's racist bias? Scholars who focus on race/ethnicity in other fields have, however, continued to use psychoanalysis in spite of, or perhaps even because of, Freud's racial bias (Eng 2001; Cheng 2001; Chow 2002).[41] Psychoanalysis should also become a consideration as soon as one acknowledges an instrumental ethnicity (whether in part or in full, whether as a complement to or a replacement of primordial ethnicity), because doing so would require one to talk about political galvanization and thus the psychological processes of identification (see Fuss 1995).[42] Although New Testament scholars who focus on (racial/ethnic) identity

40.   Despite a chapter on Ethiopians as sexual threats (2002: 77–103) and a quotation from Philo about the appearance and the passions of eunuchs (2002: 112), Byron (like many others before her) fails to read the convergence of race/ethnicity, (post)colonialism, and sexuality in the Ethiopian eunuch of Acts 8 (2002: 109–15). Marjorie B. Garber has suggested that an unexpected appearance of a transvestite figure in a text signals a 'category crisis [or irresolvable conflict] elsewhere' (1992: 17). I wonder if Garber's proposal is also true of the unexpected appearance of this sexually ambiguous Ethiopian eunuch in Acts 8.

41.   Not to be missed here is Banton's early attempt to theorize race (1959). As I mentioned, he ends up attributing the invention of race to white doubt or white anxiety. This conclusion is ironic, given Banton's insistence that one should study race in sociological rather than psychological (or economic) terms.

42.   My argument here is in direct contrast to that of G. Carter Bentley, who suggests by way of habitus (Bourdieu 1977) that ethnic identification is an unconscious process, and thus has nothing to do with instrumentality (1987).

and interpretation have been reluctant to consider this, the link between (racial/ethnic) identity and identification seems to point powerfully toward a potentially productive intersection of culture, politics, and psychoanalysis.

This disappearance (or displacement?) of psychoanalysis is even more curious and awkward in postcolonial criticism of the New Testament. It is well known that the understandings and arguments of both Fanon and Bhabha are inseparable from their investments in psychoanalysis. A quick consultation of the indexes of several important contributions to postcolonial Biblical Studies (Sugirtharajah 1998b; Segovia 2000b; Sugirtharajah 2001; Dube and Staley 2002) will reveal—for lack of a better term—an 'interesting' phenomenon. While the names of Fanon and Bhabha appear over and over again, the name of Freud and the term psychoanalysis never appear. The name of Lacan does appear but once (Sugirtharajah 2002: 239).[43] Does this mean that New Testament scholars are only parroting rather than engaging Fanon and Bhabha? Or is this a conscious or unconscious 'mimicry' (in Bhabha's subversive sense of the term) of the postcolonial masters (!) on the part of New Testament scholars? I am not saying that the interpretive lens of race/ethnicity and/or postcolonialism must inevitably involve psychoanalysis. I am only saying that those who do look at race/ethnicity and/or postcolonialism by way of Fanon and Bhabha should consider and clarify why as well as how they use Fanon and Bhabha without engagement with psychoanalysis. This is particularly important given Bhabha's recent defense of his own use of this 'peculiarly Eurocentric idea' (Bhabha and Comaroff 2002: 29–32).[44]

Community I have already talked about the different postcolonial locations (and differences within each) as well as about the psychological and political dynamics of identity and identification. I would like to follow up on those comments by suggesting the need for a critical reflection upon the meanings of both identity and community. New Testament scholars who use race/ethnicity as an interpretive optic claim identity as their specific starting points. Yet, as I mentioned, they seldom get very specific about what they mean by racial/ethnic identity. The connections among identity, identification, and community are, of course, central to any political operation, whether racial/ethnic and/or postcolonial. The identification of community has become particularly significant as discourses of race/ethnicity and postcolonialism displace nation-states from being the

43.   Boer, a Hebrew Bible scholar, does better than most within New Testament studies in this regard. His book on postcolonial biblical criticism in Australia refers to Freud in a couple of places (2001: 96, 145).

44.   Note that Said has also taken on Freud in his recent work (2003).

assumed unit of community. Furthermore, communities (racial/ethnic, postcolonial, or other) are full of internal differences and fissures. How then do communities get constructed and reconstructed? Without a careful and critical reflection on identity and community, it will be difficult to compare and contrast different diasporas and postcolonial locations. The same is true for any vision of a new interracial/ethnic alliance or a new postcolonial community that is not based solely on race/ethnicity, as Liew and Wimbush (2003) have started to articulate.

Let me briefly suggest here that the kind of interracial/ethnic comparison, or even community, suggested by Liew and Wimbush is also postcolonial in the sense that its attention will now be focused on each other as colonized racial/ethnic groups rather than their white colonizers. In other words, not only does it move beyond the white/color dyad that has long dominated race/ethnicity studies, it also helps answer Aijaz Ahmad's criticism that 'the conceptual apparatus of "postcolonial criticism" privileges as primary the role of colonialism as the principle of structuration in ... history' (1995: 6–7). Forming such a new community changes the terms of the conversation previously set by white colonizers.

Conveniently for us, as the debates over the reading of Paul and ethnicity show, the New Testament may be one helpful (re)source for us to discover—and thus better to evaluate—the complex, dynamic, and even contradictory relations involved in identity and community construction. In addition to readers who read Paul, several readers have scrutinized John's Gospel to examine how the Gospel constructs ethnic space (Swanson 2002), nation (Glass 2002), or community (Liew 2002b).

Authority Readers should notice that when I mentioned the New Testament as one (re)source for discovery and evaluation, I did not say that the New Testament is a blueprint of community construction that readers should simply copy or follow. In other words, while the New Testament may help me think and see, I do not necessarily let it think or see for me. I have already mentioned how biblical authority has been questioned in the more recent anthologies that read the Bible with the interpretive category of race/ethnicity. Biblical authority has also been a question within postcolonial studies of the Bible. Sugirtharajah, for example, seems to see liberation hermeneutics as a part of but also apart from postcolonial biblical criticism, precisely because of the way liberation hermeneutics prices and privileges biblical authority (2002: 103–23). In contrast, Sugirtharajah advocates a form of postcolonial biblical criticism that recognizes and respects religious plurality by not assuming or affirming biblical superiority or authority (2002: 191).

As Sugirtharajah realizes, this question of biblical authority goes even deeper (2002: 206). Literary scholars who work with literary canons have suggested that canonization works by repetition (Eng 1998: 14). That is to say, the canonical capital of a literary text goes up with every conversation on, commentary on, or criticism of that text, even if what one says about that text is negative. What we have here is something in some way the opposite of what Antonio Gramsci says about hegemony (1971). For Gramsci, the difference between hegemony and ideology lies precisely in the difference between calm practices and clamorous protests. That is to say, when articulation is needed to defend or argue for a position, that position is already exposed as contestable ideology. Hegemony (that highest form of ideology), on the other hand, is what we do in silence and live out as 'it-goes-without-saying'. It is taken for granted, it is understood as a given, it is simply assumed; there is no question raised or any inquisition made. Conversely, a literary text has no canonical status as long as no one talks about it, but it becomes more canonically entrenched the more it is discussed, cited, or criticized. This canonization-as-repetition argument is supported by Sugirtharajah's own work on the Bible in the Third World, particularly if one pays attention to how the cultural capital of the Bible changes through the precolonial, colonial, and the postcolonial period (2001).

What then might a New Testament scholar do if she or he wants to resist or subvert biblical authority, whether from an optic of race/ethnicity and/or postcolonialism? Is this essentially a hopeless endeavor? Is there any other way in addition to the 'give-up-the-texts' suggestion of Sugirtharajah (2002: 206–207)? I would like to suggest that New Testament scholars who are intentional in cultivating the space-clearing effect and affect of interdisciplinary work and theory (like those on race/ethnicity and/or postcolonialism) are also achieving this same purpose. Here 'space clearing' refers to not only the carving out of an opening not presently allowed by political or 'practical' considerations but also to a displacing of both biblical texts and traditional biblical scholarship. Akin in a way to Wimbush's discussion of changing the key and the time of Biblical Studies to the black present (2001b), using race/ethnicity and/or postcolonialism as an interpretive category should lead to an extensive and intensive detour that takes one to and through a different land(scape). This different place is one filled with different names, texts, concerns, traditions, and procedures. By the time one (re)turns to the biblical text, what and how one sees will also have become different because of all the differences that one has encountered along the way. Equally if not more importantly, at the end one cannot be sure if race/ethnicity and/or postcolonialism is a lens through which one interprets the Bible, or whether the Bible is a lens through which one investigates race/ethnicity and/or postcolonialism. In other words, theory is for me neither a luxury nor an indulgence. The special status of the Bible as privileged object of study will not be displaced if one simply undertakes theory as another technique to 'apply' to biblical interpretation, and rush through the journey.

Scriptural In(ter)ventions at One Racial/Ethnic and Postcolonial Intersection

To illustrate one way an interpretive optic of race/ethnicity *and* postcolonialism may address my concerns above, I want to look at the biblical interpretation and in(ter)ventions found in Theresa Hak Kyung Cha's *Dictée*.[45] In addition to its canonical status within Asian American literature, I am choosing *Dictée* because it is truly a multiracial/ethnic and postcolonial text. Cha is an Asian/American of Korean descent, but within the pages of *Dictée* one will also find words in Chinese, English, and French, as well as drawings and photographs. China, France, and the USA have not only been colonizing Korea in different forms and at various times, they have also been in a complicated web of colonial relations among themselves. How does the Bible function in this diglossic (Ferguson 1972), heteroglossic (Bakhtin 1981: 263), or simply but by no means simple multiracial/ethnic and postcolonial (con)text?

First, Cha transports or translates what she finds in the Bible onto or into a new (con)text not for the sake of 'application' or 'illustration' but in a spirit of interruption and opposition. In a 'chapter' focusing on her mother as a 'woman warrior' who fights for survival rather than glories in martyrdom, Cha cites from the Authorized Version (KJV) rather unexpectedly the entire episode of Jesus being tempted in the wilderness by the devil (1995: 50–53). This citation of Matthew 4.1–11 is both framed and fragmented by Cha's description of a dream or hallucination of heaven that her mother experiences while living under Japan's colonial rule and falling ill in Manchuria. The Matthean Jesus, as we know, secures angelic service by overcoming three temptations by the devil. Jesus refuses to eat, to jump from the temple top, or to worship the devil on a mountain top. In contrast, Cha's mother refuses three times the angelic service of heavenly food and ends up being pushed from heaven back down to earth by an angel. Time and space will not allow me to do a detailed interpretation of Cha's use of this Matthean passage. I will simply suggest that Cha is here

---

45. Cha's *Dictée* (or dictation in French) has much to do with learning and reading language(s). The issue of language is, of course, an important one in terms of both the racial/ethnic and the postcolonial optic. In yet another way that might be significant for New Testament studies, dictation involves the fluidity between what is spoken and what is written; as Eun Kyung Min suggests, dictation is a process in which 'the audible turns visible and the visible becomes audible' (1998: 309). For a study of the orality and the textuality of the New Testament, see Kelber 1997.

protesting or questioning the biblical rhetoric or logic that privileges hunger for heavenly or 'spiritual' food over earthly food. For Cha, survival on earth may well be equally or even more meaningful than martyrdom for the reward of entering heaven. In other words, she circumscribes, disrupts, or recontextualizes the dictates of a Gospel text. After all, unlike the Matthean Jesus, who is articulate in his refusal of the devil as well as assured of his identity as the 'Son of God', Cha or Cha's mother is a female transnational traveler whose speech is often denied and whose identity is in flux. In Cha's multiracial/ethnic and postcolonial (con)text, even biblical citation does not dictate but is displaced and transformed by means of a transporting, translocating, or translating act.[46]

Second, Cha also displaces the Bible by placing it as but one text in a vast 'library' of texts (written or otherwise). To put it in a term made popular by Dipesh Chakrabarty (2000), the Bible is 'provincialized' in Cha's multiracial/ethnic and postcolonial (con)text. In the last 'chapter' of *Dictée*, Cha narrates a story that is simultaneously similar and dissimilar to the story of Jesus meeting the Samaritan woman at the well in John 4 (1995: 167–70). It is dissimilar because this meeting at the well does not result in the Samaritan woman at the well going to evangelize her townsfolk upon meeting a Jewish man. Instead, it ends with a woman at the well giving a girl some medicine to take back to the girl's neighboring village to cure the girl's ailing mother. It is dissimilar because Cha seems to be mixing the story of John 4 here with at least two other texts: (1) an ancient Korean shamanistic myth about a young princess who, by virtue of marriage and the birth of seven sons, receives healing water from her husband's well to make her mother well from a deadly illness; and (2) the ancient Greek myth about Demeter and her rest at an Eleusian well in her search of her daughter, Kore(a?), who has been abducted by Hades into the underworld because Kore(a?), unlike Cha's mother who refuses to eat other-earthly food, has eaten a few seeds in Hades (the underside of the US empire?). I am going to sidestep most of the interpretive issues surrounding this specific episode within *Dictée*, but I do want to make several brief observations.

Cha's practice of interweaving texts (biblical, Greek, and Korean) here points to an interracial/ethnic (or even postcolonial) and inter(con)textual coalition or conflation, which results in an in(ter)vention that deconstructs any simple binarism between nativism and Christianity. It also exposes (again) the gender-specificity of the New Testament text by putting the emphasis on a mother–daughter relationship. Unlike the male Johannine

---

46. Said has talked about how a theory might be transformed as it travels over time and space (1982). What we see in Cha is that the same is true of the 'traveling Bible'. In a new context, the biblical text is literally transformed or 're-accent[-]uated' (Bakhtin 1981: 5).

Jesus, whose experience of rebirth and resurrection is full and permanent, the female Kore, the nation Korea, as well as Cha('s mother) can never have a complete and unproblematic return or recovery after their experience of violence. We know Kore ends up splitting her time between Hades in the winter and earth in the spring, and Korea ends up being divided into North and South. Similarly, *Dictée* tells us that Cha('s mother), after being naturalized as a US citizen, has an extremely dissatisfactory 'return' trip to (South) Korea. For Cha, being a postcolonial Korean American is different from being a postcolonial in Korea.

Furthermore, Johannine scholars have understood this well-meeting scene between Jesus and the Samaritan woman in terms of betrothal, marriage, and/or family (see Fehribach 1998: 45–81). These variations depend on whether one focuses on John 4.1–7 as a type scene of a man and a woman meeting at a well, 4.13–16 where Jesus offers his 'living water' or sperm, and/or on 4.28–30, 39–42, where the Samaritan woman witnesses to her townsfolk and (re)produces (spiritual) children for Jesus. All these 'well' meanings, or heterosexually loaded innuendo, of John 4 are, however, removed within Cha's interweaving text.

Finally, Cha's practice of interweaving texts points to competing texts and traditions not only alongside but also inside any dictate. If the Korean myth on Princess Pari Gongju is a competing tradition that is separable from the Bible, such a neat separation cannot be made between the Demeter/Kore myth and the Gospel texts. The Greek myth is, of course, associated with the ancient mystery religion of Eleusis and thus in competition with the Gospels in the first four centuries of the Common Era (L. Martin 1987: 62–72). However, a different picture arises if one considers their common emphasis on transworld travels and rebirth as well as the fact that the Greek myth and the mystery both predated the Gospels but continued to be circulated and celebrated in the same geographical and cultural zones of the Gospels. In this light, one will be hard pressed to deny the influence that this and other ancient Greek myths might have on the Gospels. Rather than setting up binary and mutually exclusive entities or communities, Cha is more interested in detecting and disclosing the seldom-acknowledged heterogeneity within each. It is well known, for instance, that even the Korean myth to which Cha seems to refer has multiple and contrasting versions.

Cha's biblical in(ter)ventions will become even more explicit when, instead of repeating the biblical dictate that 'in the beginning was the Word' and 'the Word was made flesh' (John 1.1, 14), she inscribes that her own 'words [were] made flesh' (1995: 18). Not only that, she further insinuates that there are multiple beginnings as well as multiple words or texts with her two introductory invocations of the muses: 'Beginning *wherever* you wish, tell even us' (1995: 7, 11; emphasis mine). What this randomness registers, I would argue, is the psychoanalytic idea of a permanent loss. In the theory of psychoanalysis, every attempt to return is inevitably a(nother) displacement. One can never return to an origin(al) that is lost. Cha's biblical in(ter)ventions seem to suggest that 'originality', like canonicity, is a consequence of repetitions or 'cultural citations' (Cheng 2001: 149). Such an understanding deconstructs not only the authority of the Bible, but also those of history and the vernacular.

What Cha seems to recognize in *Dictée* is how forms of domination take place at the intersections or the cross-roads. At the same time, what Cha is good at in *Dictée* is precisely intervening and interrogating at the intersections. She does so, as we have seen, by interrupting the story of Jesus' temptation in Matthew 4. She also does so by interweaving the story of Jesus meeting a Samaritan woman at a well (John 4) with other stories. It is important to remember that for Cha these intersections and interweavings point to differences and contradictions rather than similarities and conformity. In fact, I suspect part of the reason why Cha picks Matthew 4 is because of the conflicts and contradictions inherent in that episode. Jesus and the devil are both quoting from the Hebrew Bible to make claims and counterclaims in a war of holy words, or a dispute over Scripture(s). What we find there then is a great illustration that neither Matthew nor the Hebrew Bible is 'a monolithic entity in which all of its statements point in one direction' (Snodgrass 1996: 118). Sugirtharajah has commented at length on what he calls 'heritagist' readings of the Bible that aim to emphasize similarities and build consensus between one's own heritage and the Bible while at the same time give the colonizers a taste of the exotic (2002: 55–62).[47] What we find in Cha is instead a hybridity or an impurity that may promote understanding but never understates difference. Perhaps it is more accurate for me to say that it is an impurity that promotes understanding precisely by not understating difference.

47. I am thus surprised that Sugirtharajah ends by affirming Mahatma Gandhi as a model of postcolonial biblical criticism (2002: 192–93). It seems to me, at least as Sugirtharajah presents it, that Gandhi's is but another 'heritagist' biblical interpretation. Despite the difference that Sugirtharajah attempts to draw (2002: 204–205), both Gandhi and the earlier 'heritagists' emphasize how different things and traditions are actually complementary with or illustrative of each other. In contrast to Cha, Gandhi's type of 'heritagist' reading looks more to me like a benign form of multiculturalism that plays up an assimilative consensus and downplays cultural dissonance. In other words, it is precisely the kind of non-nativist but benign hybridity (Chow 1998: 155), or the kind of 'universalist ... humanist ... [and] enlightened unity' (Bhabha 2000: 139) that Sugirtharajah means to critique by quoting Chow and Bhabha (2002: 194, 196). For a couple of more nuanced readings of Gandhi's ideology, see van der Veer 1993: 39–43 and Lelyveld 1993: 189–93.

Conclusion

Cha's *Dictée* is for me an illustration of cutting-edge (biblical) scholarship. Cutting-edge scholarship is scholarship that literally cuts at the edges. It initiates intervals and carves out space at the brim, so that it can invent and invest in intersections. This type of scholarship works at and with the margins, borders, boundaries, and yes, even extremities. It does not seek to become the center, but it also does not leave the center undisturbed. By cutting at the edges, it transports and translates differences. This always impure practice thus also becomes cutting to the center and is often declared to be illegitimate. Over a decade ago, Felder started to 'trouble the waters' by using race as an interpretive category to study the New Testament (1989). In the mid-1990s, postcolonialism becomes intersected with New Testament studies. Since then, race/ethnicity, postcolonialism, and the New Testament have been intersecting, interrupting, and interacting with each other. I have suggested that there are more in(ter)ventions and intersections we need to instigate, investigate, and integrate that have much to do with race/ethnicity and postcolonialism. Hall is right when he, at the end of the twentieth century, updated Du Bois' statement—which Du Bois made at the beginning of the twentieth century and with which I began this essay—by suggesting that 'the capacity to *live with difference* is, in my view, the coming question of the twenty-first century' (1993: 361). In contrast to what Henry Louis Gates, Jr., calls the 'gospel impulse' to simplify (1992: 141), I would suggest that an imperative for New Testament scholarship is to multiply, pluralize, and impurify.

I will close with one final thought on race/ethnicity, postcolonialism, and New Testament studies. It should be clear by now, I hope, that all of the above have to do with the issue of knowledge and power. This issue of knowledge and power involves, however, not only the use of knowledge to exercise (racial and colonial) power; it also involves the (racial and colonial) power to limit access to knowledge. The (postcolonial) questions for us then are not just what areas of knowledge qualify as legitimate New Testament scholarship but also who gets to learn and develop New Testament studies. These two questions are obviously interconnected: changing the contents of New Testament studies is contingent upon access to those studies. Since New Testament scholarship has historically drawn its scholars from the generally (though not always or completely, as I have repeatedly emphasized) privileged culture of white colonizers, they have been less able or willing (again, not just unable or unwilling) to bring up questions of race/ethnicity and colonial domination in their studies. What this means for me is thus the need to reinforce rather than reverse the trend of intentionally recruiting racial/ethnic minorities and postcolonials into our own profession (see also Segovia 1996). Doing so will mean, of course, that we pay attention to *read* the politics and policies as well as the material factors that are always already embedded in our institutions and societies.

Bibliography

Adam, Ian, and Helen Tiffin
   1990   *Past the Last Post: Theorizing Post-Colonialism and Post-Modernism* (Calgary: University of Calgary Press).
Ahmad, Aijaz
   1995   'The Politics of Literary Postcoloniality', *Race and Class* 36: 1–20.
Alexander, Philip S.
   2001   'Hellenism and Hellenization as Problematic Historiographical Categories', in Troels Engberg-Pedersen (ed.), *Paul Beyond the Judaism/Hellenism Divide* (Louisville: Westminster John Knox Press): 63–80.
Appadurai, Arjun
   1993   'Number in the Colonial Imagination', in Breckenridge and van der Veer 1993a: 314–39.
Ardener, Edwin
   1989   *The Voice of Prophecy and Other Essays* (ed. Malcolm Chapman; New York: Basil Blackwell).
Ashcroft, Bill, Gareth Griffiths, and Helen Tiffin
   1998   *Key Concepts in Post-Colonial Studies* (New York: Routledge).
Back, Les, and John Solomos (eds.)
   2000   *Theories of Race and Racism: A Reader* (New York: Routledge).
Bagnall, Roger S.
   1988   'Greeks and Egyptians: Ethnicity, Status, and Culture', in Richard Fazzini and Robert S. Bianchi (eds.), *Cleopatra's Egypt: The Age of the Ptolemies 305–30 B.C.E.* (Brooklyn: Brooklyn Museum): 21–27.
Bakhtin, Mikhail
   1981   *The Dialogic Imagination* (trans. Caryl Emerson and Michael Holquist; Austin: University of Texas Press).
Balibar, Étienne, and Immanuel Wallerstein
   1991   *Race, Nation, Class: Ambiguous Identities* (trans. Chris Turner; New York: Verso).
Banks, Marcus
   1996   *Ethnicity: Anthropological Constructions* (New York: Routledge).
Banton, Michael P.
   1959   *White and Coloured: The Behaviour of British People Towards Coloured Immigrants* (London: Jonathan Cape).
   1979   'Analytical and Folk Concepts of Race and Ethnicity', *Ethnic and Racial Studies* 2: 127–38.
   1998   *Racial Theories* (2nd edn; New York: Cambridge University Press).
Barclay, John M.G.
   1996   '"Neither Jew nor Greek": Multiculturalism and the New Perspective on Paul', in Brett 1996a: 197–214.

Barker, Francis, Peter Hulme, and Margaret Iversen (eds.)
    1994   *Colonial Discourse/Postcolonial Theory* (New York: Manchester
                University Press).
Barker, Martin
    1981   *The New Racism* (London: Junction).
Barth, Fredrik
    1969   'Introduction', in Fredrik Barth (ed.), *Ethnic Groups and Bound-
                aries: The Social Organization of Cultural Difference* (Boston:
                Little, Brown): 9–38.
Baucom, Ian
    1999   *Out of Place: Englishness, Empire, and the Locations of Identity*
                (Durham, NC: Duke University Press).
Bauman, Zygmunt
    1989   *Modernity and the Holocaust* (Malden: Blackwell).
Bentley, G. Carter
    1987   'Ethnicity and Practice', *Comparative Studies in Society and History*
                29: 24–55.
Betts, Raymond F.
    1998   *Decolonization* (New York: Routledge).
Bhabha, Homi K.
    2000   'The Vernacular Cosmopolitan', in Ferdinand Dennis and Naseem
                Khan (eds.), *Voices of the Crossing: The Impact of Britain on
                Writers from Asia, the Caribbean and Africa* (London: Serpent's
                Tail): 133–42.
Bhabha, Homi K., and John Comaroff
    2002   'Speaking of Postcoloniality, in the Continuous Present: A
                Conversation', in Goldberg and Quayson 2002: 15–46.
Blackburn, Robin
    1997   *The Making of New World Slavery: From the Baroque to the
                Modern, 1492–1800* (New York: Verso).
Blu, Karen L.
    1980   *The Lumbee Problem: The Making of an American Indian People*
                (New York: Cambridge University Press).
Boer, Roland
    1999   *Knockin' on Heaven's Door: The Bible and Popular Culture* (New
                York: Routledge).
    2001   *Last Stop Before Antarctica: The Bible and Postcolonialism in
                Australia* (The Bible and Postcolonialism, 6; Sheffield: Sheffield
                Academic Press).
Bourdieu, Pierre
    1977   *Outline of a Theory of Practice* (New York: Cambridge University
                Press).
Boyarin, Daniel
    1994   *A Radical Jew: Paul and the Politics of Identity* (Berkeley:
                University of California Press).
    1997   *Unheroic Conduct: The Rise of Heterosexuality and the Invention of
                the Jewish Man* (Berkeley: University of California Press).

Breckenridge, Carol A., and Peter van der Veer
    1993b   'Orientalism and the Postcolonial Predicament', in Breckenridge
             and van der Veer 1993a: 1–19.
Breckenridge, Carol A., and Peter van der Veer (eds.)
    1993a   *Orientalism and the Postcolonial Predicament: Perspectives on South
             Asia* (Philadelphia: University of Pennsylvania Press).
Brett, Mark G.
    1996b   'Interpreting Ethnicity: Method, Hermeneutics, Ethics', in Brett
             1996a: 3–22.
Brett, Mark G. (ed.)
    1996a   *Ethnicity and the Bible* (Leiden: E.J. Brill).
Bromley, Yulian V.
    1974   'The Term *Ethnos* and Its Definition', in Yulian Bromley (ed.),
             Soviet Ethnology and Anthropology Today (Paris: Mouton): 55–72.
Brooten, Bernadette
    1999   'Stendahl, Krister (1921–)', in Hayes 1999: 2.505–506.
Bullard, John M.
    1999   'Deissmann, Adolf (1866–1937)', in Hayes 1999: 1.264–65.
Butler, Judith
    1990   *Gender Trouble: Feminism and the Subversion of Identity* (New
             York: Routledge).
Byron, Gay L.
    2002   *Symbolic Blackness and Ethnic Difference in Early Christian
             Literature* (New York: Routledge).
Campbell, Jan
    2000   *Arguing with the Phallus: Feminist, Queer, and Postcolonial Theory:
             A Psychoanalytic Contribution* (New York: Zed).
Cha, Theresa Hak Kyung
    1995   *Dictée* (Berkeley: Third Woman).
Chakrabarty, Dipesh
    2000   *Provincializing Europe: Postcolonial Thought and Historical Differ-
             ence* (Princeton: Princeton University Press).
Chamberlain, M.E.
    1999   *Decolonization* (2nd edn; Malden: Blackwell).
Chapman, Malcolm
    1992   *The Celts: The Construction of a Myth* (New York: St. Martin's).
Cheng, Anne Anlin
    2001   *The Melancholy of Race: Psychoanalysis, Assimilation, and the
             Hidden Grief* (New York: Oxford University Press).
Childs, Peter, and Patrick Williams
    1997   *An Introduction to Post-Colonial Theory* (New York: Prentice Hall/
             Harvester Wheatsheaf).
Chow, Rey
    1993   *Writing Diaspora: Tactics of Intervention in Contemporary Cultural
             Studies* (Bloomington: Indiana University Press).

1998   *Ethics After Idealism: Theory-Culture-Ethnicity-Reading* (Bloomington: Indiana University Press).

2002   *The Protestant Ethnic and the Spirit of Capitalism* (New York: Columbia University Press).

Chrisman, Laura

2003   *Postcolonial Contraventions: Cultural Readings of Race, Imperialism and Transnationalism* (New York: Manchester University Press).

Clark, Peter Yuichi

2002   'Biblical Themes for Pastoral Care Revisited: An Asian American Rereading of a Classic Pastoral Care Text', *Semeia* 90/91: 291–314.

Coggins, R.J., and James L. Houlden (eds.)

1990   *A Dictionary of Biblical Interpretation* (Philadelphia: Trinity International).

Comaroff, Jean, and John Comaroff

1991   *Of Revelation and Revolution: Christianity, Colonialism, and Consciousness in South Africa* (2 vols.; Chicago: University of Chicago Press).

Cooper, Frederick, and Ann Laura Stoler (eds.)

1997   *Tensions of Empire: Colonial Cultures in a Bourgeois World* (Berkeley: University of California Press).

Cowe, S. Peter

1999   'Armenian Biblical Interpretation', in Hayes 1999: 1.57–60.

Curtin, Philip D.

1990   *The Rise and Fall of the Plantation Complex: Essays in Atlantic History* (New York: Cambridge University Press).

Curtis, L. Perry

1971   *Apes and Angels: The Irishman in Victorian Caricature* (Washington: Smithsonian Institute).

De Waal, Alex

1994   'Genocide in Rwanda', *Anthropology Today* 10: 28–29.

Dharwadker, Vinay

1993   'Orientalism and the Study of Indian Literatures', in Breckenridge and van der Veer 1993a: 158–85.

Dobrin, Sidney I.

1999   'Race and the Public Intellectual: A Conversation with Michael Eric Dyson', in Olson and Worsham 1999a: 81–126.

Donaldson, Laura E.

1996a   'Postcolonialism and Biblical Reading: An Introduction', *Semeia* 75: 1–14.

1999   'The Sign of Orpah: Reading Ruth Through Native Eyes', in Sugirtharajah 1999b: 20–36.

Donaldson, Laura E. (ed.)

1996b   *Postcolonialism and Scriptural Reading* (*Semeia* 75; Atlanta: Society of Biblical Literature).

Drake, St. Clair, and Horace R. Cayton
    1945   *Black Metropolis: A Study of Negro Life in a Northern City* (New York: Harcourt, Brace and Company).

Du Bois, W.E.B.
    1996   *The Souls of Black Folk* (1903; reissued New York: Penguin).

Dube, Musa W.
    1999   'Postcolonial Biblical Interpretation', in Hayes 1999: 2.299–303.
    2000   *Postcolonial Feminist Interpretation of the Bible* (St. Louis: Chalice Press).

Dube, Musa W., and Jeffrey L. Staley (eds.)
    2002   *John and Postcolonialism: Travel, Space and Power* (Sheffield: Sheffield Academic Press).

Duncan, Dawn
    1994   'Pushing the Post-Colonial Boundaries: Freeing the Irish Voice in Brian Friel's *Translations*', *Working Papers in Irish Studies* 3: 1–10.
    2002   'A Flexible Foundation: Constructing a Postcolonial Dialogue', in Goldberg and Quayson 2002: 320–33.

Dussel, Enrique
    1996   *The Underside of Modernity: Apel, Ricoeur, Rorty, Taylor, and the Philosophy of Liberation* (ed. and trans. Eduardo Mendieta; Atlantic Highlands: Humanities).

Dyer, Richard
    1988   'Whiteness', *Screen* 29: 44–64.

Edelman, Diana
    1996   'Ethnicity and Early Israel', in Brett 1996a: 25–55.

Eng, David L.
    1998   'Queer/Asian American/Canons', in Lane Ryo Hirabayashi (ed.), *Teaching Asian America: Diversity and the Problem of Community* (Lanham: Rowman & Littlefield): 13–23.
    2001   *Racial Castration: Managing Masculinity in Asian America* (Durham, NC: Duke University Press).

Epstein, Steven
    1987   'Gay Politics, Ethnic Identity: The Limits of Social Constructionism', *Socialist Review* 43/44: 9–49.

Esler, Philip F.
    1996   'Group Boundaries and Intergroup Conflict in Galatians: A New Reading of Galatians 5:13–6:10', in Brett 1996a: 215–40.

Espiritu, Yen Le
    1992   *Asian American Panethnicity: Bridging Institutions and Identities* (Philadelphia: Temple University Press).

Fanon, Frantz
    1961   *The Wretched of the Earth* (trans. Constance Farrington; New York: Grove).
    1967   *Black Skin, White Masks* (trans. Charles Lam Markmann; New York: Grove).
    1970   *Toward the African Revolution* (trans. Haakon Chevalier; New York: Grove).

Fehribach, Adeline
    1998   *The Women in the Life of the Bridegroom: A Feminist Historical-Literary Analysis of the Female Characters in the Fourth Gospel* (Collegeville: Liturgical Press).
Felder, Cain Hope
    1989   *Troubling Biblical Waters: Race, Class, and Family* (Maryknoll: Orbis Books).
    1991b   'Preface', in Felder 1991a: ix-xi.
    1991c   'Introduction', in Felder 1991a: 1-14.
    1999   'Afrocentric Biblical Interpretation', in Hayes 1999: 1.13-16.
Felder, Cain Hope (ed.)
    1991a   *Stony the Road We Trod: African American Biblical Interpretation* (Minneapolis: Fortress Press).
Ferguson, Charles A.
    1972   'Diglossia', in Pier Paolo Giglioli (ed.), *Language and Social Context: Selected Readings* (Harmondsworth: Penguin): 232-51.
Foucault, Michel
    1970   *The Order of Things: An Archaeology of the Human Sciences* (New York: Pantheon).
    1997   *'Il faut défendre la société': Cours au Collège de France (1975-1976)* (Paris: Seuil/Gallimard).
Fuss, Diana
    1995   *Identification Papers* (New York: Routledge).
Garber, Marjorie B.
    1992   *Vested Interests: Cross-Dressing and Cultural Anxiety* (New York: Routledge).
Gates, Henry Louis, Jr.
    1992   *Loose Canons: Notes on the Culture Wars* (New York: Oxford University Press).
Gilman, Sander L.
    1985   *Difference and Pathology: Stereotypes of Sexuality, Race, and Madness* (Ithaca: Cornell University Press).
    1993   *Freud, Race, and Gender* (Princeton: Princeton University Press).
Gilroy, Paul
    1993   *The Black Atlantic: Modernity and Double Consciousness* (New York: Verso).
    2000   *Against Race: Imagining Political Culture Beyond the Color Line* (Cambridge: Harvard University Press).
Glass, Zipporah
    2002   'Building Toward "Nation-ness" in the Vines: A Postcolonial Critique of John 15.1-8', in Dube and Staley 2002: 153-69.
Glazer, Nathan, and Daniel P. Moynihan
    1975   'Introduction', in Nathan Glazer and Daniel P. Moynihan (eds.), *Ethnicity: Theory and Experience* (Cambridge: Harvard University Press): 1-26.

Goldberg, David Theo
    1993   *Racist Culture: Philosophy and the Politics of Meaning* (Cambridge: Blackwell).
    2002   'Racial Rule', in Goldberg and Quayson 2002: 82–102.
Goldberg, David Theo, and Ato Quayson (eds.)
    2002   *Relocating Postcolonialism* (Malden: Blackwell).
Goss, Robert E., and Mona West (eds.)
    2000   *Take Back the Word: A Queer Reading of the Bible* (Cleveland: Pilgrim).
Gramsci, Antonio
    1971   *Selections from the Prison Notebooks* (2nd edn; trans. Quinton Hoare and Geoffrey Nowell Smith; New York: International).
Gunew, Sneja
    1993   'Multicultural Multiplicities: Canada, USA, Australia', *Meanjin* 52: 447–61.
Hall, Stuart
    1988   'New Ethnicities', *Black Film, British Cinema* 7: 27–31.
    1993   'Culture, Community, Nation', *Cultural Studies* 7: 349–63.
Hallett, Judith P., and Marilyn B. Skinner (eds.)
    1997   *Roman Sexualities* (Princeton: Princeton University Press).
Halley, Janet E.
    2000   '"Like Race" Arguments', in Judith Butler, John Guillory, and Kendall Thomas (eds.), *What's Left of Theory: New Work on the Politics of Literary Theory* (New York: Routledge): 40–74.
Haraway, Donna J.
    1991   *Simians, Cyborgs, and Women: The Reinvention of Nature* (New York: Routledge).
Harvey, David
    1989   *The Condition of Postmodernity* (Cambridge: Blackwell).
Hawley, John C. (ed.)
    2001   *Postcolonial, Queer: Theoretical Intersections* (Albany: State University of New York Press).
Hayes, John H.
    1999   *Dictionary of Biblical Interpretation* (2 vols.; Nashville: Abingdon Press).
Helmreich, Stefan
    1993   'Kinship, Nation, and Paul Gilroy's Concept of Diaspora', *Diaspora* 2: 243–49.
Hesse, Barnor
    2002   'Forgotten Like a Bad Dream: Atlantic Slavery and the Ethics of Postcolonial Memory', in Goldberg and Quayson 2002: 143–73.
Huie-Jolly, Mary
    2002   'Maori "Jews" and a Resistant Reading of John 5.10–47', in Dube and Staley 2002: 94–110.
Hyam, Ronald
    1990   *Empire and Sexuality: The British Experience* (New York: Manchester University Press).

Ignatiev, Noel
    1995   *How the Irish Became White* (New York: Routledge).
Jenkins, Richard
    1986   'Social Anthropological Models of Inter-Ethnic Relations', in John
                Rex and David Mason (eds.), *Theories of Race and Ethnic Relations*
                (New York: Cambridge University Press): 170–86.
Jennings, Theodore W., Jr., and Tat-siong Benny Liew
    2002   'Mistaken Identities but Model Faith: Rereading the Centurion, the
                Chap, and the Christ in Matthew 8:5–13', Paper presented at the
                Annual Society of Biblical Literature Meeting, Toronto, Canada.
Just, Roger
    1989   'Triumph of the Ethnos', in Elizabeth Tonkin, Maryon McDonald,
                and Malcolm Chapman (eds.), *History and Ethnicity* (New York:
                Routledge): 71–88.
Kelber, Werner H.
    1997   *The Oral and the Written Gospel: The Hermeneutics of Speaking and
                Writing in the Synoptic Tradition, Mark, Paul, and Q* (Bloomington:
                Indiana University Press).
Kelley, Shawn
    2002   *Racializing Jesus: Race, Ideology, and the Formation of Modern
                Biblical Scholarship* (New York: Routledge).
Khare, Ravindra S.
    1992   'The Other's Double—The Anthropologist's Bracketed Self: Notes
                on Cultural Representation and Privileged Discourse', *New
                Literary History* 23: 1–23.
Kim, Daniel Y.
    1998   'The Strange Love of Frank Chin', in David L. Eng and Alice Y.
                Hom (eds.), *Q & A: Queer in Asian America* (Philadelphia: Temple
                University Press): 270–303.
King, C. Richard (ed.)
    2000   *Post-Colonial America* (Urbana: University of Illinois Press).
Kolko, Beth E., Lisa Nakamura, and Gilbert B. Rodman (eds.)
    2000   *Race in Cyberspace* (New York: Routledge).
Kuan, Jeffrey Kah-jin
    1999   'Asian Biblical Interpretation', in Hayes 1999: 1.70–76.
Lelyveld, David
    1993   'The Fate of Hindustani: Colonial Knowledge and the Project of a
                National Language', in Breckenridge and van der Veer 1993a: 189–
                214.
Liew, Tat-siong Benny
    2001   '(Cor)Responding: A Letter to the Editor', in Stone 2001: 182–92.
    2002a   'Introduction: Whose Bible? Which (Asian) America?', *Semeia* 90/
                91: 1–26.
    2002b   'Ambiguous Admittance: Consent and Descent in John's Commu-
                nity of "Upward Mobility"', in Dube and Staley 2002: 193–224.

Liew, Tat-siong Benny, and Gale A. Yee (eds.)
    2002   *The Bible in Asian America* (*Semeia* 90/91; Atlanta: Society of
             Biblical Literature).
Liew, Tat-siong Benny, and Vincent L. Wimbush
    2003   'Contact Zones and Zoning Contexts: From the L.A. Riot to a New
             York Symposium', *Union Seminary Quarterly Review* 56: 21–40.
Lloyd, David
    1991   'Race Under Representation', *Oxford Literary Review* 13: 62–94.
McLeod, John
    2000   *Beginning Postcolonialism* (New York: Manchester University
             Press).
Martin, Clarice
    1989   'A Chamberlain's Journey and the Challenge of Interpretation for
             Liberation', *Semeia* 47: 105–35.
Martin, Dale B.
    2001   'Paul and the Judaism/Hellenism Dichotomy: Toward a Social
             History of the Question', in Troels Engberg-Pedersen (ed.), *Paul
             Beyond the Judaism/Hellenism Divide* (Louisville: Westminster John
             Knox): 29–62.
Martin, Luther H.
    1987   *Hellenistic Religions: An Introduction* (New York: Oxford Uni-
             versity Press).
Matlock, Barry
    1998   'Almost Cultural Studies', in J. Cheryl Exum and Stephen D.
             Moore (eds.), *Biblical Studies/Cultural Studies: The Third Sheffield
             Colloquium* (Sheffield: Sheffield Academic Press): 433–59.
Mehta, Uday
    1997   'Liberal Strategies of Exclusion', in Cooper and Stoler 1997: 59–86.
Memmi, Albert
    1965   *The Colonizer and the Colonized* (trans. Howard Greenfeld; Boston:
             Beacon).
    2000   *Racism* (trans. Steve Martinot; Minneapolis: University of Minne-
             sota Press).
Miles, Robert
    1989   *Racism* (New York: Routledge).
Min, Eun Kyung
    1998   'Reading the Figure of Dictation in Theresa Hak Kyung Cha's
             Dictée', in Sandra Kumamoto Stanley (ed.), *Other Sisterhoods:
             Literary Theory and U.S. Women of Color* (Urbana: University of
             Illinois Press): 309–24.
Mohanram, Radhika
    1999   *Black Body: Women, Colonialism, and Space* (Minneapolis: Uni-
             versity of Minnesota Press).
Moore, Stephen D.
    2001   *God's Beauty Parlor: And Other Queer Spaces in and Around the
             Bible* (Stanford: Stanford University Press).

Moose, George L.
    1978   *Toward the Final Solution: A History of European Racism* (New York: Fertig).

Morgan, Robert
    1999   'Bultmann, Rudolf Karl (1884–1976)', in Hayes 1999: 1.148–49.

Nakamura, Lisa
    2002   *Cybertypes: Race, Ethnicity, and Identity on the Internet* (New York: Routledge).

Nanos, Mark D.
    2002   *The Irony of Galatians: Paul's Letter in First-Century Context* (Minneapolis: Fortress Press).

Nguyen, Viet Thanh
    2002   *Race and Resistance: Literature and Politics in Asian America* (New York: Oxford University Press).

Novick, Peter
    1988   *That Noble Dream: The 'Objectivity Question' and the American Historical Profession* (New York: Cambridge University Press).

Nussbaum, Martha C., and Juha Sihvola (eds.)
    2002   *The Sleep of Reason: Erotic Experience and Sexual Ethics in Ancient Greece and Rome* (Chicago: University of Chicago Press).

Olson, Gary A., and Lynn Worsham
    1999b   'Staging the Politics of Difference: Homi Bhabha's Critical Literacy', in Olson and Worsham 1999a: 3–39.

Olson, Gary A., and Lynn Worsham (eds.)
    1999a   *Race, Rhetoric, and the Postcolonial* (Albany: State University of New York Press).

Omi, Michael, and Howard Winant
    1994   *Racial Formation in the United States: From the 1960s to the 1990s* (2nd edn; New York: Routledge).

Ong, Aihwa
    1999   *Flexible Citizenship: The Cultural Logics of Transnationality* (Durham, NC: Duke University Press).

Osborne, Grant R.
    1999   'Evangelical Biblical Interpretation', in Hayes 1999: 1.357–61.

Parker, Andrew, Mary Russo, Doris Sommer, and Patricia Yaeger (eds.)
    1992   *Nationalisms and Sexualities* (New York: Routledge).

Parks, Fayth M.
    2001   'When Mighty Waters Rise: African American Folk Healing and the Bible', in Wimbush 2001a: 661–70.

Pels, Peter
    1997   'The Anthropology of Colonialism: Culture, History and the Emergence of Western Governmentality', *Annual Review of Anthropology* 26: 163–83.

Pollock, Sheldon
    1993   'Deep Orientalism? Notes on Sanskrit and Power Beyond the Raj', in Breckenridge and van der Veer 1993a: 76–133.

Prashad, Vijay
    2001   *Everybody Was Kung Fu Fighting: Afro-Asian Connections and the Myth of Cultural Purity* (Boston: Beacon).
Reed, Ishmael, Shawn Wong, Bob Callahan, and Andrew Hope
    1989   'Is Ethnicity Obsolete?', in Werner Sollors (ed.), *The Invention of Ethnicity* (New York: Oxford University Press): 226–35.
Riches, John
    1996   'Cultural Bias in European and North American Biblical Scholarship', in Brett 1996a: 431–38.
Rocher, Rosane
    1993   'British Orientalism in the Eighteenth Century: The Dialectics of Knowledge and Government', in Breckenridge and van der Veer 1993a: 215–49.
Rogin, Michael
    1996   *Blackface, White Noise: Jewish Immigrants in the Hollywood Melting Pot* (Berkeley: University of California Press).
Said, Edward W.
    1978   *Orientalism* (New York: Vintage).
    1982   'Traveling Theory', *Raritan* 1: 41–67.
    1989   'Representing the Colonized: Anthropology's Interlocutor', *Critical Inquiry* 15: 205–25.
    1993   *Culture and Imperialism* (New York: Knopf).
    2002   'In Conversation with Neeladri Bhattacharya, Suvir Kaul, and Ania Loomba', in Goldberg and Quayson 2002: 1–14.
    2003   *Freud and the Non-European* (New York: Verso).
Sanders, E.P.
    1977   *Paul and Palestinian Judaism: A Comparison of Patterns of Religion* (Philadelphia: Fortress Press).
Segovia, Fernando F.
    1995   'Toward a Hermeneutics of the Diaspora: A Hermeneutics of Otherness and Engagement', in Fernando F. Segovia and Mary Ann Tolbert (eds.), *Reading from This Place: Vol. I. Social Location and Biblical Interpretation in the Untied States* (Minneapolis: Fortress Press): 57–73.
    1996   'Racial and Ethnic Minorities in Biblical Studies', in Brett 1996a: 469–92.
    1998   'Biblical Criticism and Postcolonial Studies: Toward a Postcolonial Optic', in Sugirtharajah 1998b: 49–65.
    1999   'Hispanic American Biblical Interpretation', in Hayes 1999: 1.505–508.
    2000a   *Decolonizing Biblical Studies: A View from the Margins* (Maryknoll: Orbis Books).
    2000c   'Interpreting Beyond Borders: Postcolonial Studies and Diasporic Studies in Biblical Criticism', in Segovia 2000b: 11–34.
Segovia, Fernando F. (ed.)
    2000b   *Interpreting Beyond Borders* (The Bible and Postcolonialism, 3; Sheffield: Sheffield Academic Press).

Sharpe, Jenny
    1995   'Is the United States Postcolonial? Transnationalism, Immigration, and Race', *Diaspora* 4: 181–99.

Shohat, Ella, and Robert Stam
    1994   *Unthinking Eurocentrism: Multiculturalism and the Media* (New York: Routledge).

Silverman, Kaja
    1996   *The Threshold of the Visible World* (New York: Routledge).

Sim, David
    1996   'Christianity and Ethnicity in the Gospel of Matthew', in Brett 1996a: 171–96.

Singh, Amritjit, and Peter Schmidt
    2000   *Postcolonial Theory and the United States* (Jackson: University Press of Mississippi).

Smith, Abraham
    1995   'A Second Step in African Biblical Interpretation: A Generic Reading Analysis of Acts 8:26–40', in Fernando F. Segovia and Mary Ann Tolbert (eds.), *Reading from This Place: Vol. I. Social Location and Biblical Interpretation in the United States* (Minneapolis: Fortress Press): 213–28.

Snodgrass, Klyne
    1996   'Matthew and the Law', in David R. Bauer and Mark Allan Powell (eds.), *Treasures New and Old* (Atlanta: Scholars Press): 99–127.

Snowden, Frank M., Jr.
    1970   *Blacks in Antiquity: Ethiopians in the Greco-Roman Experience* (Cambridge: Harvard University Press).

    1983   *Before Color Prejudice: The Ancient View of Blacks* (Cambridge: Harvard University Press).

Spivak, Gayatri Chakravorty
    1985   'The Rani of Sirmur: An Essay in Reading the Archives', *History and Theory* 24: 247–72.

    1988   'Can the Subaltern Speak', in Cary Nelson and Lawrence Grossberg (eds.), *Marxism and the Interpretation of Culture* (Urbana: University of Illinois Press): 271–313.

    1990   *The Post-Colonial Critic: Interviews, Strategies, Dialogues* (ed. Sarah Harasym; New York: Routledge).

Staley, Jeffrey L.
    1999   'Fathers and Sons: Fragments from an Autobiographical Midrash on John's Gospel', in Ingrid Rosa Kitzberger (ed.), *The Personal Voice in Biblical Interpretation* (New York: Routledge): 65–85.

Steinberg, Stephen
    1981   *The Ethnic Myth: Race, Ethnicity, and Class in America* (New York: Atheneum).

Stendahl, Krister
    1976   *Paul among Jews and Gentiles: And Other Essays* (Philadelphia: Fortress Press).

Stocking, George W. Jr. (ed.)
   1991   *Colonial Situations: Essays on the Contextualization of Ethno-
             graphic Knowledge* (Madison: University of Wisconsin Press).
Stoler, Ann Laura
   1995   *Race and the Education of Desire: Foucault's History of Sexuality
             and the Colonial Order of Things* (Durham, NC: Duke University
             Press).
   2002   *Carnal Knowledge and Imperial Power: Race and the Intimate in
             Colonial Rule* (Berkeley: University of California Press).
Stone, Ken
   1999   'Gay/Lesbian Interpretation', in Hayes 1999: 1.432–34.
Stone, Ken (ed.)
   2001   *Queer Commentary and the Hebrew Bible* (Cleveland: Pilgrim).
Stylianopoulos, Theodore
   1999   'Orthodox Biblical Interpretation', in Hayes 1999: 2.227–30.
Sugirtharajah, R.S.
   1998a   *Asian Biblical Hermeneutics and Postcolonialism: Contesting the
             Interpretations* (Maryknoll: Orbis Books).
   1999a   'Cross-cultural Biblical Interpretation', in Hayes 1999: 1.231–33.
   1999c   'Vernacular Resurrections: An Introduction', in Sugirtharajah
             1999b: 11–17.
   1999d   'Thinking about Vernacular Hermeneutics Sitting in a Metropoli-
             tan Study', in Sugirtharajah 1999b: 92–115.
   2001   *The Bible and the Third World: Precolonial, Colonial and
             Postcolonial Encounters* (New York: Cambridge University Press).
   2002   *Postcolonial Criticism and Biblical Interpretation* (New York:
             Oxford University Press).
Sugirtharajah, R.S. (ed.)
   1991   *Voices from the Margin: Interpreting the Bible in the Third World*
             (Maryknoll: Orbis Books).
   1998b   *The Postcolonial Bible* (The Bible and Postcolonialism, 1; Sheffield:
             Sheffield Academic Press).
   1999b   *Vernacular Hermeneutics* (The Bible and Postcolonialism, 2;
             Sheffield: Sheffield Academic Press).
Sumida, Stephen H., and Sau-ling Cynthia Wong
   2001   'Introduction', in Sau-ling Cynthia Wong and Stephen H. Sumida
             (eds.), *A Resource Guide to Asian American Literature* (New York:
             Modern Language Association): 1–9.
Swanson, Tod D.
   2002   'To Prepare a Place: Johannine Christianity and the Collapse of
             Ethnic Territory', in Dube and Staley 2002: 11–31.
Takaki, Ronald
   1994   'Reflections on Racial Patterns in America', in Ronald Takaki
             (ed.), *From Different Shores: Perspectives on Race and Ethnicity in
             America* (2nd ed. New York: Oxford University Press): 24–35.

Trinh T. Minh-ha
1991   *When the Moon Waxes Red: Representation, Gender, and Cultural Politics* (New York: Routledge).
Van Bremen, Jan, and Akitoshi Shimizu (eds.)
1999   *Anthropology and Colonialism in Asia and Oceania* (Richmond: Curzon).
Van der Veer, Peter
1993   'The Foreign Hand: Orientalist Discourse in Sociology and Communalism', in Breckenridge and van der Veer 1993a: 23–44.
Wan, Sze-Kar
2000a   'Collection for the Saints as Anticolonial Act: Implications of Paul's Ethnic Reconstruction', in Richard Horsley (ed.), *Paul and Politics*, (Harrisburg: Trinity International): 191–215.
2000b   'Does Diaspora Identity Imply Some Sort of Universality? An Asian-American Reading of Galatians', in Segovia 2000b: 107–31.
Weaver, Jace
1996   'From I-Hermeneutics to We-Hermeneutics: Native Americans and the Post-Colonial', *Semeia* 75: 153–76.
Weinreich, Max
1999   *Hitler's Professors: The Part of Scholarship in Germany's Crimes Against the Jewish People* (New Haven: Yale University Press [1946]).
West, Cornel
1993   *Race Matters* (Boston: Beacon).
Williams, Brackette F.
1989   'A Class Act: Anthropology and the Race to Nation Across Ethnic Terrain', *Annual Review of Anthropology* 18: 401–44.
Williams, Craig A.
1999   *Roman Homosexuality: Ideologies of Masculinity in Classical Antiquity* (New York: Oxford University Press).
Wimbush, Vincent L.
1992   'Ascetic Behavior and Colorful Language: Stories about Ethiopian Moses', *Semeia* 58: 81–92.
2001b   'Reading Darkness, Reading Scriptures', in Wimbush 2001a: 1–43.
Wimbush, Vincent L. (ed.)
2001a   *African Americans and the Bible: Sacred Texts and Social Textures* (New York: Continuum).
Wong, Sau-ling Cynthia
1995   'Denationalization Reconsidered: Asian American Cultural Criticism at a Theoretical Crossroads', *Amerasia Journal* 21: 1–27.
Wong, Sau-ling Cynthia, and Rachel C. Lee (eds.)
2003   *Asian American.Net: Ethnicity, Nationalism, and Cyberspace* (New York: Routledge).

Marx, Postcolonialism, and the Bible

Roland Boer

My argument is relatively straightforward: the almost complete absence of Marxism in biblical postcolonial criticism is a legacy of the wider zone of postcolonial theory itself that has been all too keen to dump Marx. But I also want to show how the gradual forgetting of Marx in postcolonialism and postcolonial theory has distinct ramifications for the engagements with postcolonial theory by biblical critics. So, after outlining the way postcolonial theory has forgotten its own history, a history in which Marxism was the key factor, I select two biblical critics working with postcolonial theory in order not only to make the obvious point about the absence of Marx but also to indicate some of the shortfalls such an absence generates. Finally, I pick up the work of Ernst Bloch in order to locate a more political version of Mikhail Bakhtin's widely influential dialogic criticism.

Left Out: Marx and Postcolonial Theory

Postcolonial theory, understood as a particular method employed in academic circles for interpreting cultural products, especially those of the era of European colonialism, which arose in the late 1980s, seems to have forgotten two crucial dimensions of the possibility of its existence: history and Marxism.[1] One might grant that Marxism has somehow slipped out of the picture, but history? Is not postcolonial theory very much concerned with rereading the history, art, texts, and practices of European colonialism and its aftermath? Postcolonial theory's concern is, therefore, postcolonialism itself, whether we hyphenate the word in a more periodizing frame of mind or not. However, this is not the history that concerns me here: I write of the history of the theory itself, of postcolonial theory.

The rapid emergence of postcolonial theory with the work of Edward Said, Gayatri Spivak, and Homi Bhabha has effaced the long path that led to this theory. It seems to me that this obliteration has happened not so much through a willful neglect on the part of this triumvirate and their various followers as through the process of reinterpreting the older

---

1. The first part of the argument that follows is an expanded version of one that I first developed in the introduction to a recent *Semeia* volume on postcolonial theory (2001c).

theorists, the precursors to postcolonial theory. Thus, Bhabha gives extensive attention to Frantz Fanon, and Spivak identifies Marx as one of her inspirations. Others have fallen by the wayside, such as W.E.B. Du Bois and Sol Plaatje at the turn of the century, although the former has been taken up by African-American critics such as Cornel West. Bart Moore-Gilbert (1997) usefully reminds us of this longer critical history by distinguishing between postcolonial theory (that which we have now after Said, Spivak, and Bhabha) and postcolonial criticism (the longer history of the critique of colonialism). In fact, as I will argue in a moment, we need to go back to Karl Marx and Vladimir Lenin for the origins of this kind of criticism. The catch with Moore-Gilbert's distinction, however, is that the very notion of a tradition of *post*colonial criticism relies upon the more recent development of a postcolonial theory. That is to say, the idea of a history of this intellectual and political project seems to be enabled by the subsequent theory, which generates its own history. In this case the history itself, which happened without a distinct identifier such as 'postcolonial', does seem to vanish before the other history of postcolonial theory, which boils down to a version of *creatio ex nihilo*. What is needed then is a strategy for recovering this alternative history which simultaneously deals with the historical constructions of postcolonial theory.

To state what is in many respects the obvious: Marx and then Lenin first developed a critical approach to what they variously called colonialism and imperialism. If Marx traced the way (capitalism for its very survival had to expand, to 'grow'—still very much the benchmark of economic success—beyond the confines of Europe and conquer ever new colonial spaces), Lenin, especially in *Imperialism, the Highest Stage of Capitalism* (1950), developed an analysis of imperialism, or imperial capitalism, as the most advanced stage of capitalism up until that point. From a Leninist perspective, both 'World Wars' were conflicts between the European imperial powers, vying for global dominance, the struggle coming to a head in the competition for the conquest of ever more territories throughout the globe. After Lenin, the systematic theorization and critique of capitalist expansion, including colonialism, took place in the Marxist tradition. Key figures of earlier postcolonial criticism, following Moore-Gilbert's classification, such as Frantz Fanon, W.E.B. Du Bois, and C.L.R. James, were all Marxist critics of colonialism. Apart from the analysis of colonialism, there were two other vital parts of their work: the study of literature and other cultural products from their own locations and a distinct level of political involvement. For instance, James was not only intensely interested in the role of cricket as both a colonial and anti-colonial cultural force, but he was also a central figure in the process towards independence in the West Indies.

Given this history, which I have sketched far too briefly and haphazardly, how is it that the Marxist dimension of postcolonial theory has been lost? Through a simultaneous process of transformation that systematically detached various key aspects of Marxist theory from Marxism itself and then negated their political potential. The process began with Edward Said's use of Antonio Gramsci's notion of hegemony.

Two-edged, the theory speaks both of the necessary combination of consent and force and the complex patterns whereby a dominant ideological position is maintained and overthrown (see Gramsci 1971: 268, 328, 348, 365, 370, 376). As far as the necessary link between consent and force is concerned, Gramsci argues that a dominant hegemony works by articulating and spreading a specific set of cultural assumptions, beliefs, ways of living, and so on that are assumed to be 'normal', accepted by people as the universally valid way of living. Here, intellectuals, the 'organizers' of ideology, culture, philosophy, religion, law, and politics, are central to the idea and operation of hegemony. Hegemony runs deeply through any social and political formation, for the structures of knowledge and values, the filters through which society acquires form and meaning, are precisely those that are constructed and maintained by the leading class or party.

But hegemony is both a tool of analysis and of revolution. This means that any force for change must brook no rivals, no possibilities of oppositional hegemony in the construction of the new state. Consent must be at one with the use of force, the two sides of hegemony. Religion thereby forms a crucial component of consent, falling under the rubric of intellectual and moral leadership (*direzione*). Domination or coercion (*dominio*), especially over against antagonistic groups, is the inescapable obverse. By contrast, those with whom the leading group is in alliance and association work together by consent: 'The supremacy of a social group is manifested in two ways: as "domination" and as "intellectual and moral leadership". A social group is dominant over those antagonistic groups it wants to "liquidate" or to subdue even with armed force, and it is leading with respect to those groups that are associated or allied with it' (Gramsci, quoted in Fontana 1993: 141).

In the period of colonialism, such hegemony involved wholesale ideological work, ranging from racial theory, through military action and the production of belief in the superiority of the imperial centre to Said's well-known 'orientalism' (Said 1978). But Said linked this in problematic fashion to Michel Foucault's work on power, specifically the dispersed, capillary forms of power that never reside in the named and expected seats of power. One can see the connection—dispersed power and a threatened hegemony—but Foucault was not a Marxist, despite being a student of Jean-Paul Sartre and a political activist. The absence of other categories crucial to hegemony—such as class, class conflict, and the central role of political economics[2]—meant that the notion of hegemony was orphaned, drifting away from the conceptual context in which it made sense. Thus, the first step in watering down the Marxist heritage in postcolonial theory was made.

Even though Gayatri Spivak claims Marxism as part of her own theoretical and political position, it was her translation of Derrida's *Of Grammatology* (1976), and especially the long and difficult introduction that she wrote, which brought deconstruction into the mix of what was becoming postcolonial theory. The subsequent appearance of her *In Other Worlds* (1988) reinforced the prominence of Derridean deconstruction, along with Gramsci and Foucault via Said, as one of the theoretical strands available for critics wanting to forge a new approach. In its much-vaunted refusal of method, of the careful attention to the details of the text in question, in the perpetual discovery of the way texts face an incoherence that both subverts and structures the text itself, deconstruction became a useful tool in reading for the other voices, those excluded and marginalized by the dominant discourses of the European colonial powers. But a Derridean Marx—taking for a moment Spivak's effort to combine deconstruction, Marxism, and feminism seriously—is a strange Marx indeed, looking more like a slightly left-of-centre liberal, as Derrida's own *Specters of Marx* (1994) showed only too well.

The final step in the banishment of Marx from postcolonial theory came with Homi Bhabha's work, especially *The Location of Culture* (1994), which introduced Lacanian psychoanalysis along with a demarxified Bakhtin into the reading of colonial texts that range from the Bible in India to a de-fanged Frantz Fanon. Although he has become a model for so many postcolonial critics, one is never sure whether the looping and idiosyncratic style and the misreadings of Lacan are all designed to turn Lacan against himself, or whether Bhabha is covering other tracks. As more than one radical critic first mesmerized by Bhabha has found out to her or his dismay, Bhabha is a solid bourgeois writer for whom liberalism is the only possible ideological position (witness his later art and literary criticism). Yet, with Bhabha, Lacanian psychoanalysis and Bakhtin's dialogic reading strategy became part of the contradictory hybrid of postcolonial theory, and now, along with hegemony and deconstruction,

---

2. How long has it been since the economy was itself a political domain? At first glance, it seems that economics is precisely the domain of politics. Do not the various governments and political parties in the so-called 'democracies' vie with each other for the best means to facilitate economic growth, generate jobs and maintain consumer confidence? But there is never a question posed as to the type of economics that might be best. In their various ways, the governments and political parties assume that capitalism is a given, that it is not a domain of political contestation, that a political party cannot in fact say that capitalism is inimical to the well-being of the population and act accordingly.

terms such as mimicry, hybridity, and border crossing became the keys to reinterpreting the texts of colonial encounters.

So, postcolonial theory sets one looking for the wealth of subversive material that remains buried and forgotten, such as indigenous literary resistance, unexpected or unwanted appropriations of the colonizer's cultural tools, or even counter-hegemonic moments in canonical texts. Rather than the overwhelming dominance of European colonial culture, myriad moments of resistance, negotiation, and alternative uses that slid out of the colonizer's grasp become the focus of one's attention. While this is an immensely fruitful and necessary task, to the point of constructing an alternative narrative or history, I still want to ask: what next, after the resistance has been located, after the text deconstructs, after the Real has been glimpsed? Is this the kind of work that begins to make sense of the anti-colonial movements and wars of independence, or do these acts of alternative agency remain ultimately futile, absorbed into the dominant system? Is postcolonial criticism caught in a fruitful but limiting methodological mix?

However, by the time postcolonial theory achieved something of an identity and maturity, the Marxist heritage of postcolonial theory had vanished, and even Gramsci appeared less of a Marxist and more of a postcolonial critic *avant la lettre*. I am tempted to make a Lacanian point (especially in light of Bhabha's appropriation of Lacan) and suggest that the forgetting of Marx is necessary for the constitution of postcolonial criticism: in light of the enabling role of Marxism in postcolonial theory, that theory can only exist by excluding that which keeps it functioning. What is outside the system provides the glue that keeps the system running. Yet, rather than a somewhat irritated tracing of this gradual forgetting, one of the agendas for subsequent work in postcolonial theory, it seems to me, is a recovery of this tradition that has been 'left out', as Andrew Milner argues in relation to the history of cultural studies (2002).

Where's Marx? Postcolonial Biblical Studies

It should come as no surprise, then, that one is more likely to come across Groucho or Harpo Marx in the writings of biblical critics who have taken up postcolonial theory, or indeed, postcolonial critics who have written about the Bible. And those biblical critics who do work with Marxism, such as Norman Gottwald (1985, 1992, 1993, 1999), Gale Yee (1995, 1999, 2003), Ron Simkins (1999), and Richard Horsley (1999, 2001, 2002), notwithstanding his guarded essay in *The Postcolonial Bible* (1998), tend to cluster in the domain of the social sciences rather than, say, ideological or literary criticism, although David Jobling (1991, 1992a, 1992b, 1998) and I (1996, 1997, 2003) have made contributions in this area. Only Gerald West

(1999) and I (1996, 1997, 2003) (2001a; 2001b) have sought the links between Marxism and postcolonial criticism.

Apart from West's work and my own, in the increasing number of works that are beginning to appear in what might be called postcolonial Biblical Studies, I can find references to Said, Spivak, and Bhabha, and less often to Bakhtin. But neither Gramsci nor Marx rate a mention. At times, these works rightly stress the absence of considerations of the Bible in postcolonial studies, given its crucial role in European colonial expansion (see Boer 2001b; Sugirtharajah 2002). But, rather than survey the growing amount of postcolonial biblical studies, what I want to do here is take a sample of these works and see what happens methodologically. I cannot go past R.S. Sugirtharajah's recent texts, especially *The Bible and the Third World* (2001) and *Postcolonial Criticism and Biblical Interpretation* (2002). Along with Sugirtharajah's central work, I also want to include an Australian example, namely Mark Brett's recent *Genesis: Procreation and the Politics of Identity* (2000).

R.S. Sugirtharajah

Sugirtharajah has been the most voluminous writer in this area, but what interests me are his various and scattered methodological reflections. Thus, in the closing pages of *The Bible and the Third World* and in the opening pages of *Postcolonial Criticism and Biblical Interpretation* he produces the standard material on the development of postcolonial theory, listing the obligatory three (Said, Spivak, and Bhabha), but especially Said's *Orientalism* (1978). His recitation is a little more gentle than that of the Marxist, Arif Dirlik. Thus, over against Sugirtharajah's 'Utilizing the space offered by the Western academy in the 1980s ...', I prefer Dirlik: '"When exactly ... does the 'postcolonial' begin?" queries Ella Shohat in a discussion of the subject. Misreading this question deliberately, I will supply here an answer that is only partially facetious: "When Third World intellectuals have arrived in First World academe"' (1997: 52).

Marx himself appears but a handful of times, and then only in the briefest fashion, in both books. Thus, in *The Bible and Third World*, we find him battling it out with poststructuralism in terms of the 'mutually incompatible critical categories' (2001: 246) of postcolonialism. The other occurrence comes in a criticism of liberation theology's use of Marx: 'Marx's dialectical materialism failed to perceive the potentiality for revolution in religion' (2001: 264). That he pairs Marx up with Karl Barth, as the 'two Karls', is as convenient a dismissal as might be found—Barth could not find room for revelation in religion, he suggests, rather astonishingly. In fact, Sugirtharajah likes it so much that he repeats it in *Postcolonial Criticism and Biblical Interpretation* (2002: 116). Apart from this aside, Marx turns up in a footnote that links him with M.M. Thomas's argument for the beneficial effect of British colonialism (Sugirtharajah 2002: 41). And that is it as far as Marx is concerned. Sugirtharajah unwittingly sums up the situation in his own work best: 'the fortunes of Marxist criticism took a deep dive' (2002: 15).

We do not need to look far to find the implications for Marx's dive on the way to his own definition. Sugirtharajah suggests three historical conditions for the emergence of postcolonial criticism: the failure of socialism; the rise of global capitalism and the market economy, which resulted in the disruption of both metropolitan and village economies; and the loss of political momentum among Third World countries (2001: 247). While we may grant the first point—although the failure of 'actually existing socialism'[3] might be a better description—the second I find most astounding. Did global capitalism and the market economy first arise with the revolutions in the former communist countries of Eastern Europe? This would date global capitalism from the years 1989–1990; I suspect it has been around for a little longer than that. And the metropolitan and village economies were very much integrated in the intricate systems of capitalism well before then. What is wanting here is an analysis that takes into account the mutations in capitalism, which may be analyzed in the terms of Michael Hardt and Antonio Negri as an acephalous 'empire' in which there is no central power (2000) or in terms of the regulation school, with the financialization of the market and the emergence of 'regimes of accumulation' (Boyer 1990).

However, there is another narrative operating in Sugirtharajah's threefold historical periodization, and that is the demise of Marxism itself. Each of the points may read as alternative versions of this same story: Marxism is finished, in terms of the political economics of nation-states, as the source of opposition to capitalism itself and as the only viable political option for many Third World countries. In its place comes postcolonialism, on which the hope of the future rests. Or, to put it in Dirlik's terms, the term 'postcolonial', through its alternative period-ization, effectively erases the revolutionary pasts of the places from which it emerges and about which it speaks (1997: 163–85). The postcolonial may therefore also be described as the 'post-revolutionary'. And so it becomes possible to read Itumeleng Mosala's explicitly Marxist biblical criticism of the book of Esther (1992) as postcolonial instead: Vashti's model of revolt becomes an agenda for multiculturalism in which diasporic communities can both celebrate their ethnic identities and embrace the cultural heritage of their new homes.

---

3. The paradox of 'actually existing socialism' is that this has never 'actually' existed, the states that did and do operate with socialism being a half-way house, a glimmer of socialism that fell short.

The narrative of Marxism's passing also lies behind Sugirtharajah's deliberations on liberation theology. The fact that Marx appears but once in the overlapping discussions of liberation theology in both books (2001: 264; 2002: 116) is extraordinarily curious, given Marxism's position as the preferred method for analyzing the socio-economic situation in which liberation theologians worked. Postcolonialism, suggests Sugirtharajah, is able to overcome the problems of liberation theology, namely, its 'excessive textualism, disparagement of both major and popular religions, and homogenization of the poor' (2002: 103). Only then will both liberation theology and postcolonialism be able to link arms in the battle for liberation, although by this stage it is a thoroughly demarxified brand of liberation theology.

And yet, postcolonialism, at least in Sugirtharajah's formulation, shares with Marxism the combination of theory and practice, or praxis; it is, in other words, a method that comes out of and entails a distinct political practice, like feminism, or gay and lesbian criticism. 'The task of postcolonialism is ensuring that the needs and aspirations of the exploited are catered to, rather than being merely an interesting and engaging avenue of inquiry' (2001: 275; see 2002: 40). No comment here on the intellectual as vanishing mediator, the one who speaks and writes on behalf of others, or 'caters' for them, from a place of privilege while erasing his presence in the process (see Boer 2001c).

In the end, Sugirtharajah would like to find the source of such a theoretical politics in the Third World. Marxism, then, is but one of many Eurocentric approaches with which Sugirtharajah wishes to dispense. He makes little, if nothing, of Lacanian psychoanalysis, or of Derridean deconstruction, or even of dialogic readings that came by way of Bakhtin—all of them central to much postcolonial theory. Instead, unlike 'other critical categories which are in vogue today, postcolonialism's original incarnation was in the form of imaginative literature, in the writings of Indians, Africans and Latin Americans' (2001: 272; see also 1998c: 91–94; 2002: 14–21).[4] Indeed, Sugirtharajah's great contribution to postcolonial theory and biblical studies is to show how deeply the Bible was enmeshed in both colonialism and the myriad ways in which it was appropriated, reinterpreted, and resisted. The breadth of his survey is stunning, running all the way from the Peshitta to contemporary vernacular hermeneutics, from Tertullian to Ananda Coomaraswamy (see 1998b: 16–18; 1998c; 2001; 2002). I can also understand the political

---

4.   Further: 'I define postcolonial criticism as a textual and praxological practice initially undertaken by people who were once part of the British, European and American Empires, but now have some sort of territorial freedom while continuing to live with burdens from the past and enduring newer forms of economic and cultural neo-colonialism' (2001: 246).

need for such a move, but I wonder at the absence of any sense of a dialectical relation between colonizer and colonized. Elsewhere, I have argued that the possibilities of anti-colonialism and postcolonialism came, in part at least, from the contradictory nature of European imperialism, providing colonized peoples with the physical, economic, and conceptual tools—individual subjectivity and agency; collective identity in a nation-state; racial and ethnic identity—that made anti-colonialism possible in the first place (see Boer 2001a: 180–93).

Mark Brett

Instead of the encyclopedic range of Sugirtharajah's work, preferring synoptic sweeps over the field, Mark Brett's *Genesis* book tacks close by the biblical scroll of the same name. The contrasts runs in other directions as well: instead of the Third World intellectual in the old colonial center, Brett works on the colonial fringe, an uneasy and ambivalent Australian with white settler background. As for the book itself, Brett's reading strategy is 'inspired especially by postcolonial theory' (2000: 5), and the issue that draws him in is the tension between social structures and individual agency. Hence the significant place accorded to anthropology, and the long defense of intention, broken down into explicit and indirect communicative intention, as well as motive.

At the same time, postcolonial theory emerges from a welter of other approaches that one would be tempted to describe as pluralist, were it not for his emphasis on methodological differences and the need to find points of commensurability from different reading perspectives. So we find: postmodernism; Nonconformist Protestantism; historical study, especially that of Kenneth Hoglund (1992); the narrative poetics of Robert Alter and Meir Sternberg; pragmatic and structuralist linguistics (especially of Henri de Saussure); anthropology, particularly of a structuralist bent; Kenneth L. Pike's linguistics; deconstruction; and, of course, postcolonial theory. Marx appears very obliquely, in the reference to Christopher Hill's book on Bunyan and the Baptists, in *A Turbulent, Seditious and Factious People* (1988). Hill is a Marxist historian, but one requires personal communication from Brett himself in order to locate the hidden reference. In fact, the tradition in which Brett works is the same Baptism of Norman Gottwald and Jorge Pixley, as well as Raymond Williams. Williams ended up being an atheist, while Gottwald and Pixley are Marxist biblical scholars, but Welsh Baptist chapels were, among other things, centers of some of the major miners' strikes of the nineteenth and twentieth centuries. It is significant, however, that postcolonial theory connects more readily with this tradition of Brett than Marxism.

Agency is one of the crucial categories for postcolonial theory, and Brett cites both Mary Douglas on Numbers (1993) and the work of James Scott on covert resistance (1990). But he relies most heavily on Homi Bhabha 'in assuming that some kind of agency is necessary in any resistance to a dominant culture' (Brett 2000: 23). Indeed, Bhabha provides Brett with the means for distinguishing between a deconstruction of free-play and libertarian pessimism and that of postcolonialism, where the agency of resistance comes from a 'hybrid inter-subjectivity' (p.23). Not necessarily aware of its own work, such an intersubjectivity brings together both Israelite and non-Israelite materials in contesting colonial power in the Persian period.

What we have, then, is a postcolonial deconstruction—described most fully as a 'subversive and artful hybridity' (p.23)—that comes through Bhabha rather than Spivak. But the methodological spoor that Brett tracks in Bhabha is not that of Lacan but of Bakhtin. There is but one reference to Bakhtin's *The Dialogic Imagination* (1981), and yet Brett's description of intentional hybridity may as well have come from this book: 'intentional hybridity is a blending of two or more voices, without compositional boundaries being evident, such that the voices combine into an unstable chorale—sometimes speaking univocally, but more often juxtaposing alternative points of view such that the authority of the dominant voice is put into question' (p.22). The vast difference is that whereas Brett, following Bhabha, postulates a distinct redactor responsible for the undermining voice, Bakhtin saw such 'voices' emerging in the writings of a single author. There was no need for more than one writer to speak with more than one voice.

We are a long way from Marx, which is entirely Brett's prerogative, although Slavoj Žižek does make a brief entry on the question of ideology (p.21). The connection is oblique, although not as much as the one that swirls around Bakhtin himself. Whether or not Bakhtin was Vološinov is perhaps not as relevant here as the debate itself—was Bakhtin the guardedly innocuous nom de plume of a more political Vološinov, or was Vološinov the cover for Bakhtin's critical Marxism? For it was only when Bakhtin was freed from the troublesome shackles of Marxism, with all the associations of Soviet orthodoxy and the robot-like subservience to the Great Cause, that he could be taken up in the Western academy as a dissident liberal within the enemy ranks (hence Bhabha's great liking for Bakhtin). Which is not to say that Bakhtin's dialogic readings are not political, for in the end we find him favoring the quiet subversive voice, the one that speaks not too loudly for fear of reprisal, a covert textual whisper here and there.

So, in the case of Genesis, Brett identifies a tension or conflict between a voice that expresses an ethnocentric, exclusivist position concerned with the dominance of one group over another (males, priests, genealogically pure Judahites over everyone else), and a voice that quietly and subtly opposes this position, urging instead an inclusivist approach that does not operate by means of domination. The hypothesis he wants to test is that such a conflict took place in the Persian period (537–331 BCE), under Persian governors. The debate is in fact between the position represented in Ezra and Nehemiah and the one he finds in Genesis. But it is more than this, for the dominant position of Genesis is similar to the one we find in Ezra and Nehemiah. It is only the quieter, subversive voice of Genesis that challenges this—an editor working carefully through the material of Genesis in order to make his point, always seeking to avoid the heavy hand of the censors.

Now, there are specific political reasons and implications of such an argument for both the particular and general contexts in which Brett works: the use of texts such as Genesis within the churches on issues ranging from gay and lesbian involvement to indigenous rights, and the wider national debates over refugees, terrorism, and the inability of the Australian government to understand what 'justice' means in relation to Aboriginal peoples. In these contexts, I stand by Brett's positions over against the forces of reaction. And yet, the way he reads for the dialogic voices in Genesis may also be understood, if we take a more Marxist line, as the normal function of ruling class ideology, which is precisely to manage the range of objections and criticisms directed at it so as to be better rulers by offering what appears to be a more comprehensive approach that does not stifle debate. This means that the tensions and problems Brett finds represented in the text are not so much ones of dominating and subversive voices but of different positions within a ruling class situation, even if the voice he finds in Genesis runs against that of Ezra for explicitly economic reasons. For it is interesting that Brett spends little time with the notion of a Priestly editor, passing over that debate in a couple of pages.[5] The exclusion is symptomatic, to my mind. For most of the scholarship that stresses the Persian era for texts like Genesis indicates that the only viable class or class fraction that could have done any editing of texts would have been priestly scribes. This means that—given Brett's wish to locate Genesis within a particular historical debate—a more comprehensive hypothesis is that here we have a dialogue between priests or priestly groups.[6]

---

5. To be fair, Brett does refer to a number of works on the Priestly redactor: Douglas (1993), Rendtorff (1996), Joosten (1996), Knohl (1995), and Grünwaldt (1992).

6. In a response to an earlier form of this criticism, given at a panel of the Bible and Critical Theory Seminar (Brisbane, 5 April 2001), Brett seeks to dissociate the notion of the holy seed, and indeed the position of Ezra, from that of a properly Priestly position:

> I doubt whether my reading of Levi in Genesis 34 as a character who is violently and hypocritically manipulating the distinctively Priestly practice of circumcision is really compatible with Boer's picture of a self-critical priest, subtly pointing out

Disinterring Ernst Bloch

However, rather than dismiss Bakhtin and even Bhabha as bourgeois critics, I want to suggest a different line, one that takes account of the importance of Ernst Bloch and recasts the dialogic relation in class terms. Apart from the fascinating narrative of Bloch's critical legacy—passing through liberation theology to become a key figure in Utopian studies (see Moylan 1997)—he provides a distinctly Marxist version of the strategy that Brett applies to Genesis. And it is not that we need to plunder Bloch's work for the possibilities they might contain for biblical studies, for Bloch is one of those extraordinary Marxists who wrote a book on the Bible, *Atheism in Christianity* (1972), as well as finding it one of the great sources for *The Principle of Hope* (1995).

The key feature Bloch wishes to introduce into biblical criticism—this in the 1950s and 1960s—is the category of class, since the Bible, he suggests, is very much a text of both those who labor and those who live off that surplus labor and do none themselves. In all its variety and contradictions, there are stories in the Bible which have become homely in the smallest of peasant households, but also those used by the overlords and religious professionals. And it is not just that such class differences indicate a different reading strategy, different assumptions about the various narratives, poetry, and statements: the texts themselves tend in either direction, their content and form speaking with a double voice, one that is and is not folly for the rich and powerful. The Bible is then a text riven with class conflict: not a conflict that may be read in terms of bourgeoisie and proletariat alone but in terms of the basic Marxist category of class difference, however that may be articulated historically, between oppressors and oppressed, rulers and ruled.

The litmus for such a method of reading—which is very much part of Bloch's famous Utopian hermeneutics—is the conflict between the Reformer Martin Luther and the peasant leader Thomas Müntzer. While the former could invoke Paul and the cross of Christ as the lot of all, the latter called upon the Exodus and the Bible's anger 'against the Ahabs and Nimrods' (Bloch 1972: 23). But the deepest affinity of the Bible, despite its

the excesses of his colleagues. And I am persuaded by enough of Mary Douglas' work on Leviticus and Numbers to assert that Ezra's ethnocentric discourse concerning the 'holy seed' is not actually Priestly; it is more likely that this discourse is a distortion of Priestly language in the service of imperial interests. In line with Douglas' work on P, I have argued that the sly redactors of Genesis are setting out to undermine the notion of the 'holy seed'. But Genesis has no interest in the cult of holiness, i.e., the text has no interest in the defining characteristic of Priestly tradition. At most, one could offer the hypothesis that the traditions of Genesis have been adapted to a Priestly cause. (2002: 129) 'adaptability to select master-ideologies' (1972: 24), is to ordinary, uneducated people, who took the stories as their stories, something the clergy and rulers could not do.

For what Bloch seeks to do in *Atheism in Christianity* is to uncover both the way in which ruling class ideologies have been imposed on the text and to examine the patterns and strategies of subversive slave talk. The interlacings, overlays, and myriad complexities of such materials require readings that are attentive to the subtle shifts and changes that have taken place. Thus, Bloch is not interested in submissive varieties of slave talk— and so the Psalms do not appear—but rather texts whose subversive voice is either early or late, of the first strata or at some later stage of usage. The one that survives is the masked text: 'it wears its mask, rather, from below, and wears it freely, as a first form of alienation, a characteristic change of ground' (1972: 14). Well before James Scott (1990) made a similar argument, for Bloch such texts have a double function, a 'sly irony', appearing to appease the rulers while openly criticizing and lampooning them. 'Men often spoke in parables, saying one thing and meaning another; praising the prince and praising the gallows to prove it' (1972: 15).

As an example of the complexity of such readings, Bloch offers an interpretation of Korah's rebellion in Numbers 16, a text that, as it is now, speaks of a Priestly rebellion, centering on the issue of ritual and incense, which is crushed through divine intervention. As the story stands, it is an account of a 'premature palace revolution' (1972: 80) within the Priestly upper class, but what catches Bloch's attention is the way the revolt is dealt with: God opens the ground which swallows them up as an example to anyone else who would rebel, who would burn incense before the Lord. This is not a God of war, waging a fight for survival, but a God of 'white-guard terror' (1972: 80), one who emerges from the redactor's pen. For Bloch, an echo of political rebellion reverberates through the text. Not only does the punishment itself signal this, but the perpetual recurrence of the Israelites' grumbling throughout the chapter indicates for Bloch a subversive, rebellious, anti-Yahweh voice that has been turned into something else—the sign of disobedience and recalcitrance on the part of the people themselves.

The dialogic reading strategy is similar to that of Bakhtin, Bhabha, Scott, and Brett, but the Marxist in Bloch leads in another direction, seeking the traces of subversion and rebellion in class and economic terms. In Bloch's hands such biblical detective work becomes a political tool, the various traditions and layers of the Bible full of politics and economics. Although he finds major elements at the ideological center of the Bible, especially the Exodus and the Apocalypse, he assumes that by and large the dominant textual traditions are those of official power, Priestly establishment, and institutions—the ones who write, copy, and preserve texts. But also the ones who impose ideas, political and economic domination, and negative representations of the people. It is here that Bloch locates the alternatives, the possibility of opposing the hierocratic system of control and oppression. So, he focuses on the murmuring of the people against Moses, the trenchant prophetic critique of political economics, the early forms of Christianity rejected and persecuted by the early church, such as Gnostics, Ophites, and so on, who championed the serpent in the Garden, saw the God of the Hebrew Bible as an evil power, a demiurge who sought to ensnare human beings within this world. These things indicate for Bloch a healthy revolutionary force or tradition in the Bible. All of this leads Bloch to posit a distinct, although highly diverse, thread, potentially revolutionary, anti-ruling class, anti-powerful, anti-wealth, that appears in many different guises throughout the Bible. And this stands over against the texts of the oppressor, in which Baal and Yahweh become one, where the literary elites work tirelessly as ideologues for the ruling class.

However, Bloch's effort to locate a continuous thread echoes in many respects Brett's effort to find a coherent alternative voice in Genesis. In both cases there is a failure of dialogic or dialectical nerve, for properly subversive voices—those of women, the economically abused and exploited, outsiders and heretics—are inevitably piecemeal and fragmentary, with no necessary coherence, if they get any chance of appearing at all. For in the Bible it is hard enough for a subversive voice to be heard, particularly in a document that is itself the product of a scribal elite working in a profoundly patriarchal society and culture. Bloch is more enthusiastic than I am in finding such voices, but he is determined to locate what it is that fed the burning revolutionary spirits of Müntzer and company. I cannot help but wonder whether the truly subversive voices have not been entirely effaced from the text, although Bloch would argue that such an effacement is never complete, that traces are always left behind, but above all that there is more there when you know how and where to look, especially in those myths that have later been papered over with more acceptable ideological positions.

Bloch is well aware of the complexities, layers, varying voices to be found in the Bible, and I would agree that a dialectical reading is able to deal with such contradictory complexity better than any other approach. However, what is needed is an even more sophisticated dialectical reading that accounts even better for the twists, foldbacks, curious alliances, and changing oppositions of the text, one that reads back and forth between the ideological, social, and economic contradictions that are inevitably found there.

Although in a Utopian world I can imagine a more Marxist postcolonial criticism, if not a distinctly Marxist bent to postcolonial Biblical Studies, a world in which Marxists like Bloch would have a much greater presence, I fear that the legacy of the Cold War is just a little too strong and that the perceived 'triumph' of capitalism in 1989–90 has a little too much influence. But the cost of throwing Marx out of the car window, wrapped in a paper bag to avoid ready identification, is not merely a lack of awareness of the distinctly Marxist background to postcolonial criticism but also a loss of the complexity and subtlety that Marxists such as Bloch can provide.

Bibliography

Bakhtin, Mikhail
  1981   *The Dialogic Imagination: Four Essays* (trans. C. Emerson and M. Holquist; Austin: University of Texas Press).
Bhabha, Homi
  1994   *The Location of Culture* (London: Routledge).
Bloch, Ernst
  1972   *Atheism in Christianity: The Religion of the Exodus and the Kingdom* (trans. J.T. Swann; New York, Herder and Herder).
  1995   *The Principle of Hope* (trans. N. Plaice, S. Plaice, and P. Knight; Cambridge, MA: MIT Press).
Boer, Roland
  1996   *Jameson and Jeroboam* (Semeia Studies; Atlanta: Scholars Press).
  1997   *Novel Histories: The Fiction of Biblical Criticism* (Sheffield: Sheffield Academic Press).
  2001a   *Last Stop Before Antarctica: The Bible and Postcolonialism in Australia* (The Bible and Postcolonialism, 6; Sheffield: Sheffield Academic Press).
  2001c   'Introduction: Vanishing Mediators?', in Boer 2001b: 1–12.
  2003   *Marxist Criticism of the Bible: A Critical Introduction to Marxist Literary Criticism and the Bible* (London: Continuum).
Boer, Roland (ed.)
  2001b   *A Vanishing Mediator? The Absence/Presence of the Bible in Postcolonialism* (*Semeia* 88; Atlanta: Society of Biblical Literature).
Boyer, Robert
  1990   *The Regulation School: A Critical Introduction* (trans. Craig Charney; New York: Columbia University Press).
Brett, Mark
  2000   *Genesis: Procreation and the Politics of Identity* (London: Routledge).
  2002   'Self Criticism, Cretan Liars and the Sly Redactors of Genesis', in I.R. Kitzberger (ed.), *Autobiographical Biblical Criticism: Between Text and Self* (Leiden: Deo Publishing): 114–32.
Derrida, Jacques
  1976   *Of Grammatology* (Baltimore: The Johns Hopkins University Press).
  1994   *Specters of Marx: The State of the Debt, the Work of Mourning, and*

the New International (trans. Peggy Kamuf, with an introduction by Bernd Magnus and Stephen Cullenberg; New York: Routledge).

Dirlik, Arif
1997   *The Postcolonial Aura: Third World Criticism in the Age of Global Capitalism* (Boulder, CO: Westview).

Douglas, Mary
1993   *In the Wilderness: The Doctrine of Defilement in the Book of Numbers* (Sheffield: JSOT Press).

Fontana, Benedetto
1993   *Hegemony and Power: On the Relation between Gramsci and Machiavelli* (Minneapolis: University of Minnesota Press).

Gottwald, Norman
1985   *The Hebrew Bible: A Socio-Literary Introduction* (Philadelphia: Fortress Press).
1992   'Sociology of Ancient Israel', in *The Anchor Bible Dictionary*, VI: 79–89.
1993   *The Hebrew Bible in Its Social World and Ours* (Semeia Studies; Atlanta: Scholars Press).
1999   *The Tribes of Yahweh: A Sociology of Liberated Israel 1050–1250* (reprint; Sheffield: Sheffield Academic Press).

Gramsci, Antonio
1971   *Selections from the Prison Notebooks* (eds. Quentin Hoare and G. Nowell Smith; London: Lawrence & Wishart).

Grünwaldt, K.
1992   *Exil und Identität: Beschneidung, Passa und Shabbat in der Priesterschrift* (Frankfurt: Anton Hain).

Hardt, Michael, and Antonio Negri
2000   *Empire* (Cambridge, MA: Harvard University Press).

Hill, Christopher
1988   *A Turbulent, Seditious and Factious People: John Bunyan and His Church* (Oxford: Oxford University Press).

Hoglund, Kenneth
1992   *Achaemenid Imperial Administration in Syria-Palestine and the Missions of Ezra and Nehemiah* (Atlanta: Scholars Press).

Horsley, Richard
1998   'Submerged Biblical Histories and Imperial Biblical Studies', in Sugirtharajah 1998a: 152–73.
1999   *Bandits, Prophets and Messiahs: Popular Movements in the Time of Jesus* (Harrisburg, PA: Trinity Press International).
2001   *Hearing the Whole Story: The Politics of Plot in Mark's Gospel* (Louisville: Westminster John Knox).
2002   *Jesus and Empire: The Kingdom of God and the New World Disorder* (Minneapolis: Fortress Press).

Jobling, David
1991   'Feminism and "Mode of Production" in Israel: Search for a Method', in David Jobling, Peggy L. Day, and Gerald T. Sheppard

(eds.), *The Bible and the Politics of Exegesis* (Cleveland: Pilgrim Press): 239–51.

1992a   '"Forced Labor": Solomon's Golden Age and the Question of Literary Representation', *Semeia* 54: 57–76.

1992b   'Deconstruction and the Political Analysis of Biblical Texts: A Jamesonian Reading of Psalm 72', *Semeia* 59: 95–127.

1998   *1 Samuel* (Collegeville, MN: The Liturgical Press).

Joosten, J.

1996   *People and Land in the Holiness Code* (Leiden: E.J. Brill).

Knohl, I.

1995   *The Sanctuary of Silence: The Priestly Torah and the Holiness School* (Minneapolis: Fortress Press).

Lenin, V.I.

1950   *Imperialism, the Highest Stage of Capitalism* (Moscow: Foreign Languages Publishing House).

Marx, Karl, and Friedrich Engels

1976   *The German Ideology* (Moscow: Progress).

Milner, Andrew

2002   'Left Out? Marxism, the New Left, and Cultural Studies', *Arena Journal* 19 (new series): 85–98.

Moore-Gilbert, Bart

1997   *Postcolonial Theory: Contexts, Practices, Politics* (London: Verso).

Mosala, Itumeleng

1992   'The Implications of the Text of Esther for African Women's Struggle for Liberation in South Africa', *Semeia* 59: 130–141.

Moylan, Tom

1997   'Bloch against Bloch: The Theological Reception of *Das Prinzip Hoffnung* and the Liberation of the Utopian Function', in Jamie Owen Daniel and Tom Moylan (eds.), *Not Yet: Reconsidering Ernst Bloch* (London: Verso): 96–121.

Rendtorff, Rolf

1996   'The *Ger* in the Priestly Laws of the Pentateuch', *Supplements to Vetus Testamentum* 36: 245–56.

Said, Edward

1978   *Orientalism* (London: Routledge & Kegan Paul).

Scott, James

1990   *Domination and the Arts of Resistance: Hidden Transcripts* (New Haven: Yale University Press).

Simkins, Ron

1999   'Patronage and the Political Economy of Ancient Israel', *Semeia* 87:123–44.

Spivak, Gayatri Chakravorty

1988   *In Other Worlds* (New York: Routledge).

1999   *A Critique of Postcolonial Reason: Toward a History of the Vanishing Present* (Cambridge, MA: Harvard University Press).

Sugirtharajah, R.S.
    1998b   'Biblical Studies after the Empire: From a Colonial to a Postcolonial Mode of Interpretation', in Sugirtharajah 1998a: 12–22.
    1998c   'A Postcolonial Exploration of Collusion and Construction in Biblical Interpretation', in Sugirtharajah 1998a: 91–116.
    2001   *The Bible and the Third World: Precolonial, Colonial and Postcolonial Encounters* (Cambridge: Cambridge University Press).
    2002   *Postcolonial Criticism and Biblical Interpretation* (Oxford: Oxford University Press).
Sugirtharajah, R.S. (ed.)
    1998a   *The Postcolonial Bible* (The Bible and Postcolonialism, 1; Sheffield: Sheffield Academic Press).
West, Gerald
    1999   *The Academy of the Poor: Towards a Dialogical Reading of the Bible* (Sheffield: Sheffield Academic Press).
Yee, Gale
    1995   'Ideological Criticism: Judges 17–21 and the Dismembered Body', in Gale A. Yee (ed.), *Judges and Method: New Approaches in Biblical Studies* (Minneapolis: Fortress Press).
    1999   'Gender, Class and the Social Scientific Study of Genesis 2–3', *Semeia* 87: 177–192.
    2003   *Poor Banished Children of Eve* (Philadelphia: Fortress Press).

'VERY LIMITED IDEOLOGICAL OPTIONS': MARXISM AND BIBLICAL STUDIES IN POSTCOLONIAL SCENES

David Jobling

My task is to examine the intersection of a triad of discourses: postcolonialism, Marxism, and Biblical Studies. Each of these is a highly complex discourse, emerging from and indicating a complex of socio-political sites. As I was pondering, in preparation for the conference session out of which this volume emerges, how I might usefully venture into such complicated and controverted territory, I read in Gerald West's *The Academy of the Poor* a quotation from Takatso Mofokeng which reframed what I wanted to say. Mofokeng notes how attempts among young South African Blacks 'to disavow the Christian faith and consequently to be rid of the obnoxious Bible' have not succeeded,

> largely due to the fact that no easily accessible ideological silo or storeroom is being offered to the social classes of our people that are desperately in need of liberation. African traditional religions are too far behind most blacks while Marxism, is to my mind, far ahead of many blacks, especially adult people. In the absence of a better storeroom of ideological and spiritual food, the Christian religion and the Bible will continue for an undeterminable period of time to be the haven of the Black masses par excellence. (Mofokeng 1988: 40, quoted in West 1999: 87–88)

The immediately following sentence in Mofokeng begins, 'In this situation of very limited ideological options', and I have taken my title from it.

There is one thing I need to explain before proceeding. This volume contains two essays on postcolonialism, Marxism, and Biblical Studies, Roland Boer's as well as mine.[1] I have had access to Boer's essay before finalizing my own, and, though responding to him is not my main purpose, I have written very much in cognizance of his important argument, and do to some extent respond to it. His presenting so well a fairly classic Marxist line of argument has given me the freedom to do something else.

---

1. The cause of this lies entirely in my own forgetfulness and dilatoriness, but the outcome is a happy one. Undated page references to Boer in what follows are to his essay in this volume.

A Reading of Mofokeng

The quotation from Mofokeng implies an angle on each of my triad of discourses, with their socio-political sites. To determine these angles as precisely as possible, we need to note the particular place and time in which he wrote, the South Africa of 1988. He was, with his comrades, still engaged in the struggle against apartheid.[2]

A. Writing in 1988, Mofokeng does not use the word 'postcolonialism' (though he makes in his essay much use of the vocabulary of colonialism). The discourse we now know as postcolonialism was not very audible in the South Africa of 1988. Of the classic works discussed by Boer (Said 1978; Spivak 1988; Bhabha 1994; see Boer: 4–6), only Said's was available. In fact, it was not until the 1990s that 'postcolonialism' really became the name of a discourse (and in Biblical Studies not until the late 1990s). Even with the nascent postcolonial theory that did exist in 1988, Mofokeng, with his local and immediate concerns, would, I suspect, have found relatively little point of contact.

The way I would like to put it is that postcolonialism, as an 'absent presence' in Mofokeng's text, takes the form precisely of an analysis of one particular local scene. I will revert constantly, in what follows, to the problematic of the local and the global. I shall understand postcolonialism as existing on a knife edge between a globalizing discourse (at least incipiently) and an untheorized aggregate of such local scenes as Mofokeng's. I agree with those who see 'postcolonial' as a category still inadequately theorized (and based on other untheorized categories; see below, on Aijaz Ahmad). Sugirtharajah, who has himself labored mightily on the theory, acknowledges this as recently as 2001 (Sugirtharajah 2001: 245).

I do not, however, at all see this as a negative. The situation could hardly be otherwise in the present stage of the development of postcolonialism as a discourse. This discourse gets its vigor precisely from being so closely and necessarily in touch with the local—see how effectively Sugirtharajah (2001) exploits colonial/postcolonial vignettes. Mofokeng speaks from and for people in a specific struggle for liberation from a specific colonialism, in which he sees 'very limited ideological options'. Such limited options no doubt continue to be the

---

2. Since that time he has engaged in other phases of the socio-political struggle in South Africa, including occupying the thankless location of principal of one of the universities formerly set aside for Blacks, now 'liberated' but still serving only Blacks and chronically underfunded.

norm in local postcolonial situations, in contrast to the wide resources available in academic, usually Western, centers where postcolonial discourse is often created. Beginning with such a local situation, one of which I am less ignorant than I am of most, enables me to give an initial 'local' bias to my remarks, and I consider this desirable.

B. At the time Mofokeng wrote, Marxism was defined (aside from some measure of academic interest in universities) by the South African Communist Party (SACP; up to 1953, CPSA), which had been a significant factor in national politics since its foundation in 1921.[3] From 1950 it was a banned organization. During the period when opposition to apartheid had to be organized mainly from outside the country, SACP was extremely active in tandem with the African National Congress, to the extent that it became hard to distinguish the membership of one from the other. People within South Africa experienced the clandestine working of SACP mostly through its trades union arm SACTU (South African Congress of Trade Unions); hence Marxism was a factor much more in urban than in rural environments.

SACP historically followed an ideological line very much defined from Moscow.[4] During the closing stages of struggle, in the 1980s, the Party gained considerably in membership, and it is to this increased prominence that Mofokeng is responding.[5]

C. 'The Christian religion and the Bible' were variously implicated in the South African struggle—as bastions of the racist regime, as bastions of opposition to it, and as sites for some people, particularly anglophone, of a hoped-for but impossible neutrality. Outside observers tended to be astonished at the extent to which the struggle took place *within* Christianity and *over* the Bible, as both or all sides laid claim to these. The enormous role of church groups in local coalitions in the 1980s, particularly under the auspices of the United Democratic Front, has often been credited as a significant factor in the relatively smooth transition from the apartheid to the democratic regime.

The name I initially gave to the third discourse in my triad was 'Biblical Studies'. But this is not a term that Mofokeng uses. He speaks of 'the Bible' and harnesses it to 'the Christian religion', as if these presented

---

3. My understanding of these matters comes mainly from Ellis and Sechaba 1992.

4. Ellis and Sechaba (1992: 52–59) discuss the struggle in the 1960s and 1970s between Moscow and Beijing for influence in Africa, and how this soured relations between the ANC and SACP in exile and Maoist-inclined Tanzania under Julius Nyerere.

5. Since 1990, SACP has moved away from its traditional orthodoxy, but nonetheless has lost influence. In 1990, the specifically communist SACTU was dissolved and replaced by the more broadly-based COSATU (Congress of South African Trades Unions).

themselves to him as much the same thing, or as parts of the same thing. This raises two big issues.

First, what sort of thing is 'Biblical Studies'? What location(s) does it indicate? In the debates out of which this volume comes, we tend to speak of it as something rather definite within our socio-political scene. For example, Boer, discussing global socialist resistance to capitalism in *The Postcolonial Bible* (1998: 45), asks 'how can Biblical Studies be a part of all this?'[6] This strikes me as an odd question. Does he think, perhaps, that the Society of Biblical Literature ought to make a pronouncement? Don't hold your breath! I have myself tried to suggest what 'Biblical Studies' means in a global context (and in a context of globalization), concluding that it can only be a shifting aggregate of localities which one must negotiate politically as best one can (Jobling 1993: 105–109). Mofokeng's formulation reminds me that, to be of much use in postcolonial contexts, we biblical scholars will need consciously to relate ourselves to a much wider range of practices around 'the Bible' than can be comprehended by 'Biblical Studies'.

A second and even bigger issue is raised by Mofokeng's linking of 'the Christian religion and the Bible'. I find it interesting that Gerald West has recently been passionately arguing that—precisely in South Africa—'the Christian religion and the Bible' are not and should not be the same thing (e.g., 2004: 41–42). West's concern is to highlight the importance of a history which is only beginning to be told, of how various Africans were able to separate the Bible from the message of the missionaries and do things with it which the missionaries did not foresee. He sees this history as having enormous implications for how African Biblical Studies should now unfold.

Much as I sympathize with West's aim, it still seems to me that the Bible's location is often—surely *most* often—some form of church. I believe that we need, precisely those of us who tend to define ourselves primarily in terms of Biblical Studies, to take very seriously Mofokeng's expression 'the Christian religion and the Bible'. That, from his location, is how it looks (or looked), and the same would surely be true for many other locations similar to his. His expression projects a vast socio-political location and a set of practices within that location, namely all the churches and all the things they do with the Bible!

These observations make it hard for me to retain 'Biblical Studies' as part of my working triad, along with postcolonialism and Marxism. Despite the awkwardness, I shall say 'the Bible/Christianity', letting the

---

6. In the earlier part of his essay, it is true, Boer says a good deal about the churches as locations for Australian Biblical Studies, but by the end 'Biblical Studies' seems to have pried itself loose from the churches.

stroke stand for all the identities, partial identities, and non-identities between different Bibles and different churches.

Mofokeng puts Marxism and the Bible/Christianity (along with African traditional religions) conceptually *on a par*. They are to be compared in terms of their serviceability to those engaged in local colonial/postcolonial struggle. He gives to my threefold intersection a specific geometry: local sites set the agenda 'from below', while Marxism and the Bible/Christianity are on a level with each other, 'above', as potential generative spaces for the working through of the agenda. He conjures for me, then, 'postcolonialism' as an aggregate of local and particular struggles which address Marxism and the Bible/Christianity with the appeal and the demand: 'Take us seriously, which means, start from us!'

Living as I do in a place of many silos, I enjoy Mofokeng's use of the silo as a metaphor! It suggests an environment where the ideological and spiritual resources can *ferment*, become active and productive. This becomes the point of comparison between Marxism and the Bible/ Christianity. Which offers more resources for a situation *in ferment*? Mofokeng invites Marxism and the Bible/Christianity to see themselves in a *receptive* situation, literally as *receptacles* for the 'ideological and spiritual' resources of those in struggle.

In Mofokeng's comparison, the Bible/Christianity appears as *more* serviceable than Marxism. But only *for now*. At another stage, he implies, Marxism might be more serviceable. Even now, Marxism may be more serviceable for the young, the Bible/Christianity for the old. (One could imagine other similar differentiations, based on level of education, urban or rural location, or the like.)

Especially in view of the 'limited ideological options', the quotation from Mofokeng begs the question of whether there are other potential silos which might be put, in specific situations, alongside the ones he mentions. In his particular scene he finds the local traditional religions unpromising, but they may not be so everywhere. And what of other major world religions? In many parts of Africa, and to some extent even in South Africa, Islam/the Quran would come to mind. From a Western perspective it is easy for us to imagine some options related to secular postmodernism. Mofokeng, from his time and space, sees only Marxism and the Bible/ Christianity as options sufficiently advanced. But he raises for me the more general question of where people engaged in particular struggles may turn for resources. We may anticipate that in most localities the options will be limited, compared with the cornucopia we know.

Among the theoretically available silos we must now include 'post-colonialism' itself, understood as an attempt at comprehensive theory. Its advocates might wish that if Mofokeng were writing now he would include it as a promising option! What would make it widely serviceable? This is the question which it seems to me postcolonial critics need to ask themselves. The question which lies behind the rest of this essay is, what relationships does postcolonialism need to have with Biblical Studies and Marxism, particularly the latter, in order to increase its potential as a silo?

Local and Global

Having used it to establish a point of view, I now turn away from the particularity of the opening quotation from Mofokeng and expand the discussion by using the categories of the local and the global. I draw to some extent on my first foray into the arena of postcolonialism, when my immediate topic was globalization (Jobling 1993).

Postcolonialism in most of its forms retains a closeness to the local. But it is confronted in my triad by two inveterately globalizing mindsets, those of Marxism and the Bible/Christianity, both of which have a terribly hard time *not* claiming a privileged view of the whole. I and others have argued that the Bible/Christianity is constituted in a fundamental way by a global imperative (Jobling 1993: 101–105; see also Dube 1998). From the two testaments I may cite, representatively, Isaiah 45.22 and Matthew 28.19. Marxism has the same globalizing tendency, especially in its Moscow-line form. Hence postcolonial critics question Marxist pretensions to map the history of colonial peoples on their behalf (e.g., Said's critique of Marx on India, 1978: 153–6) and highlight the collusion of the Bible/Christianity in the global aspirations of colonialism (e.g., Sugirtharajah 1998a). From a postcolonial perspective, both equally represent the attempt to impose global ideologies developed in the West.

Yet paradoxically it is in exactly this same respect that postcolonialisms find Marxism and the Bible/Christianity serviceable. Local situations, to maintain their energy and to expand their options, need some sort of organized view of the outside world which confronts them. So it is their instincts and resources to think and strategize and act globally that make Marxism and the Bible/Christianity potentially useful. It is interesting that Mofokeng sees as capable of offering advanced ideological resources for his people precisely these two globalizing systems, while he rejects, as 'too far behind', the local phenomenon of African traditional religions. Local struggles need structures of mediation capable of linking them together, of keeping them in touch with a whole 'globe' of local struggles. The universality of the worldwide church and of international socialism offer such mediating possibilities. Yet both are apt to be intolerant of local variation. From the perspective of postcolonialisms, only the finest of lines separates the critique of and the need for Marxism and the Bible/Christianity.

How to reach out to these global resources without losing any of the sharpness of the local issues? I would raise two general issues. The first is that postcolonialism, at least as an academic discourse, will find it nearly impossible to avoid identification with the West as long as it is based so much in Western universities (see Jobling 1993: 99). Boer (p. 171) also alludes to this problem. In part, surely, it is unavoidable. In many places in the world there is such a crippling lack of resources as to render such an academic discourse unfeasible; in many places those engaging in it would face actual political danger. So I am not inclined to be as dismissive as Boer of Sugirtharajah's comment about 'Utilizing the space offered by the Western academy'.[7] One of the things which we in the West can and must at least do is to provide auspices, sites of meeting.[8] Nonetheless, the centering of postcolonial discourse in Western institutions poses an enormous problem. It cannot but greatly diminish the closeness to local struggles, and serviceability to them.

The second issue is the extent to which postcolonialism should aspire to global theorizing at all. Given that forums are needed, and that all available resources should be exploited to find them, including Western ones, does this mean that a common ideological base is what people in local struggles should be looking for when they get together? A colleague of mine in Saskatoon, Nettie Wiebe, is extremely active in Via Campesina, a thriving organization formed by marginalized agriculturalists from many parts of the world. To questions I asked her about its ideology, and how this might relate, or not, to the ideology of international socialism, she replied very firmly that Via Campesina resists any overt move towards ideological unification, not only when it comes from existing outside models but even when it is generated from within. Here is an organization which already far transcends the 'micropolitics' in which Boer finds so little hope (1998: 43–44) but which feels it must resist global models.

Reaching out to the global resources of the Bible/Christianity might seem an odd thing to do, given that the Bible/Christianity has tended heavily to be on the wrong side of colonial/postcolonial struggle. But it is very understandable given the great structural power which the churches still wield in many parts of the world. It is also necessary to remember that local churches have very often been in the forefront of change when national or international churches have resisted it. (Many of us can tell stories of how we have been able to use church funds and facilities to do work of which we would not have welcomed too close a scrutiny by church bodies!)

Much more paradoxical is the issue of reaching out to Marxism. This is the main topic of Boer's essay in this volume, and I have little to add to

---

7. Boer does not provide a reference for this quote.

8. In Biblical Studies, the Society of Biblical Literature has provided such a site in its consultation on the Bible in Africa, Asia, and Latin America.

what he has said. The structural resources available from the Marxist side have, of course, greatly diminished since the fall of the Soviet Empire. Still, they are far from non-existent—*some* form of socialism is still a significant presence in a great many parts of the world. And the *conceptual* resources available from the Marxist side are, as Boer indicates, still enormous. Marxism has generally (though not without exception) been on the right side of colonial/postcolonial struggles, and, as Boer rightly insists, it has been basically instrumental in defining what postcolonialism *is*.

Postcolonialism's 'forgetting' of its own Marxist history is perhaps not quite the conspiracy that Boer makes it. If this were a formal response to his essay, I would want to do some closer reading of his 'triumvirate' of postcolonial villains in this regard: Said, Spivak, and Bhabha—especially Spivak (though, strictly speaking, I do not believe one can have a female in a triumvirate). Boer allows too little for the facts that since 1990 communism has lost its main global center and that some of the sites of postcolonial struggle have had little Marxist history. But I have to agree with him when he suggests that the occlusion of what really makes it tick (i.e., Marxism) has tended to become constitutive of postcolonial theory.

I must sadly agree with Boer's strictures (pp. 171–74) on Sugirtharajah—whose work in general, of course, I value extremely highly—in respect of his treatment of Marxism. The fact that he comes from a country with one of the longest experiences of communist government (at the regional and local levels) hardly surfaces in his work. He does not seem interested in compatriot Marxists like Aijaz Ahmad. Again, to return for a moment to South Africa,[9] I have to agree with Boer (p. 172, with reference to Sugirtharajah 2001: 251–52) that Sugirtharajah's claiming the work of an Itumeleng Mosala for postcolonialism, without reference to Marxism, suggests a definite blindness.[10]

In a word, to the extent that postcolonialism is hiding (from itself and others) the resources of the Marxist tradition, it is narrowing the ideological options (limited, as we have seen) of people in struggle.

Postcolonialism faces, it seems to me, a number of dangers. Given how much of its base resides in Western universities, it risks not only losing some of its closeness to local struggles but also becoming another intellectual fad within the Western globalizing machine. An opposite danger is that it make itself into a kind of counter-globalization, by conceiving the world in terms of only a single struggle between 'developed' and 'undeveloped' regions. Much the best critique that I know of this sort

---

9. Let me here acknowledge the very great value I have found in Sugirtharajah's work on Bishop Colenso (2001: 110–39; see Jobling 2003).

10. I did notice one reference in Sugirtharajah (2001: 198) to the Marxist Arif Dirlik, who is important for Boer. Dirlik is a native of Turkey, but has pursued his academic career in the USA.

of thinking comes from Aijaz Ahmad (1992). From his own postcolonial location Ahmad comments superbly on the interactions of different communisms (particularly Soviet and Maoist) with processes of decolonization over the last half-century. He mounts a sharp critique of various postcolonialisms, those which are aggregates of incompatible nationalisms, those based on non-theorized constructs like 'Third World' or 'non-alignment', those which divide the world into oppressor nations and victim nations, with scant attention to class division and struggle *within* both kinds of nation.[11]

This leads to the final danger, that postcolonialism may be insufficiently exposed to fundamental criticism, either from without or within (see the brief comments of Horsley 1998: 153–54). I know of no substantial critique of postcolonialism that has been generated from within Biblical Studies. Nor is there any among the left-leaning Western churches, due to a desire for solidarity which has its dubious side (a mixture of self-loathing and ecstasy tends to come over Christians I know when they are reminded for the hundredth time that the churches of the 'developing world' are actually 'growing'). To reject Marxism is to lose the likeliest source of fundamental criticism like Ahmad's, which, if Boer is right, is in fact really postcolonial *self*-criticism.

The State of the Debt

Boer challenges postcolonial studies to acknowledge its debt to Marxism. Biblical Studies must do no less. Those of us for whom the Bible's operative vision is of a divine 'option for the poor' must confess that only Marxism and its offspring have given political form to that vision.[12] But the debt is theoretical as well as political. It is Marxist theory which can explain to us why *this* biblical vision is—and must be—only one among several competing biblical social visions.[13] The greatest theoretical debt which Biblical Studies owes to Marxism, in my opinion, is the understanding of historical modes of production (MPs). Postcolonialism also has a great deal to learn from MP theory. So I want in this section to discuss my triad, but with MP theory standing in the place of Marxism as a whole.

---

11. I can think of no more salutary reading, for the likely audience of this volume, than Ahmad's book.

12. Perhaps we should add also its precursors, with reference to things like the Radical Reformation (see Boer, p. 177, with references to Ernst Bloch 1972).

13. See particularly Boer's remarks (pp. 177ff. on Bloch's understanding of the Bible as a class-riven text.

'Mode of production' is a concept of the utmost comprehensiveness. Based on the model of base and superstructure, it extends the latter to include every aspect or 'sector' of the workings of a society (law, art, religion, etc.) considered in terms of the systems of implication that bind them together. The concept has become fairly well known in Biblical Studies, largely through the work of Norman Gottwald (1993; consult the index). To the basic scheme of MPs posited by Marx and his successors— primitive commune, Asiatic, slave-based, feudal, capitalist, and socialist— Melotti (1977) provides the best introduction. Recent theory (for which see Jameson 1981: 32–33, 89–100, building on Althusser and Balibar 1970) has moved in a radically new direction, in particular by abandoning the idea that a given society at a given time must exemplify just one of the modes. Rather,

> every social formation or historically existing society has in fact consisted in the overlay and structural co-existence of *several* modes of production all at once, including *vestiges and survivals of older modes of production*, ... as well as *anticipatory tendencies* which are potentially inconsistent with the existing system but have not yet generated an autonomous space of their own. (Jameson 1981: 95; emphasis mine, except for 'several')

For Hebrew Bible Studies I adopt (following Meyers 1991: 142) a 'household' MP for premonarchical Israel.[14] For monarchical Israel, and also for the empires by which Israel was from time to time dominated, I follow Gottwald (1993: xxv–xxvii) in accepting Marx's 'Asiatic' mode but renaming it 'tributary' (many important examples are not Asian). These two, household and tributary, together with the slave-based MP (relevant mainly to the New Testament), provide a most effective large-scale historical framework for the Bible. The structure of my Hebrew Bible Introduction course is provided by the conflicting ideologies of tributary and household MPs operative in canon-formation in the Persian period; we read the whole canon in terms of this conflict. The dominant Priestly party works out of the ideology of the tributary MP, as expressed in the Jerusalem theology, while the Deuteronomic party keeps alive the prophetic tradition, a continued presence (what Jameson calls a 'vestige' or 'survival') of Israel's ancient household MP. Though this approach entails a degree of simplification, it is remarkably effective in providing beginning students with an initial road map for the whole canon.

Important as MP theory is to historical Biblical Studies, its contribution to the history of biblical interpretation is no less vital. It raises a necessary

---

14. The 'primitive commune' is not relevant to Israel, and is in any case based on now outmoded anthropology. Meyers envisages households of an average of 10–12 people probably covering three generations, self-sufficient for most necessities (see esp. Ch. 6).

caveat to all suggestions of analogy between the biblical world and later ages, including our own. Analogies between ancient times and the present, of course, abound in Biblical Studies, but any proposed analogy needs to be brought to the bar of MP theory, in order to test the limits of 'translating' between societies which worked in fundamentally different ways.

Melotti's book, the handiest introduction to MP theory, is called *Marx and the Third World*, which immediately suggests the importance of the theory for postcolonial studies. Modern colonialism is a history of the forcible meeting between different MPs whose consequences, aside from sheer oppression and exploitation, have included all kinds of total misunderstanding between colonizers and colonized. The Bible, which brings into the mix yet other MPs, may simply add to the incomprehension, but it may facilitate 'translation' between colonizer and colonized when the MP of a colonized group corresponds to one of the Bible's MPs.[15] But these matters need to be thought through systematically, rather than being offered as untheorized analogies. Writing in *The Postcolonial Bible*, Fernando Segovia, for example, claims 'many and profound similarities' among empires ancient and modern (1998: 57), while Richard Horsley finds analogies between the Roman Empire and current imperialism sufficient to enable us to draw lessons from Paul's situation to our own in a fairly direct way (1998: 162–72). Perhaps such suggestions would survive close examination, but my initial reaction is that of Susan VanZanten Gallagher (1996: 230) in response to another collection of postcolonial essays: 'applying postcolonial theory to the Babylonian, Persian, or Roman conquests, the Johannine community's expansionist vision, or any biblical pericope is anachronistic and ahistorical'.[16]

I do not want to minimize the tactical value of such analogies. They may give impact to our work as we try to mobilize support from, for example, churches. But even at this level we need to 'come clean'. Although the Bible offers paradigms of resistance within the tributary and slave-based modes, it does not, by definition, have one word to say about resistance to capitalism, and we must be ready to say so. But the situation has a positive side. Capitalism, like any MP, continues to be 'inhabited' by all the MPs that preceded it—not least because ancient texts like the Bible continue to exert power within it. This should encourage us to present responsible 'translations'. In each case, we have to ask how words of power spoken within one pervasive mindset are capable of being heard within another.

---

15. This would be the proper basis on which to assess the uncanny resemblances which Bishop Colenso thought to find between the Zulu and the ancient Israelites. See Sugirtharajah 2001: 127–30.

16. This same volume of *Semeia* contains an exemplary application of MP theory in the context of postcolonial Biblical Studies; see Berquist 1996.

Let me give an example which I have used (both in North America and in South Africa) in connection with 'Jubilee 2000', the international initiative to cancel the debt of poor countries. Among the biblical texts dealing with debt-remission, the framers of the initiative chose Leviticus 25 (where the word 'Jubilee' actually occurs) over the other most prominent text, Deuteronomy 15. The ideological basis for biblical debt-remission is that God is the ultimate owner of everything. But I believe we are dealing with different MPs. Leviticus translates divine ownership, through the logic of the tributary MP, into control of everything by the state. Deuteronomy translates it, through the logic of the household MP, into the gift by God of a patrimony to each family. Both books agree that God owns everything, but working from different theologies they posit different consequences.[17] What might 'God's ultimate ownership of everything' mean within late capitalism, what is it *capable of meaning*? Until we know how to answer such a question, we should be sparing of analogies.[18]

The application of MP theory to our immediate situation is a controversial issue on which I diverge somewhat from Boer. What many call 'late capitalism', capitalism in its global stage, is different enough from the capitalism that Marx analyzed to be thought of as a new mode of production requiring a critique going beyond Marx. For such a critique we need the resources of postmodernism, ambiguous as they often seem. Marxism is just as vulnerable to the postmodern critique of 'grand narratives' as is Christianity or anything else. It has been just as guilty of taking a 'colonial' attitude to local issues and needs as any other system. The best discussion of these issues is by Jameson (1991), who always manages to negotiate a fine line between affirming (in accord with MP theory) that late capitalism is still the old enemy—a dominant, alienating MP—and discerning its special features, especially its decenteredness.

There is not much to which Boer is blind, but—though he knows his Jameson better than anyone—he is blind to Derrida.[19] In his essay in this

---

17.   The Deuteronomic legislation is actually much more advantageous to the poor than the Levitical. It is a greater constraint on the accumulation of wealth that the rich are obliged to restore the economic balance every seven rather than every fifty years! Perhaps related to this is the fact that we hear so much less now about 'Jubilee 2000'. Did it invest too heavily (if you will pardon the metaphor) in a round number? Does anyone want to wait until 2050 for another widely visible initiative for debt-remission?

18.   I do not regard Biblical Studies, as currently constituted, as at all capable of answering this question. We need the help of others, among whom I would include not only political theorists (Marxist and otherwise) but also theologians.

19.   There is much in Boer's treatment of these issues with which I am very much in sympathy, for example, his remarks on Bakhtin and hybridity (in relation to the work of Mark Brett; p. 175). He just seems to have an aversion to Derrida! But can anyone except Derrida effectively respond to Boer's later *cri de cœur*, 'I can't help but wonder whether the truly subversive voices have not been entirely effaced from the text' (p. 179)?

volume he says: 'But a Derridean Marx—taking for a moment Spivak's effort to combine deconstruction, Marxism and feminism seriously—is a strange Marx indeed, looking more like a slightly left-of-centre liberal, as Derrida's own *Specters of Marx* (1994) showed only too well' (p. 169). I know a fair number of left-of-center liberals, and without exception they are far more threatened by Derrida than by any form of Marxism! What Derrida does in *Specters* is what I have called a deconstruction of Marx on behalf of Marx (Jobling forthcoming). We need to preface what he says about Marxism with his famous acknowledgment of his own debt: 'deconstruction would have been impossible and unthinkable in a pre-Marxist space' (Derrida 1994: 92).[20] He demonstrates in the text of Marx the traces of all the tragic history of later Marxisms and communisms, but he also demonstrates Marx's amazing and almost unique openness to self-criticism and then himself shows how Marxist self-criticism might and must now be practiced.[21]

Just as biblical scholars under capitalism, in order to have any adequate understanding of their own project, must 'go to school' with Marx and Marxism, so traditional Marxists under late capitalism must go to school with the philosophers of postmodernism. A more familiar way of putting this point might be to contrast a traditional socialist economic critique with a critique of 'kyriarchy', the grand system of institutionalized domination and subordination in the western tradition, within which subsystems of domination based on gender, class, race, age, etc., mutually reinforce each other.[22] For theorists of kyriarchy, socialism in its traditional forms is discredited by its failures in the areas of gender, ecology, etc. Boer responds on socialism's behalf by saying that the kyriarchal model can support no more than a micropolitics and that late

---

20.   The discerning will have noticed that I borrow the title of this section, 'The State of the Debt', from Derrida's subtitle.

21.   I cannot refrain from quoting Marx, from *The Eighteenth Brumaire*:

> Proletarian revolutions ... criticise themselves constantly, interrupt themselves continually in their own course, come back to the apparently accomplished in order to recommence it afresh, deride with unmerciful thoroughness the inadequacies, weaknesses and paltrinesses of their first attempts, seem to throw down their adversary only in order that he may draw new strength from the earth and rise again more gigantic before them, recoil ever and anon from the immensity of their own aims, until the situation has been created which makes all turning back impossible. (Quoted from Burns 1982: 120–21)

22.   The term kyriarchy was proposed by Elisabeth Schüssler Fiorenza (1994: 14). I somewhat extend its range of meaning. These alternative foci of resistance to global capitalism are juxtaposed in *The Postcolonial Bible*. For international socialism, Boer (1998) seems to speak with a lone voice. Resistance to 'kyriarchy' is mentioned explicitly only by Ringe (1998: 136), but it hovers over the work also of Segovia and Horsley.

capitalism is quite well able to cope with micropolitics (1998: 43–44). I want to stand with Boer in his paying renewed attention to international socialism, but any socialism to which I can give my allegiance must be one that has heard the critiques of kyriarchy, especially socialist kyriarchy!

Boer is right that MP theory implies a critique of excessive concentration on the local, and his misgivings about micropolitics have to be taken seriously. The economic instance is still basic, and it is still a dominant and alienating global MP that we all face. But the dissolution of the old class structure is not just a myth propagated by the rich for their own interests, nor just a piece of self-deception by apolitical postmodernists. The response that seems to be called for is a globalizing of the local in ways which can still draw on the traditional socialist model but which understands the 'local' as something more complex than trades unions 'locals'. How do we bring together sites of struggle which are not only invisible to each other but which might not even be recognized by each other as sites of struggle?[23]

Hybridity of Biblical Studies and Marxism

On a visit to South Africa, I had the chance to attend a day-long workshop sponsored by the Jubilee initiative, at which activists from churches, trades unions, and university were brilliantly led through the complexities of the global economy by a union official of whose religious connection, if any, I know nothing. At the very end, at the point of exhaustion for him and most of the audience, the leader asked me to do a 20-minute impromptu on the biblical Jubilee. Put on the spot, I found myself giving not my Marxist-historical-deconstructive critique of the Jubilee initiative (for a fragment of this, see above) but an upbeat Jubilee sermon! This was the closest I have ever been to Mofokeng's location and the particular conjunction out of which he was writing—Marxism and the Bible/Christianity in a South African postcolonial scene.

Did that day happen *more* on account of Marxist influences or *more* on account of biblical or Christian influences? I do not believe that the

---

23. See my earlier remarks about Via Campesina. If I may insert here a 'local' remark of my own, my own location on the American (specifically the Canadian) prairie does not seem very visible to postcolonialists. We are experiencing rural depopulation and impoverishment on a massive scale, as the descendants of the pioneers who—with imperial sponsorship— drove the indigenous inhabitants off the land are themselves being driven off it by global agribusiness. The college from which I recently retired is in imminent peril of being forced 'off the land' and out of existence, since the hinterland can no longer afford the support, albeit subsistence-level, that it has traditionally given us. Yet a collection like *Reading from This Place* (Segovia and Tolbert 1995), whose scope suggests some aspiration to comprehensiveness, has no optic for this particular site of struggle.

question would have at all occurred to those who were there. Heirs of a particular history of local Marxism and/or of a particular history with the Bible and various churches, people with common interests met to tackle particular problems. Reflecting on the experience, the word that came most readily to my mind was one emerging from the postcolonial debates—hybridity. Whatever our individual profiles, we operated that day as a hybrid Christian-Marxist group.

I want to suggest that the way for Biblical Studies (and for Marxism) to be serviceable to local sites of struggle is through a hybrid relationship. Certain forms of hybridity (not so called) between Marxism and Christianity already have, of course, a substantial history. In Europe, it often takes the name 'Christian-Marxist dialogue'.[24] Closer to postcolonial concerns is the Latin American tradition exemplified by Miranda (1974). To be effective hybrids, biblical scholars need to understand their own location, including any presence there of Marxist or socialist tradition. In some locations it may be hard to find, but in others it will be substantial. My own location is a privileged one in this respect: the province of Saskatchewan has had the most years of socialist government of any place in North America, at least in the last fifty years or so. From our own location, and from this sort of awareness, we can co-operate with other biblical scholars in their particular locations.

We should work hard to avoid any kind of containment from one side or the other, being mindful of the containing tendencies endemic to both Marxism and the Bible/Christianity. But we should not look for a specious equality—the roles will be different. As I reflect further on my South African day, I am struck by the fact that the substance of what we did, the global economic analysis, was provided by the Marxist tradition, while the Bible provided just the epilogue. And yet the epilogue was felt to be necessary, perhaps to link the economics to other dimensions of human existence. One task that may fall to Biblical Studies, in this period after the fall of the Soviet Empire, is to *represent* Marxism in locations where it is weak or absent. It may be necessary to provide the basics of Marxism to our students as part of our biblical teaching. My own experience of doing this I have described above; I regularly have to deal with students who are

---

24. By no means pursued only from the Christian side; notable among Marxist treatments are those of Garaudy (1968), who was head of the French Communist Party, and Girardi (1968). One can point to a long tradition of positive Marxist interest in the Bible. Boer, who is engaged in a study of this tradition, reminds me (private correspondence) that when Ernst Bloch was working on the Bible and communism, 'the Bible still formed ... the world view of the peasants with whom the communists were working'. He mentions also Walter Benjamin's interest in the history of biblical interpretation, continued in Jameson 1981: 30–31 (and passim).

startled by my introducing the name 'Marx', as a name essential to our work, in the first session of a Biblical Studies class!

There is a story about a Christian and a Marxist who get into conversation on a train. The Christian claims that all the Marxist ideals are enshrined in the Bible and in Christian faith. 'Maybe so', replies the Marxist, 'but you have had two thousand years to try to make it work. Now it's our turn.'[25] This is a story that both Marxists and biblical scholars would do well to ponder. Neither protagonist denies the overlap of Marx and the Bible. The Marxist points to the historical failure of Christianity (of which most forms of Christian involvement in colonialism are a prime example), but now that the charge of historical failure hangs so heavily also over Marxism, perhaps the ball is back in the Bible's court. Or, better, perhaps it is now the turn of the hybrid of Biblical Studies and Marxism.

Bibliography

Ahmad, Aijaz
    1992   *In Theory: Classes, Nations, Literatures* (London: Verso).
Althusser, Louis, and Étienne Balibar
    1970   *Reading Capital* (trans. Ben Brewster; New York: Pantheon).
Berquist, Jon L.
    1996   'Postcolonialism and Imperial Motives for Canonization', *Semeia* 75: 15–35.
Bhabha, Homi
    1994   *The Location of Culture* (London: Routledge).
Bloch, Ernst
    1972   *Atheism in Christianity: The Religion of the Exodus and the Kingdom* (trans. J.T. Swann; New York: Herder and Herder).
Boer, Roland J.
    1998   'Remembering Babylon: Postcolonialism and Australian Biblical Studies', in Sugirtharajah 1998b: 24–48.
Burns, Emile (ed.)
    1982   *The Marxist Reader: The Most Significant and Enduring Works of Marxism* (New York: Avenel).
Derrida, Jacques
    1994   *Specters of Marx: The State of the Debt, the Work of Mourning, and the New International* (trans. Peggy Kamuf, with an introduction by Bernd Magnus and Stephen Cullenberg; New York and London: Routledge).

---

25. I heard this story over forty years ago from Paul Oestreicher, who has since become a prominent peace activist and the founding Chair of Amnesty International, and is now Canon Emeritus of Coventry Cathedral. He presented it as his own experience. I have since heard it in other forms from other people, but no doubt similar events can happen more than once!

Dube, Musa W.
    1998   'Savior of the World but not of This World: A Postcolonial
                Reading of Spatial Construction in John', in Sugirtharajah 1998b:
                118–35.
Ellis, Stephen, and Tsepo Sechaba
    1992   *Comrades Against Apartheid: The ANC and the South African
                Communist Party in Exile* (London: James Currey; Bloomington:
                Indiana University Press).
Gallagher, Susan VanZanten
    1996   'Mapping the Hybrid World: Three Postcolonial Motifs', *Semeia*
                75: 229–40.
Garaudy, Roger
    1968   *From Anathema to Dialogue: A Marxist Challenge to the Christian
                Churches* (trans. Luke O'Neill; New York: Vintage).
Girardi, Giulio
    1968   *Marxism and Christianity* (trans. Kevin Traynor; New York:
                Macmillan).
Gottwald, Norman K.
    1993   *The Hebrew Bible in Its Social World and in Ours* (Atlanta: Scholars
                Press).
Horsley, Richard A.
    1998   'Submerged Biblical Histories and Imperial Biblical Studies', in
                Sugirtharajah 1998b: 152–73.
Jameson, Fredric
    1981   *The Political Unconscious: Narrative as a Socially Symbolic Act*
                (Ithaca, NY: Cornell University Press).
    1991   *Postmodernism, or, The Cultural Logic of Late Capitalism* (Dur-
                ham, NC: Duke University Press).
Jobling, David
    1993   'Globalization in Biblical Studies/Biblical Studies in Globalization',
                Biblical Interpretation 1: 96–110.
    2003   'Colenso on Myth or Colenso *as* Myth: A Response to Timothy
                Larsen', in Jonathan A. Draper (ed.), *The Eye of the Storm: Bishop
                Colenso and the Crisis of Biblical Interpretation* (London and New
                York: T&T Clark International): 64–75.
    Forthcoming 'Jerusalem and Memory: On a Long Parenthesis in Derrida's
                Specters of Marx', in Yvonne Sherwood (ed.), *Derrida's Bible* (New
                York: Palgrave Macmillan).
Melotti, Umberto
    1977   *Marx and the Third World* (trans. Pat Ransford; London:
                Macmillan).
Meyers, Carol
    1991   *Discovering Eve: Ancient Israelite Women in Context* (Oxford:
                Oxford University Press).
Miranda, José Porfirio
    1974   *Marx and the Bible: A Critique of the Philosophy of Oppression*
                (trans. John Eagleson; Maryknoll: Orbis Books).

Mofokeng, Takatso
    1988   'Black Christians, the Bible and Liberation', *The Journal of Black Theology* 2: 34–42.

Ringe, Sharon H.
    1998   'Places at the Table: Feminist and Postcolonial Biblical Interpretation', in Sugirtharajah 1998b: 136–51.

Said, Edward
    1978   *Orientalism* (London: Routledge & Kegan Paul).

Schüssler Fiorenza, Elisabeth
    1994   *Jesus: Miriam's Child, Sophia's Prophet: Critical Issues in Feminist Christology* (New York: Crossroad).

Segovia, Fernando F.
    1998   'Biblical Studies and Postcolonial Studies: Toward a Postcolonial Optic', in Sugirtharajah 1998b: 49–65.

Segovia, Fernando F., and Mary Ann Tolbert (eds.)
    1995   *Reading from This Place*. Vol. 1, *Social Location and Biblical Interpretation in the United States*; Vol. 2, *Social Location and Biblical Interpretation in the Global Perspective* (Minneapolis: Fortress).

Spivak, Gayatri Chakravorty
    1988   *In Other Worlds* (New York: Routledge).

Sugirtharajah, R.S.
    1998a   'A Postcolonial Exploration of Collusion and Construction in Biblical Interpretation', in Sugirtharajah 1998b: 91–116.
    2001   *The Bible and the Third World: Precolonial, Colonial and Postcolonial Encounters* (Cambridge: Cambridge University Press).

Sugirtharajah, R.S. (ed.)
    1998b   *The Postcolonial Bible* (The Bible and Postcolonialism, 1; Sheffield: Sheffield Academic Press).

West, Gerald O.
    1999   *The Academy of the Poor: Towards a Dialogical Reading of the Bible* (Sheffield: Sheffield Academic Press).
    2004   'From the Bible as *Bola* to Biblical Interpretation as *Marabi*: Tlhaping Transactions with the Bible', in Jonathan A. Draper (ed.), *Orality, Literacy, and Colonialism in Southern Africa* (Semeia Studies, 46; Atlanta: Society of Biblical Literature).

INDEX OF AUTHORS